EDITED BY
**COLIN GRABOW
& INU MANAK**

THE CASE
AGAINST THE
JONES ACT

CATO
INSTITUTE

Print ISBN: 978-1-948647-98-4
eBook ISBN: 978-1-948647-99-1

Cover design: Faceout Studios, Tim Green.

Library of Congress Control Number: 2020939557

Printed in the United States of America.

CATO INSTITUTE
1000 Massachusetts Avenue NW
Washington, DC 20001
www.cato.org

Contents

List of Abbreviations and Acronyms   v

List of Illustrations   vii

Foreword   ix
Anne O. Krueger

Introduction   xiii
Inu Manak

Demystifying the Jones Act

1. The Jones Act: A Burden America Can No Longer Bear   3
   Colin Grabow, Inu Manak, and Daniel J. Ikenson

2. Three Myths about the Jones Act   15
   Rob Quartel

3. Rust Buckets: How the Jones Act Undermines   23
   U.S. Shipbuilding and National Security
   Colin Grabow

4. What the Trump Administration Can Learn from the Jones Act   37
   Bryan Riley

The Costs of the Jones Act

5. Dragging the Anchor: A Look at the Myriad Costs   45
   of the Jones Act
   Daniel J. Ikenson

6. By Land or by Sea: Does the Jones Act Cause Land-Based   59
   Transport Congestion?
   Thomas Grennes

7. The Environmental Case for Jones Act Reform   67
   Timothy Fitzgerald

8. A Shift Toward Murkiness: How Conflicting Transportation   77
   Policies Have Forced Unsupervised Oligopolies on Jones Act
   Trades in the Past 23 Years
   Manuel Reyes

9. The Jones Act: A Costly Failure   85
    Steve Ellis

10. Reform the Foreign Dredge Act to Create   89
    American Jobs and Save Taxpayer Money
    Howard Gutman and Andrew G. Durant

Reforming the Jones Act

11. Needed: A Cost-Benefit Analysis of the Jones Act   103
    Ted Loch-Temzelides

12. Time to Mobilize the Dispersed Costs of the Jones Act   109
    Nicolas Loris

13. Reforming the Jones Act for American Energy Consumers   115
    James W. Coleman

14. Why the Jones Act's U.S. Citizenship Quota Should Be Repealed   119
    Daniel Griswold

15. Reforming the Jones Act: What the United States   125
    Can Learn from Canada
    Taylor Jackson

16. Updating the Jones Act for the 21st Century   143
    Keliʻi Akina

17. Looking Back, Looking Forward: 149
    The Historical Lessons for Reform
    Colin Grabow and Logan Kolas

Conclusion   163
Colin Grabow

Notes   173

About the Editors   217

About the Contributors   219

Abbreviations and Acronyms

CBP	Customs and Border Protection
CETA	Comprehensive Economic and Trade Agreement (Canada–European Union)
CFIUS	Committee on Foreign Investment in the United States
CRS	Congressional Research Service
CSIS	Center for Strategic and International Studies
DHS	Department of Homeland Security
DOT	Department of Transportation
EPA	Environmental Protection Agency
FMC	Federal Maritime Commission
GAO	Government Accountability Office
GATT	General Agreement on Tariffs and Trade
GHG	greenhouse gas
ICC	Interstate Commerce Commission
LNG	liquefied natural gas
MARAD	Maritime Administration
NAFTA	North American Free Trade Agreement
NATO	North Atlantic Treaty Organization
NDU	National Defense University
OECD	Organisation for Economic Co-operation and Development
OTA	Office of Technology Assessment
RO/RO	roll-on/roll-off
RRF	Ready Reserve Force
STB	Surface Transportation Board
TEU	twenty-foot equivalent unit
TSA	Transportation Security Administration
USACE	U.S. Army Corps of Engineers
USITC	U.S. International Trade Commission
VLCC	very large crude carriers

Illustrations

Figures

Figure 3.1   Jones Act oceangoing ships   24

Figure 11.1   Economic surplus   105

Tables

Table 4.1   Low tariffs do not deter manufacturing growth   40

Table 7.1   Tonnage and emissions shares of U.S.
              freight traffic, by mode, 2016   69

Table 7.2   Estimated direct and external costs by freight
              Transport mode, cents per ton-mile   72

Table 7.3   Net annual avoided environmental costs,
              millions of dollars   75

Table 10.1   Change in hopper and cutter capacity,
              Belgian-Dutch companies, compared to the
              largest U.S. dredging company, 2004–2017   92

Table 10.2   Trailing suction hopper dredge capacity,
              Belgian-Dutch companies, compared to the
              U.S. fleet, 2017   94

Table 10.3   Cutter suction dredge capacity, Belgian-Dutch
              companies, compared to the U.S. fleet, 2017   95

Foreword

Anne O. Krueger

There is almost no economic policy or policy change that can be made without harming some members of society. In many cases, either compensation is given to the losers or several measures are passed at once so that everyone gets something.

Some policies start or are perpetuated from the pressure of lobbyists when there are few identifiable big winners (special interests) but a large number of losers. While the small number of large gainers can organize and lobby, the cost per consumer is small and opaque. Consumers usually cannot identify each other and organize, and so the cost per consumer goes virtually unnoticed.

Even for sugar, where protection is very high, the costs per consumer per year are no more than a few dollars, and there is little public protest, although sugar producers gain a lot.

The Jones Act is an exception to these generalizations. Passed a century ago, the law benefits almost no one: its presumed beneficiaries are mostly losers; it harms national security; it has driven many shipbuilding firms into bankruptcy; it has caused the size of the U.S. domestic merchant fleet to shrink; and it results in American consumers paying higher prices on most of the goods they consume that are not produced locally.

The Jones Act restricts shipping between American ports, or two points within the United States (called cabotage), to vessels that are U.S.-flagged, deemed U.S.-built, and are at least 75 percent U.S.-owned and -crewed. The proponents and defenders of the Jones Act claim that the purpose of these restrictions is to build and maintain a shipping capacity in the event that it is needed for national security.

In fact, it has done the opposite. In the past century, the U.S. share of worldwide shipping has fallen. Water transport within the United States has shrunk relative to that of land and air: there are few ships of oceangoing size built in the United States because of high costs, and their numbers have declined over time (from 257 in 1980 to 99 as of December 2019). Because shipbuilding is so expensive, shipping companies keep their ships in service long beyond their economic service life and American-owned ships are older and therefore less safe and less fuel-efficient than fleets of other countries.

The Jones Act is one piece of legislation that has harmed almost everyone, including American mariners (who face diminished employment opportunities and are often forced to work on old ships); American shipbuilders (many of whom have gone bankrupt); and American consumers. The requirement that 75 percent or more of mariners be American is partly defended on the grounds that foreign mariners might constitute a security threat when they are in American ports, but oceangoing vessels with foreign crews regularly dock here anyway. While U.S. mariners' wages are higher than those of crews on foreign-flagged ships, there are few jobs for American mariners because so many goods either arrive from overseas on foreign ships or are transported over land because of the high costs that the Jones Act inflicts on waterborne transport.

Water transport would be cheaper than land transport (as it is in other countries) if the Jones Act did not restrict it because there would be more competition, which would lower costs. More water transport would reduce congestion on land (especially along the East and West Coasts), as it would displace some rail and truck traffic. Road and air transport are also more environmentally damaging than water traffic.

The Cato Institute and the authors of the chapters in this volume deserve hearty congratulations for focusing on the Jones Act and its consequences. Many harmful policies raise costs in ways that are, or at least in principle could be, visible to consumers. But the Jones Act spreads invisible harm around to almost everyone. Even the best-informed consumers cannot ascertain how much more their purchases cost because the goods were transported by road rather than water. Also, there are costs to mitigating environmental damage.

The chapters in this volume provide a comprehensive estimate of the reach of the Jones Act's harm and show how ineffective and destructive the effects of the act are. There are economies of scale in shipbuilding: the U.S. industry suffers because large vessels are not built, as shipyards have shrunk and many forced into bankruptcy.

American ports struggle to handle large vessels because the required dredging is not worth it due to high costs imposed by the Jones Act and a related restrictive coastwise law, the Foreign Dredge Act of 1906. Smaller ships raise the cost per unit of goods transported and also prevent oceangoing vessels from foreign countries from docking here.

The number of American mariners has fallen as the volume of waterborne freight has diminished because of the shift to road transport. The noncontiguous American states and territories subject to the Jones Act pay two or three times the cost for obtaining their goods than they would otherwise have to. In Puerto Rico's case, a direct comparison of water freight costs between it and neighboring islands shows that Puerto Rico pays approximately twice as much for water transported goods as its neighbors.

The loss of shipbuilding capacity (especially for larger ships), the shrinkage of the fleet, and the reduction in the number of qualified American mariners have all followed from the Jones Act. These effects and many more are carefully documented in this volume.

The authors have also been careful to describe alternatives to the Jones Act that would be far less harmful to national security and the American economy and ease the dislocation for the few who would be negatively affected. Given the broad sweep of the act's damage, it is to be hoped that concern for the public good will be sufficiently aroused in policymakers so they will begin undoing the damage from this act and craft viable legislation that will allow for the building of a more efficient transportation capability that will produce large benefits for consumers, national security, and the environment.

When a policy harms those it is supposed to be serving, it should be altered. I hope that the evidence in this volume convinces readers that the Jones Act should be repealed.

Anne O. Krueger

Senior Research Professor of International Economics,
School for Advanced International Studies, Johns Hopkins University

December 3, 2019
Washington, DC

Introduction
Inu Manak

Prohibition goes into effect. A radio station in Pittsburgh becomes the first to offer regular broadcasts. F. Scott Fitzgerald's *The Great Gatsby* is published, as well as the first set of stories by A. A. Milne featuring Winnie-the-Pooh. Audiences see the first motion picture with sound. Charles Lindbergh successfully completes the first trans-Atlantic flight. The Nineteenth Amendment to the U.S. Constitution is ratified, giving women the right to vote. What do all these things have in common? They took place in the 1920s.[1]

This was the same time that Section 27 of the Merchant Marine Act of 1920, more commonly referred to as the Jones Act, was passed in Congress. Authored by Sen. Wesley Jones (R-WA), the Jones Act is a weight upon the United States whose burden continues to grow with each passing year.[2]

What is the Jones Act? It's a law that restricts cabotage, which is defined as "trade or transport in coastal waters or airspace or between two points within a country."[3] The Jones Act mandates that vessels transporting goods within the United States must meet four conditions:

- Be *U.S.-built,* meaning that all major components of a vessel's hull[4] and superstructure[5] must be fabricated in the United States, and the vessel must be entirely assembled in the United States.[6]
- Be *U.S.-crewed,* with at least all officers and 75 percent of the crew comprised of U.S. citizens, with the balance comprised of those eligible to work in the United States.
- Be *U.S.-owned,* with at least 75 percent U.S. ownership, and owned by U.S. companies that are controlled by U.S. citizens.
- Be *U.S.-flagged,* requiring vessels to be registered in the United States and to fly the U.S. flag. A vessel must follow the regulatory requirements of its jurisdiction and is subject to inspection by its state of nationality.

The stated purpose of the Jones Act was to ensure adequate domestic ship-building capacity and a ready supply of ships and merchant mariners that can serve as an auxiliary in times of war or other national emergencies. But has it lived up to these objectives?

This volume tackles this question through an assessment of the key assumptions typically made by supporters of the Jones Act. First, we delve into some of the Jones Act's founding myths and the false narrative they have helped perpetuate. Second, we evaluate the costs and assess the impact of the Jones Act on business, consumers, and the environment. And finally, we offer some ideas for a way forward.

In "The Jones Act: A Burden America Can No Longer Bear," Colin Grabow, Inu Manak, and Daniel J. Ikenson provide an overview of both the history and consequences of the Jones Act, showing that it has realized few of its promised benefits. Sheltered from foreign competition, U.S. commercial shipbuilders have become noteworthy only for the ludicrously high prices of the tiny number of ships they produce. This produces a severe disincentive to purchase new ships and has resulted in a withered fleet incapable of meeting the country's economic needs. For instance, no livestock carriers exist in the Jones Act fleet, so cattle ranchers in Hawaii are forced to make do with so-called "cowtainers"— essentially modified shipping containers not used by any other country—or to even send their cows to the West Coast aboard airplanes.[7]

Rob Quartel spells out the "Three Myths about the Jones Act"—that the key purpose of the Jones Act is to bolster national security, that it is critical to the U.S. shipbuilding industry, and that it provides an efficient modern fleet, as well as a maritime infrastructure at the ready disposal of both the military and American shippers. He dispels each of them. In fact, U.S. shipyards have precipitously declined, with approximately 300 closing up shop since 1983.[8] In 1980 there were 257 Jones Act oceangoing ships of at least 1,000 gross tons.[9] This number declined to 193 in 2000,[10] and by the end of 2019 stood at 99.[11] Furthermore, the ships that do exist are significantly older than those found in the fleets of other countries.

Bringing a laser focus to the most persistent myth, Colin Grabow explains in "Rust Buckets: How the Jones Act Undermines U.S. Shipbuilding and National Security," that instead of ensuring an adequate supply of U.S.-flagged ships and a ready pool of mariners to crew them, the Jones Act has contributed to the decline of both, and may have done more to harm national security than to support it. Notably, a 2017 report by the Maritime Administration found that the United States would face a projected shortfall of 1,839 mariners under a sustained wartime scenario, "even under the assumed condition of all those mariners being available and willing to sail."[12]

Bryan Riley rounds out the first section by outlining the protectionist elements of the Jones Act and explains why policies designed to boost the U.S. industrial base are doomed to fail in "What the Trump Administration Can Learn from the Jones Act." As economist and Nobel Laureate Joseph Stiglitz once explained, a study of the Jones Act undertaken by the Council of Economic Advisers during the Clinton administration estimated that each job saved by the law costs Americans $250,000. When asked if there was an economic argument to support the Jones Act, he stated, "Other than an argument of certain special interests, no."[13]

Next, Daniel J. Ikenson turns to the economic costs of the Jones Act in "Dragging the Anchor: A Look at the Myriad Costs of the Jones Act," and brings our attention to both the direct and indirect costs of the law. He identifies six conceptual categories: transportation, environment, infrastructure and repairs, lost wages and lost output, foregone domestic revenues, and foregone export revenues, to illustrate why the costs of the Jones Act are often understated and fail to capture its broader economic impact. A 2019 study by economists from the Organisation for Economic Co-operation and Development gets us closer to a comprehensive analysis of the Jones Act by also taking sectors with upstream and downstream linkages with cabotage services into account. That study estimates that repeal or even partial liberalization of the law, through removal of its domestic-build requirement, could increase U.S. economic output by up to $135 billion and create $64 billion in additional domestic value added.[14] These latter gains are largely the result of benefits to industries that would see their transportation costs reduced, thus boosting their output and domestic value added.

In "By Land or by Sea: Does the Jones Act Cause Land-Based Transport Congestion?," Thomas Grennes explains how the Jones Act has led to the "abandonment of the ocean" by making U.S.-flagged ships uncompetitive. Building a

Jones Act–eligible vessel is incredibly costly. For example, it is four times more expensive to build a tanker in a U.S. shipyard compared to foreign shipyards and up to five times more expensive to build a containership.[15] Liquefied natural gas carriers can be built in Asian shipyards for $180 million, but building comparable Jones Act–eligible vessels are estimated to cost $700 million.[16] What we are left with is increased land-based transport congestion, where the United States stands out as an anomaly among other countries.

In "The Environmental Case for Jones Act Reform," Timothy Fitzgerald explains how the Jones Act affects more than just shipping by scrutinizing the law's environmental impact. He looks at three scenarios and estimates that reforming the Jones Act would avoid environmental costs ranging from $102 million to $8.2 billion.

Manuel Reyes shifts our attention to an outsized victim of the Jones Act, Puerto Rico, in "A Shift Toward Murkiness: How Conflicting Transportation Policies Have Forced Unsupervised Oligopolies on Jones Act Trades in the Past 23 Years." He shows how the Jones Act concentrates business among a few carriers, in effect creating oligopolies. This is most obvious in the Puerto Rico trade, where carriers have even been convicted of price fixing and collusion. Notably, a 2012 report by the Federal Reserve Bank of New York found that shipping a container from New York to Puerto Rico, a route subject to the Jones Act, cost $3,063.[17] Using non–Jones Act ships, the cost of shipping a container a comparable distance, to the Dominican Republic from New York, costs $1,504, and to Jamaica, $1,687.[18] Economist and Nobel Laureate Paul Krugman has also observed that the island's economic problems have been "exacerbated by the Jones Act."[19]

Steve Ellis shows how the decline of coastal shipping provides evidence to support Jones Act critics in "The Jones Act: A Costly Failure." He notes that the downward trend in U.S. coastal shipping has also precipitated a competition among U.S. ports to attract foreign shipping instead. However, even the expansion of U.S. ports has been held back due to the Jones Act and related restrictions on the use of foreign dredging.

Howard Gutman and Andrew Durant take a deep dive into the issue of port infrastructure by looking at how a related law, the Foreign Dredge Act of 1906, has stifled another aspect of the U.S. maritime economy in "Reform the Foreign Dredge Act to Create American Jobs and Save Taxpayer Money." They explain why the Foreign Dredge Act has produced a significant bottleneck in updating port infrastructure and argue that opening up the dredging market to foreign competition could help the United States complete port projects on time and more cost-effectively.

Finally, the volume turns to an assessment of options for reform or repeal of the Jones Act, starting with Ted Loch-Temzelides, who argues in "Needed: A Cost-Benefit Analysis of the Jones Act," that what's been missing from the Jones Act debate is an honest accounting of its costs and benefits. While the U.S. International Trade Commission has conducted several assessments of the Jones Act, with varying estimates, the last report was released in 2002 and no updated estimates have been provided since then.[20]

In "Time to Mobilize the Dispersed Costs of the Jones Act," Nicolas Loris highlights the law's various dispersed costs, using the experience of a rum producer in Hawaii to illustrate how American families and business bear the brunt of the Jones Act's costs. Furthermore, the high costs of Jones Act transport serve to encourage the purchase of foreign products instead of similar domestic ones. A 2013 Government Accountability Office report noted numerous examples of businesses in Puerto Rico purchasing products that included jet fuel, animal feed, fertilizer, corn, potatoes, oil, and gas from foreign sources instead of the U.S. mainland due to the expense and limited availability of Jones Act shipping.[21]

James W. Coleman, meanwhile, explains in "Reforming the Jones Act for American Energy Consumers" how the Jones Act specifically hurts the U.S. energy boom's growth potential and notes some of the Jones Act's perverse consequences for this key sector. For example, the Jones Act fleet has no liquefied petroleum gas carriers or liquefied natural gas carriers. This helps explain why Puerto Rico and New England import gas by ship from Trinidad and Tobago—and even Russia—instead of domestically.[22] And the law's damage doesn't stop there. A 1999 Government Accountability Office report found that it was three times more expensive to ship oil from Alaska to the Gulf Coast than to the U.S. Virgin Islands (which has a Jones Act exemption) despite the voyage taking twice as long.[23]

Taking a look at the less discussed U.S.-crewed requirement of the Jones Act, Daniel Griswold explains "Why the Jones Act's U.S. Citizenship Quota Should be Repealed." He argues that this provision not only drives up the cost of

U.S. shipping, but that it also unfairly discriminates against U.S. residents who are noncitizens but who are otherwise authorized to work in the United States. A 2011 Government Accountability Office report found that in 2009, "maritime crew made about 5 million entries into U.S. ports on commercial cargo and cruise ship vessels," with the overwhelming majority being foreigners. Despite this, "there have been no reported terrorist attacks involving seafarers on vessels transiting to U.S. seaports."[24] U.S. Coast Guard officials have also argued "that they saw no security benefit associated with reducing the number of foreign shippers entering U.S. waterways and ports" because the Coast Guard has "protocols/procedures in place to help ensure safety of the United States from ships coming into U.S. port."[25]

Looking beyond the Unites States, Taylor Jackson asks what we can learn from our neighbor to the north in "Reforming the Jones Act: What the United States Can Learn from Canada." Exploring the history of cabotage restrictions in Canada, he highlights four main features from which the United States might draw, including a more liberal licensing regime, greater transparency, increasing competition in shipping through liberalization of cabotage restrictions in trade agreements, and the establishment of a commission to evaluate the costs and benefits of current cabotage laws, with suggestions for reform.

Next, with a call to action, is Keli'i Akina, whose personal experience of living in Hawaii, one of the noncontiguous states particularly impacted by the law, brings the Jones Act close to home. In "Updating the Jones Act for the 21st Century," he calls for a pragmatic approach to reform coupled with a grassroots effort to educate the public on the costs of the Jones Act and to engage in active discussions on a way forward.

The volume concludes with an exploration of the origins of the Jones Act by Colin Grabow and Logan Kolas in "Looking Back, Looking Forward: The Historical Lessons for Reform." They trace the evolution of U.S. maritime cabotage laws, juxtaposing that experience with the United Kingdom, which opted to liberalize its own cabotage regime. The contrast in outcomes between these two approaches is revealing, and it offers a stark reminder of the adverse impacts of entrenched protectionism, as well as lessons for a way forward.

The resounding conclusion of these essays is that the Jones Act not only raises the costs of shipbuilding but has also presided over the decline of the U.S.

maritime industry. It is a textbook example of cronyism, where concentrated benefits and dispersed costs have saddled American businesses and consumers with a considerable financial burden.

The essays in this volume are in large part the product of a conference held at the Cato Institute in Washington, DC, on December 6, 2018, entitled, "The Jones Act: Charting a New Course after a Century of Failure." Bringing together a diverse range of knowledge on the Jones Act from some of the leading experts on this topic, each of the presenters were asked to contribute to this book by addressing an aspect of the Jones Act relevant to their respective fields. Their submissions were then workshopped on December 7, 2018, and the final product is a result of that exchange. Additional contributors were brought in to round out the subject matter covered to ensure a comprehensive treatment of the topic.

The editors would like to thank the conference participants for their insightful contributions, and the fruitful discussions they have raised. The papers also benefitted from thoughtful questions from the conference audience, as well as comments from a number of academics and practitioners in the field, whose feedback was invaluable. We would also like to thank Logan Kolas for excellent research assistance throughout the course of this project.

To learn more about the Cato Institute's Project on Jones Act Reform, visit our website at www.cato.org/jonesact.

We hope that this volume sparks a broader discussion on reforming the Jones Act. As this book hits print, it is the 100th anniversary of the Jones Act. Let's ensure it does not continue for another 100 years.

Demystifying the Jones Act

1. The Jones Act: A Burden America Can No Longer Bear

Colin Grabow, Inu Manak, and Daniel J. Ikenson

Section 27 of the Merchant Marine Act of 1920 has been a fixture of U.S. law and an imposition on the U.S. economy for 100 years. Better known as the Jones Act, the law was presented as a plan to ensure adequate domestic shipbuilding capacity and a ready supply of merchant mariners to be available in times of war or other national emergencies.[1] The law aims to achieve those objectives by restricting domestic shipping services to vessels that are U.S.-built, U.S.-owned, U.S.-flagged, and U.S.-crewed. A century of evidence supports the conclusion that the Jones Act has failed in its main objectives. And it has failed at considerable cost to the U.S. economy.

Despite these costs and the absence of any measurable benefits, the Jones Act has persisted for 100 years. Why? The answer is complex, but it boils down to the same causes that explain the persistence of rent-seeking behavior more generally. The small number of beneficiaries, which primarily include domestic shipyards and some labor unions, are more powerfully motivated to preserve the status quo than are the far more numerous adversely affected interests in seeking its repeal.

Supporters of the status quo claim that those costs, on the rare occasions they are even acknowledged, are justified by the benefits associated with the Jones Act, which include—most importantly—preservation of a robust, competitive domestic shipbuilding industry to undergird U.S. national security. But such claims are farcical. Over the years, U.S. shipbuilding capacity has atrophied, the active fleet has aged—in some cases into obsolescence—and the number of merchant mariners has dwindled.

Nevertheless, there is a "bootleggers and Baptists" element in play that adds another layer of complexity to repeal efforts. Jones Act supporters have been successful at cloaking their scheme in national security arguments. When all

3

else fails and it becomes obvious that the Jones Act's restrictions significantly burden the economy in a variety of perverse ways, proponents lean on a national security rationale that is entirely without merit. Jones Act opponents—even those advocating limited reforms—are portrayed as unpatriotic, which is evidence enough for some policymakers to tune out arguments based on logic and facts.

The Jones Act has wreaked havoc on the U.S. economy and, after nearly a century of enduring its burdens, it is time to repeal the law once and for all. We make the case for repeal by showing that the Jones Act has failed to achieve its key objectives: not only has it restricted U.S. shipping and contributed to the decline of the U.S. commercial fleet, it has also fallen short of meeting U.S. national security needs.

How the Jones Act Restricts Shipping

The Jones Act restricts foreign vessels from transporting cargo between two points in the United States—an activity known as "cabotage." Most governments have some form of cabotage restrictions.[2] The United States, however, is one of only 11 countries that fully exclude foreign vessels without exception.[3] According to the World Economic Forum, the Jones Act is the world's most restrictive example of global cabotage laws.[4]

Interestingly—or, as some would say, inevitably—in the United States, where foreign competition in cabotage services is restricted, only 2 percent of freight travels by sea. In the European Union, where cabotage among the member states is permitted, the corresponding figure is 40 percent.[5] In Australia, where vessels need not be built domestically to participate in cabotage services, coastal shipping accounts for 15 percent of domestic freight.[6] Meanwhile, after relaxing its cabotage restrictions in 1994, New Zealand experienced a decrease of approximately 20–25 percent in coastal freight rates over the subsequent six years.[7]

Although geographic and other factors account for some of the differences observed in shipping capacity and rates, protectionist cabotage—as well as domestic-build and domestic-ownership requirements—also explain a great deal of the divergences.

As a result of these restrictions, the U.S. economy endures artificially inflated shipping costs because the transport of cargo within the United States is off-limits to foreign competition. Although higher shipping rates are the most obvious cost of the Jones Act, they are merely the first in a cascade of adverse consequences unleashed by the law's restrictions.

Higher prices for waterborne transportation drive down demand for shipping services. When businesses move less cargo by water, shipping companies purchase fewer vessels. Reduced demand means that shipyards build fewer ships and, accordingly, there are fewer employment opportunities for merchant mariners.

Meanwhile, high waterborne shipping rates increase demand for alternative forms of transportation, including trucking, rail, and pipeline services, raising those modes' rates and inflating business costs throughout the supply chain. Transportation expenses—incurred to move raw materials and intermediate goods to the next stage in the production process, and final products to retailers and end-users—comprise a significant portion of the cost of goods sold. Elevated transportation costs affect nearly every business in nearly every industry, rippling through supply chains, squeezing profits, curtailing business investment, disadvantaging U.S. companies relative to their foreign competitors, and depriving U.S. households of savings that could be spent elsewhere in the economy or invested.

Meanwhile, heightened reliance on trucks and freight trains increases not only infrastructure and maintenance costs from wear and tear on roads, bridges, and rail, but it also generates greater environmental costs. Surface transportation produces more carbon emissions than ships do, and because it is used more intensively it increases the likelihood of highway accidents and train derailments involving hazardous materials. Relatedly, time wasted in growing traffic congestion—especially on highways running parallel to U.S. sea lanes—generates enormous opportunity costs from lost wages and lost output.

Significant opportunity costs also can be observed in the loss of revenues experienced when, for example, a hog farmer in North Carolina purchases corn feed from Brazil instead of from a farmer in Iowa because exorbitant delivery costs make the latter's price uncompetitive. But even though some foreign suppliers benefit by happenstance in this manner, the Jones Act has been a persistent irritant to some of our most important trade partners, serving to prevent better access for U.S. exporters to their markets.

A Fleet in Decline

The U.S. shipping industry is the first casualty of the Jones Act. Of course, the primary stated objective of the law was to ensure a vibrant shipping industry as a pillar of U.S. national security. If vibrancy and fleet size were synonymous, Americans might sleep well knowing that the U.S. fleet consists of more than 40,000 vessels. However, we might choose to sleep with one eye open after learning that barges operating primarily on the Mississippi River alone account for 55 percent of that number.

In fact, nearly 9 of every 10 commercial vessels produced in U.S. shipyards since 2010 have been barges or tugboats.[8] Among oceangoing ships of at least 1,000 gross tons that transport cargo and meet Jones Act requirements, their numbers have declined from 193 to 99 since 2000, 79 of which are deemed militarily useful.[9] Even in their expressions of support for the Jones Act, government officials concede that the U.S. shipping industry and its associated ecosystem have been depleted. Appearing before Congress in 2019, Maritime Administrator and retired rear admiral Mark H. Buzby testified that "over the last few decades, the U.S. maritime industry has suffered losses as companies, ships, and jobs moved overseas."[10]

One of the main causes of that decline is the onerous domestic-build requirement of the Jones Act, which prohibits U.S. carriers from operating vessels constructed abroad. U.S.-built coastal and feeder ships cost between $190 and $250 million,[11] whereas the cost to build a similar vessel in a foreign shipyard is about $30 million.[12] Accordingly, U.S. carriers buy fewer ships, U.S. shipyards build fewer ships, and merchant mariners have fewer employment opportunities to serve as crew on those nonexistent ships.

Meanwhile, facing exorbitant replacement costs, ship owners are compelled to squeeze as much life as possible out of their existing vessels. That means the Jones Act fleet is not only shrinking but rapidly aging. The typical economically useful life of a ship is 20 years,[13] yet half of all Jones Act–eligible containerships are more than 30 years old.[14] Excluding tankers,[15] the ships in the Jones Act fleet currently average 27 years old, a full 7 years older than the average age of a ship in the world merchant fleet of other developed countries.[16]

These increasingly decrepit vessels are not only inefficient, but dangerous. A report by a British maritime technology university found that standards and design have improved the safety of ships over the years, but older ships lack these features or are not well maintained over long periods of time.[17] As should be expected, older vessels are more prone to accidents.[18]

Likewise, the U.S. shipyards that produced these aging and increasingly unsafe vessels are in a similarly diminished state. The U.S. Maritime Administration (MARAD) last published annual data on U.S. shipyards in 2004 and noted that there were 89 private shipyards, including 4 public shipyards, 9 active yards, 15 shipyards with build positions that have not produced a ship in two years, 27 repair yards, and 34 top-side repair yards.[19] In 2015 MARAD listed the number of active shipyards at 124 but also pointed out that, of those, only 22 are "mid-sized to large shipyards capable of building naval ships and submarines, oceangoing cargo ships, drilling rigs and high-value, high-complexity mid-sized vessels."[20] This pales in comparison to shipyards in Asia. Japan, for instance, currently has more than 1,000 shipyards, and it is estimated that China has more than 2,000.[21]

Shipyards can be further distinguished by the size of the ships they build. Small and medium shipyards build small and coastal vessels, whereas major shipyards build large and high value-added products, such as containerships, very large crude carriers (VLCC), liquefied natural gas (LNG) tankers, and other large ships. There are only 7 active major shipbuilding yards in the United States, as compared to roughly 60 major shipyards (producing ships over 150 meters in length) in Europe.[22] At under one million gross tons, U.S. shipbuilders' output from 2014–2016 was less than 1 percent of China's and South Korea's shipbuilders.[23]

Not only has U.S. shipbuilding atrophied into global obscurity, but the builders that do operate have become extremely reliant on defense purchases. Of the seven major U.S. shipyards, four produce ships exclusively for the military.[24] Nearly two-thirds (98 of 150) of new vessel orders in 2014 came from the military, which accounted for 70 percent of the shipbuilding and ship-repairing industries' revenues in 2014 and 2015.[25]

The Jones Act's inability to fulfill its purpose only looks set to worsen, given its growing divergence with the realities of modern global commerce. Since its passage, the shipbuilding industry and the ships themselves have undergone vast transformations. When the Jones Act became law, the great shipyards of the world were found in Europe, supply chains were rudimentary, and the loading and unloading of ships was a labor-intensive affair requiring days to complete. Today the vast majority of shipping tonnage is built in Asia, complex global supply chains are prevalent, and global transportation has been revolutionized by the advent of the shipping container. Even the ships themselves have been transformed. Today a 1,300-foot ship with a cargo capacity of more than 18,000 TEU (twenty-foot equivalent unit, roughly equivalent to a shipping container) sails with a crew of 22 and can manage with a mere 13.[26] As recently as the 1960s, crew sizes were twice as large.[27]

Rather than swim against this tide, other countries have adapted. Although the shipyards of Europe no longer churn out large cargo ships as they once did, competition has instead forced them to find unique areas within the industry in which to specialize. As a study produced for the European Commission notes:

> Europe is active in many segments, and—notwithstanding the overall dominance of Korea, Japan and increasingly China—European companies are still dominant in a few specialized market segments such as cruise vessels (99% market share), offshore vessels (43%) and luxury yachts (65%). . . In general, these segments are characterized by a high degree of specialization and high-tech qualities, complex production processes, in combination with limited numbers of vessels of the same type that are to be built. As such Europe's position can be characterized as one of a specialized niche player.[28]

Absent competitive forces, the U.S. shipbuilding industry has not felt compelled to evolve and similarly find its own competitive niche.

Instead of specializing in the production of one, two, or several types of ships and purchasing other vessels from foreign builders more adept at their production—as U.S. firms sensibly do in other segments of the transportation sector and the economy more broadly—U.S. shipbuilders complacently settle for mediocrity across a range of commercial ship classes. This mediocrity is further confirmed by the absence of foreign demand for U.S. ships. Exports from the sector, including repair services, accounted for a mere 4.6 percent of the industry's revenue in 2014.[29]

Yet we are expected to believe that this flailing industry is doing its job to bolster U.S. national security.

Questioning the National Security Rationale

Despite its portrayal by supporters as essential to U.S. national security, the Jones Act's contributions are grossly overstated. The quality and characteristics of the Jones Act fleet are increasingly out of sync with the demands of the military. Moreover, the nature of modern warfare calls the Jones Act's utility into question.

Given the dilapidated condition of the Jones Act fleet, it should come as no surprise that it plays a minor role in supporting overseas military operations. Only a single Jones Act ship was among the 209 U.S. and foreign commercial vessels chartered to transport military materials to Saudi ports during Operations Desert Shield and Desert Storm.[30] In contrast, foreign-crewed and -flagged vessels were enlisted to transport supplies from nearby ports in Israel, Singapore, and the United Arab Emirates. Rob Quartel, a former commissioner with the Federal Maritime Commission, noted that the Jones Act had to be "partially suspended to ensure adequate fuel for the nation's defense."[31]

There is little reason to believe the Jones Act fleet has become any more capable in the years since the Gulf War's conclusion. Noting its "dwindling size," Gen. Darren W. McDew, the head of the U.S. military's Transportation Command until 2018, told Congress that this situation "demands that we reassess our approach to ensure that the [United States] retains critical national security surge sealift capabilities. We may also need to rethink policies of the past in order to face an increasingly competitive future."[32]

In contrast to domestically built Jones Act vessels, foreign-built ships have proven essential to the U.S. military's sealift capabilities. Of the 46 ships comprising the Maritime Administration's Ready Reserve Force—a fleet that helps transport combat equipment and supplies "during the critical surge period before commercial ships can be marshaled"—30 are foreign-built.[33] Though worthy to serve in the country's defense, these same ships are ineligible to engage in coastwise trade.

The irrelevance of the Jones Act to U.S. national security can also be gleaned from the growing divergence between the characteristics of its fleet and the needs of the armed forces. The military, according to the Congressional Research Service, prefers ships with speed and versatility that can "unload diverse cargos in shallow harbors lacking shore-side cranes."[34] Jones Act carriers, in contrast, prefer vessels that operate at slower, more fuel-efficient speeds; are specialized for a particular type of cargo; and are designed to operate in modern port facilities. Meanwhile, increasing specialization within the commercial shipping sector has reduced the likelihood that military requirements can be met by Jones Act ships.[35]

Other aspects of today's military further illustrate the growing divide between the Jones Act and modern realities. At the time the law was written, soldiers were typically transported to the theater of operations in troopships, which slowly ploughed the waves. Today such ships no longer exist. Instead, troops are typically flown to their destinations aboard jet aircraft at hundreds of miles per hour.[36] And with modern conventional wars typically measured in weeks or even days, there is often barely enough time to lay down a keel before hostilities have ended.

Indeed, the goal of ensuring that domestic shipyards are capable of churning out new vessels in times of war to replace losses or add to the country's firepower is also anachronistic. With the exception of some smaller vessels sunk by mines in the Korean War, the United States has not lost a ship to enemy action since World War II. Thus, the value in exacting such a heavy, ongoing toll on the country's economy to promote a domestic shipbuilding capacity—which might be needed in the event of a long, early 20th-century type of conventional war in the future—is increasingly dubious.

Another component of national security is the capacity to respond quickly and effectively to natural and manmade disasters. In this area, the Jones Act again falls short. Rather than serving as an asset in such scenarios, the law actually functions as an impediment by disqualifying ships from providing relief. Theoretically this problem could be mitigated through presidential waivers of the Jones Act, but—believe it or not—protected industries tend to lobby in opposition to any waivers, including those extended for humanitarian purposes. Keith Hennessey, who served as director of President George W. Bush's

National Economic Council, reported that following Hurricane Katrina in 2005, carriers, shipbuilders, and maritime workers lobbied the Bush administration "hard" and "at all levels" against a waiver, demanding shorter timeframes and narrower waiver scopes.[37]

After Hurricane María hit Puerto Rico in 2017, President Trump admitted to being hesitant to grant a Jones Act waiver because "a lot of people who work in the shipping industry . . . don't want the Jones Act lifted."[38] Trump agreed to a mere 10-day waiver, which was not enough time for a Norwegian ship to transport 53 containers of aid from New Orleans to Puerto Rico or for a Dutch vessel, owned by Greenpeace, to carry supplies to the beleaguered island.[39]

Finally, just as the Jones Act has contributed to a weakened response to national emergencies, it has impeded the goal of creating a ready reserve of merchant mariners. The Transportation Institute—an organization that supports the Jones Act status quo—asserts that the law "guarantees a professional and ready force of merchant mariners who are vital to America's ability to supply our military forces" and provides "manpower that the military can call upon during deployments."[40] But those claims are dubious. In recent congressional testimony, a senior union official conceded that "the pool of licensed and unlicensed mariners has shrunk to a critical level" and, absent government action, "the military will no longer be able to rely on the all-volunteer U.S. Merchant Marine as our nation's fourth arm of defense."[41] Already, McDew notes that a protracted need for mariners would "stress the labor pool beyond acceptable risk."[42]

Taking these items into consideration, it is evident that the Jones Act has not lived up to its stated goals, and most alarmingly, has failed to achieve its central objective of maintaining a strong and competitive domestic shipbuilding industry to undergird U.S. national security.

Charting a New Course

By any measure, the Jones Act has been a failure. Under its watch the U.S. shipbuilding industry has atrophied, its domestic fleet has withered, and its contribution to the military's sealift capability has underwhelmed. While failing to meet its intended objectives, the Jones Act has inflicted considerable economic harm through a variety of direct and indirect channels. Rather than serving to bolster national security, the law has stultified domestic ship-building, diminished the size of America's Merchant Marine, and hamstrung our ability to respond expeditiously and effectively to natural and manmade disasters.

Among the world's cabotage laws, the Jones Act stands out for its extreme protectionism. Only a handful of countries require ships engaged in domestic maritime services to be built domestically and none have more onerous restrictions. Moreover, there are no comparably stringent regulations of other means of transportation in the United States. The wave of deregulation that brought renewed efficiency and vitality to the rail, trucking, and airline industries in the 1970s and 1980s left the domestic maritime sector largely untouched.

Accordingly, the U.S. shipbuilding industry is a shambles. Because U.S.-built ships are vastly more expensive than those built overseas, as a result, there are far fewer of them. Indeed, over the past three decades U.S. production of cargo and tanker vessels has typically been in the low single digits[43] and currently averages a mere two to three per year.[44] The high cost of shipbuilding has contributed to an aging fleet, as there is less incentive to invest in newer ships. Typically, a ship has a total life of about 20 years, but half of the U.S. domestic containership fleet is more than 30 years old. Rather than ensure the existence of a strong domestic shipbuilding industry, the absence of competition has discouraged shipbuilders from innovating, keeping up with industry standards, or even building many new ships.

Meanwhile, the higher costs imposed on carriers are passed on to their customers—the intermediate goods-consuming producers, wholesalers, and retailers—who absorb some of the costs and pass the rest on to consumers. Because these costs are dispersed over a broad swath of interests, the per entity incidence is generally not significant enough to make repeal of the law a priority for them. Moreover, the disparate interests and concerns of these downstream entities make it more difficult to appreciate the commonality of purpose in repeal.

That such a burdensome law has evaded meaningful reform for 100 years speaks to the determination of a small, well-organized, well-connected class of producers and unions that have succeeded over the years in portraying any effort to reform or repeal the Jones Act as an affront to national security. The time has come to finally turn the tables and for Congress to repeal this onerous law.

Of course, repeal will not be easy, because after 100 years, incumbent interests, regulators, and politicians get used to the privileges of a system that benefits a concentrated few. In addition to untangling these political alliances, repeal efforts will have to contend with pushback from agencies and committees with oversight authorities that have institutional interest in protecting their jurisdictional turf. No fewer than 16 congressional committees and 6 federal agencies have some form of oversight authority.

Short of full repeal, meaningful incremental progress toward eventual repeal would include relaxation of the U.S.-build requirement so that the economy could at least benefit from the availability of a larger fleet of safer, more efficient, higher-quality vessels. Additionally, permanent Jones Act exemptions for Alaska, Hawaii, Puerto Rico, and other noncontiguous U.S. territories, where the economies are disproportionately dependent upon waterborne transportation, would mark progress. Finally, if those reforms continue to prove elusive, another meaningful incremental reform would be to ensure that the process of obtaining Jones Act waivers is made more liberal, transparent, and predictable.

One thing is certain. The Jones Act is a burden that America can no longer bear.

2. Three Myths about the Jones Act
Rob Quartel

For many Americans, President Trump's order to suspend the Jones Act in the wake of Puerto Rico's devastation by Hurricane María was the first they'd ever heard of the law. The ensuing pushback from the maritime industry—that the Jones Act promotes national security, supports a mighty domestic fleet, creates tens of thousands of American jobs—and all at little to no cost to the nation—no doubt sounded perfectly reasonable.

The industry's origin story and operating rationale, however, are indisputably false.

Myth: The Jones Act's Purpose Is to Bolster National Security

The first and most pervasive myth purported by Jones Act absolutists—whether just in error or as a deliberate conflation—is that the Merchant Marine Act of 1920 and the Jones Act (Section 27) are one and the same. It's an important, stage-setting distinction, because they're not. The result has been to imbue the Jones Act with a purpose it never had.

The Merchant Marine Act of 1920, the product of extensive congressional hearings and debate, was a set of deliberate policy choices aimed at rebuilding a failed American merchant marine and shipbuilding sector after the First World War. The so-called "Jones Act," however, is a handful of words that have taken on the mantle of sacred script—barely touched over the last century—that are embedded in the Merchant Marine Act as Section 27. These provisions were slipped in at the last minute on the floor of the Senate by Sen. Wesley Jones (R-WA), without discussion or debate, and with only the most cursory statement as an explanation.[1]

Curiously, one of Section 27's effects was to eliminate two Canadian steamship lines from serving the Alaskan market, thereby benefitting Seattle-based shipping interests.[2] According to Ernest Gruening, governor of the territory of Alaska from 1939–1953, this was no coincidence. He suggested that Section 27 was designed to "subject Alaska to steamship service owned in the city of Seattle." Senator Jones, Gruening added, "no doubt assumed, and correctly, that this would be most helpful to some of his constituents there, as indeed it proved to be, but at the expense, the heavy expense from that time on, of our citizens without voting rights in Alaska."[3]

And even if evidence exists to support the conclusion that the chief motivation behind Section 27 was to bolster U.S. national security, it is far from clear that it has actually done so. Indeed, the facts tell us a story of failure in every respect—except in the enrichment it provides to the handful of companies and investors to which its monopoly rents flow.

In the two largest overseas conflicts of the last several decades—the 1991 Persian Gulf War and the 2003 Iraq War—the active U.S. merchant fleet played only a small role in operations, and the so-called "Jones Act fleet" was essentially AWOL. Of the 459 shiploads of supplies that were carried from the United States to Saudi Arabia during the Persian Gulf War, 196 of these wartime trips were on foreign-flagged commercial vessels, a mere 62 on U.S.-flagged commercial ships, and the remainder on indigenous U.S. government assets.[4] Only one 23-year-old Jones Act ship—the *Ponce*—made the voyage. The Iraq War saw the U.S. military even less reliant on U.S.-flagged merchant vessels, which delivered a mere 6.3 percent of deployment cargo, versus 13 percent delivered during the Persian Gulf War.[5]

How does the U.S. military actually meet its overseas supply requirements? Airplanes are used to transport personnel and other high value cargo, and large, self-propelled, deep-draft deepwater ships move everything else. A handful of containerships, theoretically available through the Voluntary Intermodal Sealift Agreement subsidy program; numerous qualified deep-draft ships from our foreign allies; the National Defense Reserve Fleet, sometimes called the "Mothball Fleet" (much of which is built overseas); and the other "gray hull" ships (fast sealift, pre-positioned) that are already operating in the government fleet carry the cargo, weapons, and munitions needed to support U.S. troops.[6]

The history of modern wars objectively demonstrates that if ship capacity is crucial, the Jones Act fleet is irrelevant to national security. Furthermore, one could also reasonably argue that the Jones Act actually *undermines* it: restrictions on foreign competition, ownership, and capital investment weaken

America's shipbuilding base by reducing the demand for new ships, further raising the cost of already inefficient production, and increasing prices to an unsustainable level. All of this serves to place U.S. shipyards in a vicious cycle in which they become ever more uncompetitive. The lack of ships and the seamen's billets associated with them, meanwhile, act to reduce available qualified manpower to levels that are only marginally able to support the government's own, more plentiful and reliable ships.

The best proof may just be the facts of the case. The law has been suspended numerous times over the last 35 years for national emergencies—hurricanes, oil shortages, wars, and more—*on the grounds that it was an impediment to national security.*

Myth: The Jones Act Is Critical to U.S. Shipbuilding

By the end of World War II, the United States was the largest producer of big ships on the planet. Even 50 years ago, the United States produced more than 20 ships or more a year for global and domestic commercial markets.[7] In the last two decades, however, the industry has only averaged about 3 tankers or containerships a year, and few commercial vessels of any kind have been sold overseas. Today, the industry's competitive disadvantage is so great that a large commercial ship built in the United States can cost much more than a comparable vessel built in a foreign shipyard.

Shipbuilders and ship operators have long held that this differential comes about because American labor is paid more to support the "American lifestyle"; because Coast Guard regulations require a higher and costlier standard of construction; and, finally, because foreign shipyards receive unfair government subsidies. While many factors have contributed to the decline of the American shipbuilding industry—including global oversupply, recessions, and changing economic conditions—it is simply not true that American shipyard workers are paid more than their foreign counterparts. European and Asian shipyard workers, like others in comparable manufacturing jobs, are today regularly paid more than Americans in direct wages and benefits.[8] Nor, with minor exceptions, can the disadvantage be blamed on U.S. regulatory requirements, which conform to the same rules to which our competitors abide, as set out by international conventions and certification societies.

The foreign-subsidy argument does have some merit, but with a big caveat: the American commercial yards capable of building the large, deep-draft, self-propelled ships that the global markets and the military desire are themselves the beneficiaries of numerous subsidies, including access to high-value military contracts, government operating subsidies to impel demand, low-cost government loans to finance ship buyers—and the protection of the supposedly high-value Jones Act domestic market. But the same shipyards that complain about foreign subsidies sabotaged efforts in the 1990s to eliminate international shipbuilding subsidies.[9]

At the core of this decline is the more serious economic problem: eliminating global market competition and restricting domestic deepwater trade to scarce Jones Act–eligible ships decouples the normal price impact of competition from the market, perversely reducing demand as the unrestrained price for transportation of goods by water rises above the natural market price. Faced with the rising cost of coastwise transport, cargo owners have shifted the transport of their goods from ships to faster and ever more competitive rail and trucks.[10] Higher prices and scarce supply reduce the demand for Jones Act–eligible ships, further shrinking an already limited mix of vessels. As shipyard activity is reduced, the cost of production rises as fixed costs are spread across fewer ships. In a long-running deindustrialization cycle, American-built deep-draft vessels suitable for both commerce and military resupply voyages—self-propelled ships of more than 1,000 tons, not barges—now cost up to five times more than comparable vessels sourced in the global market.[11]

In contrast, the United States has an efficient, productive industry of barge, tug, and service-boat builders and repair yards that can compete in any global market. Interestingly, these yards supported the global shipbuilding talks in the 1990s because they felt they could compete internationally—and because it would give them the opportunity to move up to larger ships. However, due to the Jones Act, their potential growth remains stunted.

Myth: The Jones Act Provides an Efficient, Modern Fleet for Military and American Shippers

The United States does have a huge maritime and port infrastructure, thanks to its status as the world's largest beneficiary of global maritime trade. But we are defined by the world as a "port state," meaning that we lack a significant fleet.

So does the United States actually have 40,000 vessels, as claimed by Jones Act proponents? Let's take a look at the numbers that the Maritime Administration publishes.

In 1950, there were 434 U.S.-built oceangoing self-propelled vessels exceeding 1,000 gross tons in the domestic commercial fleet.[12] By 2000, the Jones Act–eligible fleet consisted of just 193 ships.[13] That number has now shrunk to 99 ships, 79 of which theoretically qualify as militarily useful. Of these, only 24 are containerships; 7 are roll-on/roll-off (RO/RO) vessels (used to move tanks and other large equipment); and only 2 are general cargo ships, both of which are smaller vessels under 3,500 gross tons.[14]

Meanwhile, the Military Sealift Command already has 127 Ready Reserve, pre-positioned, and other gray-hull ships at its disposal.[15] Moreover, if there is a shortfall, our allies can be relied upon to assist us. For example, during the 1991 Persian Gulf War, America's allies provided more than 25 percent of the shipping used to transport American military equipment because there were so few American containerships available to carry cargo on the high seas.[16] The remainder of the Jones Act fleet is comprised of barges, tugboats, tows, and service vessels, none of which would prove useful in a global conflict.

Unfortunately, U.S. fleet economics are driven by capital expenditure: the capital investment required to buy a Jones Act ship is three to five times more than the global market price because American shipyards are so much less efficient than their foreign counterparts. Financing costs are also higher because these buyers have a limited-use case; that is, the ships are too expensive to be resold on the global market, so they have to be sold to or put into use by the limited number of existing Jones Act operators.

Variable costs, such as labor, are somewhat higher, not only because American wages are higher, but because the older ships in the Jones Act–eligible fleet require a large crew. And while fuel is purchased at essentially global prices, Jones Act ships typically require more fuel for their less-efficient engines because they're kept operating decades longer than ships in other developed countries. Older ships also require more repair as they age.[17] It's obvious as well that the aging Jones Act fleet is less safe and environmentally acceptable than the younger fleets of Europe and Asia.

The predictable outcome is a competitive disadvantage for Americans who want to ship to other Americans. Unsurprisingly, the American Maritime Partnership, a leading Jones Act advocacy group, takes a different view:

> The Jones Act is . . . critical to our country's economic security. The 40,000 Jones Act vessels operating in the domestic trades support nearly 500,000 American jobs and almost $100 billion in annual economic impact. An impressive five indirect jobs are created for every one direct maritime job, which results in more than $28 billion in labor compensation. The industry moves close to 888 million tons of cargo every year, which plays an important role in relieving congestion on the nation's crowded roads and railways.[18]

An objective analysis belies these assertions. First, out of those 40,000 *vessels*, less than 100 can be categorized as deep-draft, self-propelled *ships* of more than 1,000 gross tons. The other 39,900 are barges and small service vessels rather than oceangoing ships. Only a fraction of the crewmen on such vessels are qualified to work on the deep-draft, self-propelled ships the military needs in the event of war. This Jones Act fleet of 99 ships, with a generous average of two crews of 25 for each of those vessels, can only be said to support about 3,380 active sailing jobs.[19]

The claim that 9 out of 10 American professional mariners work in the domestic trades is probably true.[20] However, all but a relative handful of these mariners work on small vessels rather than ships, and they do not answer the military's needs in overseas engagements.

So what's the real labor situation? Maritime Administrator Mark H. Buzby, an ardent advocate for the industry, has testified before Congress on numerous occasions that he is concerned that there might not be enough qualified mariners with the required "endorsements," or credentials, to sustain a prolonged activation of the entire sealift fleet beyond an initial four to six months of a sealift surge. He has estimated there to be some 11,700 able seamen, of which the military would need 3,869 to crew government-owned ships, in addition to regular commercial operations. And many of these mariners are retired, with lapsed credentials.

A working group that was convened to look at the problem estimated a shortfall of some 1,800 mariners in the event of a sustained mobilization under a best-case scenario—assuming that all mariners, active and inactive, would report voluntarily when called upon.[21] In addition, the simulation also assumed that there would be no ship losses or personnel casualties, despite the fact that such a mobilization would require uncredentialed and retired mariners to get on board.

It seems the law that destroyed the shipbuilding industry and U.S. commercial fleet has destroyed the jobs that go with them, too. The unfortunate reality is that the same law that has been central to the decline of the U.S. shipbuilding industry and U.S. commercial fleet is also the prime culprit for the shortfall of skilled and able-bodied mariners.

The Jones Act Hurts the U.S. Maritime Industry

Critically examining the common myths of the Jones Act reveals a troubling reality. Unfortunately for its supporters, the truth is that the Jones Act was never intended to support the national interest in war or commerce. In fact, it was enacted only to benefit the political clients of an insular senator from the West Coast. Its restrictions, applied broadly to the rest of the country, have led to the demise of American ships and shipbuilding and the subsequent loss of military support capacity, to the detriment of our national security.

Adding insult to injury, it has also exerted a particular burden on the residents of Alaska, Guam, Hawaii, and Puerto Rico, the last of which counts itself among the poorest U.S. jurisdictions. And it has harmed numerous other American industries along the way, from salt and mining production to timber, agriculture, and more. While the benefits have been concentrated, the costs are diffuse but potent.

Years ago, Sen. Trent Lott (R-LA), an ardent defender of the Jones Act, told the author that whatever the merits of the case, the Jones Act would not fall until Sens. John Breaux (D-LA), Ted Stevens (R-AK), Daniel Inouye (D-HI), and himself were gone. That politicians from Hawaii and Alaska support the Jones Act may seem puzzling. However, it is easily explained: while they face heavy costs, both states are also home to maritime interests that profit from the law's protectionism.[22] The fact that so few people can have such an outsized grip on the whole country points to the cronyism of the law's endurance.

Americans should not have to put up with this. Now is the time to throw off the yoke of this misguided law. In the absence of its requirements—and the

U.S.-built and U.S.-owned provisions in particular—the maritime industry will face direct competition and be better for it. American producers will demand that an increasing share of their cargo gets delivered by water. Truck and train operators will be forced to compete, and the American consumer will benefit from ever more efficient and cheaper transportation.

Our coastal towns and ports will see a resurgence of maritime trade and services, and Americans will grab a larger and larger share of transshipments from efficient international trading vessels. More ships will need more repairs, which means that more American repair workers will learn the latest technologies and eventually transfer those skills to shipbuilding itself. Shipbuilding will eventually increase the size of the fleet and the number of jobs along with it.

For too long, the U.S. maritime industry has suffered from the Jones Act. It's time to be honest about the law's failure and abandon this sinking ship.

3. Rust Buckets: How the Jones Act Undermines U.S. Shipbuilding and National Security
Colin Grabow

Jones Act supporters claim that the law's restrictions on foreign competition help foster a merchant marine and shipbuilding and repair capability that can be harnessed by the United States government in times of war.[1] This is the theory. The reality is quite different.

In the early 1990s, the Jones Act was put to the test. Following Iraq's invasion of Kuwait, the United States rushed soldiers, military equipment, and supplies to Saudi Arabia. Although this military build-up was highly successful, the Jones Act's contributions were marginal at most. Of the 281 Ready Reserve Force[2] and commercial ships chartered by the Military Sealift Command during the conflict,[3] a mere 8 were Jones Act–eligible, consisting of 1 roll-on/roll-off (RO/RO) ship, 1 heavy lift ship, and 6 tankers.[4] Of these 8, only 5 entered the Persian Gulf and only the lone RO/RO, a dilapidated ship called the *Ponce*, transported equipment from the United States to Saudi Arabia.[5]

Rather than the Jones Act ensuring even an adequate supply of U.S.-flagged ships, the United States found itself dependent on foreign-flagged vessels to transport needed equipment and supplies. The United States chartered no fewer than 177 foreign-flagged commercial ships for the Persian Gulf War. Those ships transported 21.2 percent of total dry cargo and 26.6 percent of total unit cargo (U.S.-flagged commercial ships carried 12.7 percent of total unit cargo—cargo specific to particular military units—with the balance transported by government-owned vessels).[6] So desperate was the United States for sealift capacity that it twice requested the use of a Soviet-flagged ship, the *Magnitogorsk*, but was rejected both times.

The situation was little better on the manpower front. The promised pool of Jones Act mariners to crew government-owned ships was found distressingly shallow, producing a scramble to find the needed personnel. As the U.S. military's official history of the Transportation Command's performance during Operations Desert Shield and Desert Storm points out, to crew the Ready Reserve Force required the use of retirees, cadets from the U.S. Merchant Marine Academy, and even raw recruits. This struggle for manpower, the report added, in large part reflected the decline of the U.S. commercial fleet in prior decades and concomitant reduction in seafarers.

The Persian Gulf War was no anomaly. Crew shortages also proved a headache for U.S. logisticians during the Vietnam War. Speaking at the Naval War College in 1969, the commander of the Military Sea Transportation Service,[7] Vice Admiral Lawson Ramage, called the merchant marine manpower pool "barely adequate," adding, "Crew shortages and consequent ship delays have been a continuing problem almost from the outset of the Vietnam escalation."[8]

Downward pressure on the merchant mariner pool has not abated. The Jones Act fleet continues to atrophy, currently standing at a mere 99 ships, as shown in Figure 1.

Figure 3.1

Jones Act oceangoing ships

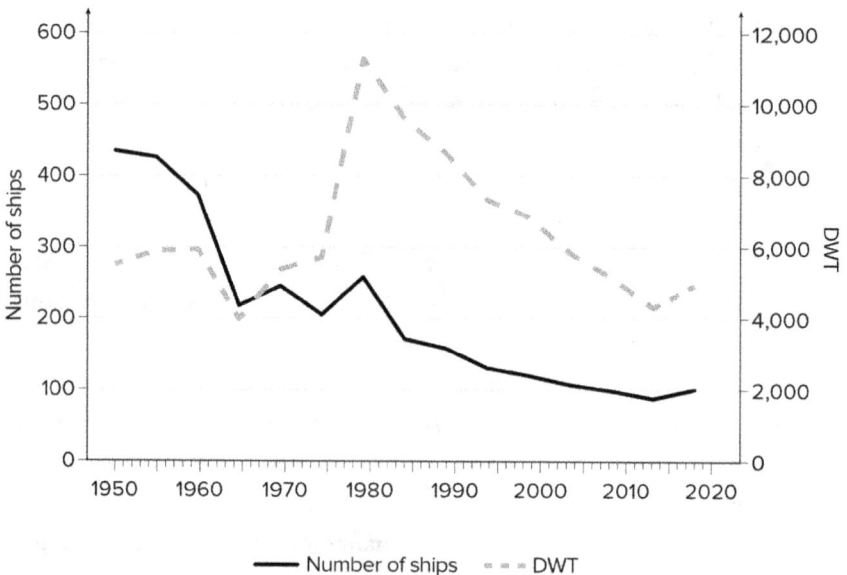

Source: Congressional Research Service, using data from U.S. Maritime Administration (MARAD).
Note: DWT = deadweight tonnage, a measure of ship cargo capacity.

The impact of the Jones Act fleet's decline on mariners was underscored by a 2017 Maritime Administration report, which warned that in a wartime scenario the United States would be at least 1,839 mariners short of the 13,607 needed to perform sustained sealift operations and crew the U.S. commercial fleet.[9] This, however, is a best-case scenario that assumes all mariners with unlimited credentials (i.e., those able to serve on any size ship operating anywhere) are available and willing to crew sealift vessels as well as the U.S.-flagged commercial fleet.

The situation is equally grim on the shipbuilding and repair front. From 1983 through 2013, approximately 300 shipyards closed[10] and shipbuilding employment fell from 186,700 in 1981[11] to 94,000 as of 2018.[12] Today a mere four shipyards in the United States are in the business of constructing large, oceangoing commercial ships.[13] One of those four, the Philly Shipyard, currently has no ships on its order book, and as of July 2019 it is down to approximately 80 employees.[14]

Little wonder that in 2018 the head of the U.S. Transportation Command, Gen. Darren W. McDew, commented that, while the Jones Act was intended to ensure a baseline level of business to support both U.S. shipping and shipbuilding, the domestic fleet's dwindling size "demands that we reassess our approach." The country, he added, may need to "rethink policies of the past in order to face an increasingly competitive future."[15]

The maritime status quo, of which the Jones Act plays a foundational role, appears increasingly untenable.

Jones Act: National Security Asset or Liability

Given these realities, it seems increasingly apparent that the Jones Act's contributions to national security are overstated and diminishing. In fact, there is considerable evidence that the Jones Act is a net national security liability.

The Jones Act's domestic-build requirement means that Americans must buy ships for domestic use that are far costlier than those constructed abroad, as U.S. commercial shipbuilding has degenerated into its current uncompetitive state. This results in fewer ships and fewer mariners to draw upon in times of war or national emergency.

However, Jones Act advocates counter that the provision is ultimately beneficial because it promotes U.S. shipbuilding. But that assertion is mistaken on at least two counts. First, as a 1985 report by the U.S. National Advisory Committee on Oceans and Atmosphere notes, "sealift requirements for the initial stages of a modern major conflict depend more on the sufficiency of U.S.-controlled shipping—and on trained U.S. crews—than on shipbuilding capacity."[16] In other words, in the critical early stages of a conflict, a country's shipbuilding capacity is less important than its ability to mobilize ships and crew—and the Jones Act's domestic-build provision results in less of each.

In addition, it is far from clear that the Jones Act has contributed to a more robust shipbuilding capacity than would otherwise be the case. Recent decades have seen substantial declines in U.S. shipbuilding measured both in terms of the number of shipyards and the workers employed there. This should be entirely expected, given the costly nature of the ships built in these U.S. yards. Such high costs reflect a longstanding qualitative gap between U.S. shipyards and their foreign peers that is a logical consequence of being "protected" from foreign competition.

A 1983 government report authored by the now-defunct Office of Technology Assessment (OTA), for example, noted that U.S. shipyards "generally employed lower levels of technology" than their foreign counterparts and had "not installed the level of modern shipbuilding technology necessary for high productivity in the construction of today's major merchant ships."[17] Comparing U.S. shipyards to those of Japan and South Korea, the report listed numerous ways in which the former fell short, which ranged from inferior levels of research and development to the reduced adoption of automation and robotics.

Two years later, a report issued by the U.S. International Trade Commission, citing shipbuilding industry observers, found that U.S. shipyards "lag behind many of [their] foreign competitors in the use of modular construction techniques, in tooling, in the degree of automation, in the use of robotics, and in the methods of processing, joining, and assembling materials." The report added that U.S. commercial shipyards "require approximately 40 to 60 percent more manhours to construct the same ship as many foreign yards."[18]

A 2001 Commerce Department study provided a similarly gloomy as-sessment, noting that productivity in the U.S. shipbuilding industry had not improved since the mid-1980s and that U.S. shipyards lagged their foreign counterparts in ship construction, design, shipyard layout, and product engi-neering. "Among shipbuilding nations," the report added, "U.S. shipbuilders rank at or near the bottom in terms of productivity, *and the gap is widening* [emphasis added]."[19] A 2009 report issued by the National Defense University (NDU) suggested the picture was little changed. Once again comparing U.S. shipbuilders to those in Asia, the report found the Asian yards offered lower prices, greater efficiency, and had higher industry best-practice ratings.[20]

Three years earlier, an NDU report had also examined the global situation and said that "a company representative [from a leading maritime consulting firm] familiar with the techniques employed by U.S. and European shipyards advised us that the U.S. shipbuilding industry is currently about fifteen years behind in implementing changes that would enhance productivity,"[21] while a 2016 NDU report noted that U.S. shipbuilding is "an average of twenty years behind international shipyards regarding advanced technology."[22]

Notably, both the OTA and 2009 NDU reports suggested that the Jones Act was at least partly culpable for the yawning gap with foreign shipyards. The OTA report noted that, owing to federal shipbuilding subsidies (since discon-tinued) as well as the Jones Act, the United States has become an anomaly in the construction of major merchant ships. As the report states:

> In many other major maritime countries, shipbuilding is viewed on a global perspective. This is not the same in the United States, where only 1 to 2 percent of the world merchant fleet is now built. The U.S. shipbuilding industry is basically quite different from that of Europe, Japan, and Korea. Those countries have built most of today's modern shipping fleets and compete for orders in a world market. The United States does not.[23]

This is completely logical. The Jones Act's U.S.-build requirement has incen-tivized American shipyards to orient themselves away from the competitive international market and toward a captive domestic shipbuilding market. This, in turn, means reduced output (a mere two or three oceangoing ships per year), less competition, and a failure to develop a specialized market niche. All of these missing elements are vital to increased productivity and lowered costs.[24] As the OTA report points out:

> Briefly stated, U.S. yards have never had sufficient volume of merchant ship orders to specialize, to become truly expert, or to develop high efficiency. Flexibility to build many different varieties of ships and other marine equipment has been maintained in U.S. shipyards. Thus, the economies of mass production have seldom been adopted.[25]

The 2009 NDU report laid at least partial blame for the lack of U.S. shipbuilding competitiveness upon "protectionist policies, such as the Jones Act, that have shielded domestic shipbuilders from the pressures of global competition," while a 2007 NDU report sounded a similar note:

> U.S. shipyards are not currently cost competitive in any of the major classes of large ships, and their annual market is limited to the six to ten large Jones Act ships destined for the domestic U.S. trade. Since the total Jones Act requirement is only a small fraction of the output of the largest Asian yards, the U.S. shipbuilding industry is locked in a cost/quantity trap, one that it appears unlikely to escape.[26]

This lack of shipbuilding competitiveness has wreaked havoc within the maritime industry, thus undermining national security. As a 2019 Congressional Research Service (CRS) report notes, the high cost of U.S. shipbuilding has prompted the Department of Defense to reconsider a plan to build sealift ships domestically and instead focus on the purchase of foreign-built substitutes.[27] "I can't afford a lot of $600 million ships. I can't really afford a lot of $400 million ships when I can go out and buy used RO/RO's for $35 to $40 million," said Secretary of the Navy Richard Spencer in May 2019.[28] The head of U.S. Transportation Command, meanwhile, explained the decision to pursue used foreign-built ships during a March 2019 congressional hearing by noting that such vessels cost $25–60 million depending on age. New domestic-built ships, he added, would cost *twenty-six times* as much.[29]

The U.S. military, in other words, has effectively been forced to look abroad to meet some of its ship construction needs because of cost inefficiencies encouraged by the Jones Act. As a 2015 NDU report states, "The Jones Act creates an environment where the U.S. government must pay a premium to buy a world-class navy."[30]

But dependence on foreign-built ships to meet U.S. sealift needs is long-standing. Of the 46 vessels in the Ready Reserve Force, only 16 were constructed in U.S. shipyards. The 60 privately owned ships that participate in the Maritime Security Program are entirely foreign-built.[31] So, the majority of the current putative sealift fleet is foreign-built and the U.S. Navy now plans to continue on the foreign-build path for the foreseeable future, given the destitute state of U.S. shipbuilding competitiveness. This is nearly the exact opposite of what Jones Act supporters claim the law was meant to achieve.

Evidence of the benefits of competition to both consumers and U.S. companies, meanwhile, is abundant throughout the economy. In other forms of transportation not subject to domestic-build requirements—which is to say, *all* other forms of transportation—U.S. firms play leading roles. Within the auto sector, Ford and General Motors are among the world's top five largest automakers[32] and the United States produces more autos than any country except China.[33] Among aircraft manufacturers, the United States is a global juggernaut, with Boeing ranked as the world's largest in 2018.[34]

That Boeing prospers in the absence of a domestic-build requirement is particularly noteworthy given the many similarities between the airline and shipping industries. Both are subject to cabotage restrictions, with foreign-registered airlines prohibited from transporting passengers or goods within the United States (with a limited exemption for Alaska).[35] Like Jones Act ships, U.S.-registered airlines are also required to have at least 75 percent U.S. ownership. Furthermore, airlines play a key role in U.S. national security, with commercial aircraft often relied upon in times of war to transport military personnel. In the Persian Gulf War, for example, more than 60 percent of the troops and 25 percent of the cargo airlifted were aboard civilian airliners.[36] In 2003 nearly 500,000 troops were transported via the Pentagon's Civil Reserve Air Fleet program.[37]

Destined to Fail

The Jones Act's glaring deficiencies do not surprise, given the incongruity between the law's objectives and the means by which it seeks to accomplish them. Based on a theoretical underpinning deeply at odds with modern maritime realities, the Jones Act's failure is merely the law reaching its inescapable conclusion.

Shipping versus Shipbuilding

A desired U.S. capability to construct and repair the large numbers of ships required in a global conflict helps explain the impetus for the Jones Act's domestic-build requirement. By preventing Americans from using foreign-built ships to conduct domestic commerce, the law provides U.S. shipbuilders with a captive market. These U.S.-built ships, however, are vastly more expensive than those produced overseas. This means that the buyers of these ships are footing the bill for what amounts to a massive subsidy to the shipbuilding sector (to the degree that demand even exists for such expensive ships).

Such extremely high price tags limit demand for ships, raise the cost of transporting cargo, and consequently make waterborne transport a less attractive option for moving goods. This, in turn, means fewer ships are available to serve the needs of the U.S. economy and to respond effectively to national emergencies. Meanwhile, U.S. shipyards—and their skilled workers—are themselves harmed as fewer ships means reduced opportunities to perform maintenance, repairs, and upgrade work. Moreover, the dearth of ships frustrates the policy goal of ensuring sufficient numbers of mariners to crew both government-owned and commercial ships in wartime.

The inherent conflict between the protection of U.S. shipbuilding and the desire for robust U.S.-flagged shipping has not escaped the notice of military logisticians. Writing in the *Defense Transportation Journal* in 1993, former commander of the U.S. Transportation Command General Duane H. Cassidy said that if he was king for a day, one of his decrees would be to decouple the U.S.-flagged shipping industry and the shipbuilding industry. "The continued yoking of these two industries stifles competition for both," Cassidy said. "Carriers, to be competitive, need to buy new ships where the market dictates, like any other U.S. business."[38]

Jones Act's Limited Wartime Benefit to U.S. Shipbuilding

One of the Jones Act's advertised benefits—a domestic capability to build large, oceangoing ships during times of war—has proven to be of limited utility. Since the Jones Act's passage, the United States has been in only one conflict, World War II, that required a large increase in shipbuilding. But even here, it is not apparent that the Jones Act contributed much to the country's shipbuilding capacity. Scant commercial shipbuilding took place in the years preceding the war, and a vast expansion of U.S. shipbuilding capacity was required to meet the country's wartime needs.[39] An emergency shipbuilding program announced by President Franklin D. Roosevelt in January 1941—nearly a year before the United States entered the war—for the construction of 260 cargo vessels, for example, necessitated approval for the construction of nine new shipyards.

In many of the other conventional military interventions, such as the 1991 Persian Gulf War, the conflict ended long before a new ship could even have been built had the necessity arisen.

Costlier Ships

When the Jones Act was passed in 1920, U.S.-built ships were estimated to be 20 percent more expensive than those built overseas.[40] Since that time, the cost premium attached to vessels constructed in the United States has risen dramatically. As a 2019 CRS report points out:

> The cost differential increased to 50% in the 1930s. In the 1950s, U.S. shipyard prices were double those of foreign yards, and by the 1990s, they were three times the price of foreign yards. Today, the price of a U.S.-built tanker is estimated to be about four times the global price of a similar vessel, while a U.S.-built container ship may cost five times the global price, according to one maritime consulting firm.[41]

The picture worsens when the time required for construction is considered. A 1981 Government Accountability Office report found that "it takes about 2 years longer to build oceangoing vessels in the United States than overseas,"[42] while a 1985 U.S. International Trade Commission study stated that "U.S.-built commercial ships take twice as long to build and cost two times as much money as many comparable foreign-built vessels."[43] This appears to still be the case, with recent ships built for the Jones Act fleet requiring 35–42 months to construct.

Given such extraordinary cost differentials and the burden they present upon the U.S. maritime sector, it is worth considering whether the Jones Act would be passed by Congress today.

Bifurcation of U.S. Shipbuilding

An important reason given for the Jones Act's U.S.-build requirement is that, presumably, it would help to ensure the existence of shipyards where vessels

31

could be built for the U.S. military.[44] But the degree of overlap between Jones Act commercial shipbuilding and naval shipbuilding is not nearly as great as many observers may believe. As a 2019 report from the Center for Strategic and Budgetary Assessment notes, "most shipyards that build larger U.S. Navy and Coast Guard ships do not generally construct commercial vessels."[45] Of the country's three major commercial shipyards, only one—General Dynamics NASSCO—constructs both large naval (noncombatant) and commercial ships. The Philly Shipyard, which has built approximately half of all large oceangoing Jones Act commercial ships since 2000, does not build any military vessels.[46]

A 2019 analysis performed by scholars at the American Enterprise Institute calculated that, for the six companies that have built naval and commercial vessels since 2000, Jones Act merchant vessels accounted for a mere 5 percent of orders (by the number of ships).[47] This finding dovetails with a 2013 Government Accountability Office report that noted the vast majority of military vessels are built at seven major shipyards, some of which "also construct a small number of commercial vessels."[48]

There is little reason to think this will change, given the increasingly distinct nature of commercial and naval shipbuilding. As a 2001 Commerce Department report notes, "The technical specialization applied to a naval vessel is not applied to commercial ships, and the technology in both fields is advancing to such an extent that the two modes of construction are growing increasingly segregated."[49]

U.S. Dependence on Foreign Ships, Components, and Know-How

Jones Act supporters may be tempted to believe that the high cost of U.S.-built ships is a small price to pay for freeing the United States of dependence on foreign shipbuilding, but this "independence" is illusory. To comply with the Jones Act's domestic-build mandate, ships must be assembled in the United States and all major components of the hull and superstructure must be fabricated domestically.[50] This means, however, that other key parts of a ship can be—and often are—produced abroad. Even the steel plating used in a vessel's construction can be of foreign origin, provided it is delivered in "standard mill shapes and size."[51]

A containership built by the Philly Shipyard last year, the *Daniel K. Inouye*, serves as a good example. While Jones Act–eligible, the ship includes numerous components sourced from foreign firms, such as the main generator engines and propeller (Hyundai Heavy Industries, South Korea); steering gear (Rolls-Royce, United Kingdom); auxiliary boiler (Alfa Laval, Denmark); propulsion engine (MAN Energy Solutions, Germany); and maneuvering thruster (Kongsberg Maritime, Norway).[52]

Beyond components, foreign know-how is also frequently required to construct many of the Jones Act fleet's large ships. In 2006, one of the few U.S. shipyards that builds large oceangoing ships, General Dynamics NASSCO, signed a partnership agreement with Daewoo Ship Engineering Company that would see the South Korean firm "provide the detail designs, support services and some of the material necessary for ship production."[53] The fruits of this agreement are readily apparent, with Daewoo serving as the design agent for the Kanaloa-class ships currently being built at the shipyard.[54] Philly Shipyard's 2018 annual report, meanwhile, highlights its "access to global shipbuilding and design expertise with partners in Asia and Europe."[55]

Yards in the United States may be engaged in limited construction of oceangoing commercial ships—albeit at frightfully high costs that would be even higher absent their access to foreign components—but it is an open question just how truly American these ships are or how meaningful the practical difference is between manufacturing these ships in the United States and buying them from foreign yards.[56]

Also implicit in the Jones Act's logic is that a premium should be placed on U.S. self-reliance for its shipbuilding and repair needs in time of war. Such thinking, however, ignores the fact that U.S. defense allies, particularly Japan, South Korea, and members of NATO, are some of the world's leading shipbuilding countries. As a 2006 NDU report points out:

> Another argument against overseas construction of naval ships is that access could be taken away, leaving the U.S. without the capacity to build ships when needed. This is unlikely since there are many yards that are allies, and it is unrealistic to assume all of them would simultaneously turn down revenues and deny access. [57]

It's also worth pondering whether in conflicts with either China or Russia (cited by the 2017 National Security Strategy of the United States of America as "challeng[ing] American power, influence, and interests"), the United States would send its damaged ships to be repaired in the nearby shipyards of allied countries in Europe and Northeast Asia rather than having them limp or be towed back across the Pacific or Atlantic Oceans.[58]

Questionable Wartime Utility of Jones Act Ships

For the Jones Act–eligible ships that are assembled in U.S. shipyards, it is unclear how much benefit they offer in a wartime scenario. Built for commercial purposes, their capabilities do not always align with those demanded by the U.S. military. As a 1984 Congressional Budget Office study noted, "[T]here is a growing dichotomy between those features that produce a commercially efficient ship and those that yield ships more useful for support of military operations."[59]

This gap between military and commercial needs appears to have only widened in the years since the Congressional Budget Office report was first authored. A 2016 NDU report, for example, noted that the ships needed to transport military personnel and cargo "do not always line up with the vessels demanded by the market for moving commercial merchandise across the waterways."[60] A 2015 CRS report, meanwhile, pointed out that "the trend toward highly specialized and larger ships in the commercial sector appears inconsistent with the military's shipping needs."[61]

This divide between military and commercial shipping needs appears particularly pronounced in terms of U.S.-built ships—the basis of the Jones Act fleet. Indeed, a 2010 CRS report flatly stated that "very few commercial ships with high military utility have been constructed in U.S. shipyards in the past 20 years."[62] Consequently, when the Military Sealift Command has the need to charter a vessel, the report added, "nearly all of the offers are for foreign-built ships."

Given such facts, it's perhaps not surprising that the CRS speculated in its 2015 report that the military value of the U.S. Merchant Marine—of which the Jones Act fleet is a key component—"may now have more to do with the crews than with the ships themselves."

Limited Ship Availability

Further evidence for the devalued importance of Jones Act ships in a national security context is the limited availability of such vessels. Despite the pressing need for sealift during the Persian Gulf War, only a single Jones Act ship, the

Ponce, was taken out of commercial service to support the military's logistical needs. The reason for this may be that the limited number of Jones Act ships had to remain at home because they were vital to the country's domestic transportation needs. This is particularly true in the case of its noncontiguous states and territories, where the fleet's container and RO/RO ships exclusively operate. Thus, pulling ships from those trades could introduce considerable havoc through the disruption of key supply linkages for the inelastic necessities that provide the basis for employing these costly ships.

It is for this reason that even defenders of the Jones Act admit to the limited wartime utility of such vessels. "Today the only [commercial] ships being build (sic) in the U.S. are those destined for Jones Act routes," admits Loren Thompson, chief operating officer of the Lexington Institute. "That is not a lot of vessels, and if war broke out most of them would already be engaged in other tasks."[63]

Conclusion

With the number of shipyards, ships, and mariners all in decline, the Jones Act can only be described as a massive policy failure. Worse, the law has produced an outcome that is perilously at odds with its stated goals. Policymakers must consider either major reform of the law or outright repeal. The law's failure was an utterly predictable consequence. Conceived in discredited protectionist fallacies, the Jones Act deprives U.S. shipbuilding of the most essential ingredient of continuous improvement and innovation: vigorous competition. The law effectively has condemned U.S. shipbuilding to second-rate status, which becomes more apparent with each passing decade. Meanwhile, a country whose geography would seemingly make it destined for maritime commercial greatness has a domestic fleet whose size and strength continues to plumb new depths.

4. What the Trump Administration Can Learn from the Jones Act
Bryan Riley

The Trump administration has proposed several policies that are intended to boost the U.S. defense and industrial base, including Buy American directives and restrictions on imported steel and aluminum.[1] The Jones Act provides a lesson on how such economic controls can backfire.[2]

The Jones Act is described by the U.S. Department of Homeland Security as a protectionist policy that is intended to promote and develop the U.S. Merchant Marine and U.S. shipbuilding.[3] Protectionist elements of the Jones Act include requirements that ships transporting goods within the United States must be U.S.-crewed, U.S.-owned, and U.S.-built. These provisions are unnecessary and counterproductive.

U.S. Crews

Jones Act defenders claim that requiring the use of U.S. crews for domestic waterborne shipping protects Americans against foreign terrorists and spies freely traversing the Mississippi River disguised as ship operators.[4] This is largely a scare tactic. With or without the Jones Act, it is illegal for someone to work in the United States without a permanent resident card (green card), a work permit, or an employment-related visa.[5] This is true whether they are transporting merchandise between U.S. ports or whether they are employed in any other job.

U.S. Ownership

The Jones Act's requirement that ships transporting goods between two points in the United States must be U.S.-owned deprives the industry of beneficial foreign investment. Areas of the economy that are open to foreign investment account for 7.1 million jobs in the United States.[6] As other analysts have pointed out, removing ownership limits would provide more opportunities for Americans who are involved in domestic waterborne transportation to benefit from job-creating foreign investment.[7] As with foreign investment in other U.S. industries, ownership of vessels providing waterborne transportation would be screened by the Committee on Foreign Investment in the United States to mitigate national security risks.[8] Additionally, it has been argued that modern ownership arrangements render the Jones Act's ownership requirement obsolete.[9]

U.S. Construction

The most criticized element of the Jones Act has been its ban on the use of foreign-built ships for domestic shipping. This is a unique regulatory barrier. No similar restrictions apply to the domestic transportation of merchandise by air, rail, or truck. As a result, Americans pay inflated prices for ships. According to a 2019 Congressional Research Service report, containerships built in the United States can cost five times more than comparable foreign-built ships.[10]

Does the Jones Act Promote Shipbuilding?

The argument made by proponents of the Jones Act is simple: the United States needs a strong shipbuilding industry, and the way to realize this goal is by freeing the industry from the obligation to compete with foreign shipbuilders.

But even if the first part of that statement is accurate, the second part is not. High tariffs don't make industries stronger, and often they actually make them weaker. As President Woodrow Wilson explained:

> One of the counts of the indictment against the so-called "protective" tariff is that it has robbed Americans of their independence, resourcefulness, and self-reliance. Our industry has grown invertebrate, cowardly, dependent on government aid. When I hear the argument of some of the biggest business men in this country, that if you took the "protection" of the tariff off they would be overcome by the competition of the world, I ask where and when it happened that the boasted genius of America became afraid to go out into the open and compete with the world?[11]

Economist Thomas Grennes noted in a research paper for the Mercatus Center that by restricting competition, the Jones Act reduces the incentive for U.S. shipbuilders to innovate.[12] More generally, as comedian Adam Carolla observed: "American car companies have never been better, and don't tell me you . . . wouldn't be putting out Matadors and Gremlins 25 years later if it wasn't for the Camry and the Sentra."[13]

Protectionist Tariffs Don't Protect Jobs

There are plenty of examples demonstrating how protectionist policies such as the Jones Act fail to protect jobs. For example, the United States imposes very high taxes on imported clothing. As of 2017, the average U.S. tariff on clothing—technically, "articles of apparel and clothing accessories"—was 13.7 percent, while the U.S. tariff on other goods was less than 1 percent.[14]

These high tariffs didn't protect the labor-intensive jobs of clothing makers. Since 1990, U.S. employment in apparel manufacturing has dropped by 88.2 percent.[15]

Similarly, as National Taxpayers Union Foundation policy analyst Andrew Wilford has pointed out, the U.S. ban on the use of foreign-built vessels for domestic shipping hasn't prevented a decline in nonmilitary shipbuilding.[16] According to the U.S. Maritime Administration, the Jones Act–eligible ocean-going vessel fleet declined from 193 to 99 ships between 2000 and the end of 2019.[17]

Planes, Trains, and Automobiles (and Trucks and Boats)

Some of the strongest transportation manufacturing industries in the United States operate in a low-tariff environment.[18] As Table 1 shows, U.S. production of aircraft, railroad rolling stock, automobiles, and heavy-duty trucks has been increasing, even though the government does not force Americans to use U.S.-built planes, trains, or automobiles when transporting cargo, as it does with ships.[19]

Moreover, the average tariff rate for imported recreational boats is just 1 percent, but 95 percent of the recreational boats sold domestically are made in the United States.[20] Clearly, American manufacturers don't require high tariffs to be successful—in fact, their success may be contingent upon low barriers that encourage them to innovate and compete.

Table 4.1 Low tariffs do not deter manufacturing growth

	Average import tariff rate, 2017 (percent)	Increase in annual production, 2000–2016 (percent)
Planes	0.0	109
Trains	1.4	62
Automobiles	1.3	44
Trucks	0.3	36

Source: Author's calculations from U.S. International Trade Commission and Bureau of Labor Statistics data. The average tariff rate was calculated by dividing the duty revenue by the import value for each good.

Shipbuilders Like Imports—Just Not for Their Customers

The Jones Act's requirement that ships transporting cargo must be U.S.-built is somewhat misleading. In fact, as the Cato Institute's Colin Grabow has pointed out, ships can be considered U.S.-made even though many of their components are imported.[21]

This turns out to be a loophole big enough to steer a ship through. All the nonmilitary oceangoing vessels assembled in the United States in recent years relied on imports, ranging from the engines to the very specifications on how to build a ship. Consider these examples of recent "U.S.-built" vessels:

- San Diego's National Steel and Shipbuilding (NASSCO) partnered with Korea's Daewoo Ship Engineering Company (DSEC) to design its commercial ships.[22] In 2016, NASSCO received a $511 million order to build two new ships.[23] Of this, $120 million reportedly went to DSEC to design the ships and provide supplies.
- VT Halter Marine's *El Coqui* containership was built with plans from European-based Wartsila Ship Design: Wartsila reported that it "has a very professional and dedicated team mainly located in Poland and Norway which is working very closely with VTHM (VT Halter) and CM (Crowley Maritime)."[24] The *El Coqui's* engines were also imported.[25]

- Norwegian-owned Philly Shipyard has produced several tankers based on a Korean Hyundai Mipo Dockyards design.[26] Four of the shipyard's American class tankers built in 2016 and 2017 rely on imported engines.[27]

However, newly built ships can fail to attain U.S.-built status if they use too much foreign steel. Two U.S. companies based in the state of Washington learned this the hard way when they ran afoul of the Jones Act.[28] The fishing company Fisherman's Finest commissioned a new ship from Dakota Creek Industries.[29] However, because 7 percent of the ship's steel was cut and bent in the Netherlands, the ship was not allowed to fish in U.S. coastal waters. A coalition of companies successfully lobbied Congress for approval of a Jones Act waiver to allow the ship to operate in the United States.[30] A better approach would be to eliminate the Jones Act's protectionist Buy American requirements.

There is nothing wrong with shipbuilders using the highest quality inputs, regardless of where they are made. The problem is that the Jones Act deprives their customers of the same opportunity.

No Legitimate National Security Justification for the Jones Act

George Will inimitably wrote: "Fomenting spurious national-security anxieties is the first refuge of rent-seeking scoundrels who tart up protectionism as patriotism when they inveigle government into lining their pockets with their fellow citizens' money."[31] A recent National Taxpayers Union Report, "Protectionism Will Not Improve National Security," explains how protectionist policies such as the Jones Act make America weaker.[32] Trade barriers undermine U.S. security by weakening the economy and creating conflict with our allies. Earlier this year, more than 1,100 U.S. economists reiterated a call from economists in 1930 who wrote: "A tariff war does not furnish good soil for the growth of world peace."[33]

Instead of lobbying to maintain government protection from competition, shipbuilders and boat manufacturers should unite to oppose an increasingly costly and dangerous trade war that is driving up their cost of steel and aluminum, while simultaneously reducing the amount of cargo for them to transport. Headlines such as these are appearing with increasing frequency:

- American shipbuilders brace for impact of tariffs on steel, aluminum[34]
- American boat makers feel the crunch from Trump tariffs[35]
- U.S. ports criticize Trump's planned steel, aluminum tariffs[36]
- Shipbuilding, LNG may feel sting from Trump tariffs[37]
- Barge traffic could be hurt by Trump tariffs, economist says[38]
- Trump's steel tariff could affect defense shipbuilders[39]

The Jones Act has reached its 100th anniversary. Instead of receiving unending protection from international competition, shipbuilders should operate in the same low-tariff policy under which manufacturers of trucks, automobiles, aircraft, and other industries are thriving. The Jones Act should not be allowed to inflict another 100 years of damage on the U.S. economy.

The Costs of the Jones Act

5. Dragging the Anchor: A Look at the Myriad Costs of the Jones Act

Daniel J. Ikenson

In 2018, the Cato Institute published "The Jones Act: A Burden America Can No Longer Bear," which was the first in a series of papers that aims to awaken Americans to the imperative of ending one of the most expensive, distortionary, protectionist—yet still ongoing—mistakes in U.S. history.[1] That paper, which appears as the first chapter in this book, examines the history of the Jones Act, describing how it was originally sold as a plan to ensure a domestic shipbuilding capacity and military access, in times of war or other national emergencies, to a reliable and diverse fleet of ships and a ready reserve of mariners to crew them.

Describing the continuous decline in the types and number of ships built in America's disappearing shipyards, the dwindling number of U.S. mariners, the government's recurring dependence on foreign sealift capacity during national emergencies, and the absence of any compelling evidence that the law actually supports national security, the paper concludes that the Jones Act has failed to serve its purpose.

In the course of that failure, the Jones Act has saddled the U.S. economy with a variety of costly problems that should have been foreseen and could have been avoided, but that have only grown worse over time. This chapter summarizes those problems and illustrates how they weigh on the economy.

Various economic studies on the costs of the Jones Act have focused predominantly on the distribution of rents among the shipbuilders (manufacturers of ships); the carriers (service companies that purchase and lease ships); and the shippers (suppliers/owners of cargo being shipped). Protecting domestic shipbuilders from foreign competition raises the cost of ships to domestic carriers. Restricting shipping routes exclusively to domestic carriers who are compelled to use domestic labor raises the cost of transportation to domestic shippers. But these are only the immediate costs of the Jones Act.

First, transportation costs, which are affected by the costs of shipbuilding, the costs of owning and operating ships, and the viability of alternative forms of transport, are passed down the supply chain to manufacturers, wholesalers, retailers, and consumers. Second, when cargo is diverted from water to highways, railways, and airways, there are additional environmental costs to consider. Third, substituting maritime transport for road and rail exacerbates wear and tear on U.S. transportation infrastructure, which raises the cost of maintenance and repairs. Fourth, when the roads become increasingly congested, the cost of lost wages and lost output due to traffic delays must be considered. Fifth, when the cost of domestic transportation is so high as to make it more economical for U.S. businesses to sell to foreign customers and purchase from foreign suppliers what they could otherwise sell or purchase domestically, those foregone domestic sales are opportunity costs that must be taken into account. Sixth, when foreign governments choose to restrict the access of U.S. exporters to their markets because the U.S. government insists on insulating its domestic shipbuilding and waterborne transportation industries from competition, those foregone revenues must also be taken into consideration.

A comprehensive analysis of the costs of the Jones Act must consider all the major costs induced by the statute's requirements that domestic cabotage be restricted to vessels that are U.S.-built, U.S.-flagged, at least 75 percent U.S.-owned, and at least 75 percent U.S.-crewed. In this chapter we will examine six broad cost categories: transportation, environmental impact, infrastructure and repairs, lost wages and lost output, foregone domestic revenues, and foregone export revenues. This chapter does not include an analysis of other costs, including those related to national security unpreparedness, dependence on foreign-flagged ships to transport materiel to war zones, the loss of life due to traffic accidents, the environmental catastrophes caused by hazardous-material derailments, or other categories of costs.

Transportation Costs

The law mandates that only U.S.-built ships can transport goods between two points within the United States (this service is known as "cabotage"). Because they face no competition from foreign shipbuilders to build vessels to serve the domestic market, U.S. shipbuilders have less incentive to produce efficiently or price competitively. The evidence overwhelmingly supports this all-too-predictable outcome.

The cost of building a ship in the United States is significantly higher than nearly anywhere else in the world. Estimates of differentials vary and depend on the type of vessel in question. According to a 2019 Congressional Research Service report:

> A 1922 government report on shipbuilding concluded that U.S.-built ships cost 20% more than those built in foreign yards. The cost differential increased to 50% in the 1930s. In the 1950s, U.S. shipyard prices were double those of foreign yards, and by the 1990s, they were three times the price of foreign yards. Today, the price of a U.S.-built tanker is estimated to be about four times the global price of a similar vessel, while a U.S.-built container ship may cost five times the global price....[2]

In some cases, the cost differential is smaller, and in other cases it's even greater. Consider these examples. In 2017, two Chinese shipyards won contracts to build nine 22,000 twenty-foot equivalent unit (TEU) containerships for a French carrier at a total cost of $1.44 billion (TEU is a twenty-foot equivalent unit of container capacity).[3] That averages out to $160 million per ship, or $7,273 per TEU. In 2018, Hyundai Merchant Marine signed a $2.8 billion contract with South Korean shipbuilders for 20 ships with a collective cargo capacity of 396,000 TEUs—a cost of $140 million per ship, or $5,800 per TEU.[4] In early 2019, Philly Shipyard delivered the second of two 3,600 TEU Jones Act ships to carrier Matson, under a contract totaling $418 million—a cost of $209 million per ship, or $58,056 per TEU.[5] On a per-TEU basis, these U.S.-built ships were 8 times more costly than those built in China and 10 times more costly than those built in South Korea.

In recent years, the United States has become a major global supplier of oil and natural gas. But U.S. shipyards cannot build and sell oil tankers or liquefied natural gas (LNG) ships at competitive prices. Domestically built tankers are estimated to be about four times the price of foreign-built tankers, and there is limited capacity in U.S. shipyards to build them anyway. Meanwhile, the price of a U.S.-built LNG carrier is estimated to be $700 million, which is nearly four times the $180 million it costs to purchase one built in an Asian shipyard.[6] No LNG carriers have been built in the United States since 1980.[7]

That's instructive. The key differential in shipbuilding costs is volume. The captive Jones Act shipbuilding market is small, with only two or three large oceangoing ships typically built per year.[8] Building fewer ships prevents U.S. shipyards from realizing economies of scale, which is essential to reducing unit costs.

In contrast, U.S. barge production is vibrant, with U.S. shipyards delivering approximately 1,000 barges and 70 tow/push boats per year, which provides scope for economies of scale. The existing barge fleet includes nearly 4,000 tow/push boats and about 22,000 barges operating on the Mississippi River system alone.[9] Why? Barges operating on U.S. internal waterways face competition from rail and trucks, which puts pressure on barge producers to keep costs down and so helps keep up the demand for barges.

Given the high prices needed to cover the enormous costs of U.S.-built ships, why would U.S. carriers even bother to purchase them? To be sure, they don't buy very many. But if and when they do, it is because the Jones Act's restrictions on cabotage services provide enough artificial incentive for U.S. carriers to defy the economics. With no foreign competition permitted to serve this market, Jones Act carriers are free to charge exorbitant rates to recoup the excessive costs of acquiring and operating their statutorily mandated U.S.-built ships. In addition to the higher capital costs inherent in purchasing higher priced American vessels, there are also higher costs of operating them.

Numerous examples show the freight rates charged by these carriers to be double or even triple those charged to ship similar volumes over similar distances in voyages involving a foreign port, where the Jones Act does not apply. Consider shipping rates between the continental United States and Puerto Rico. According to a 2012 report from the Federal Reserve Bank of New York, it costs an estimated $3,063 to ship one TEU of household and commercial goods from the East Coast of the United States to Puerto Rico; the same shipment costs $1,504 to ship to nearby Santo Domingo, Dominican Republic, and $1,687 to ship to Kingston, Jamaica—destinations that are not subject to Jones Act restrictions.[10]

Moreover, the shipping costs to Puerto Rico from the East Coast only represent a fraction of the transportation costs for shippers transporting goods from, say, the West Coast. Those shippers must first get their cargo to one of the few ports offering Jones Act service to Puerto Rico (Jacksonville; Houston; or Pennsauken, New Jersey). This must necessarily be done by land, as waterborne container service does not exist between the West Coast and the Gulf of Mexico or between the West and East Coasts. In contrast, West Coast shippers can put their cargo on the water in nearby ports, such as Seattle or Los Angeles, and have it transported by water to Santo Domingo or Kingston.[11]

The small Jones Act fleet, beset by high shipbuilding costs, includes a mere handful of containerships and has almost totally abandoned the coastwise trade along the Atlantic, Gulf, and Pacific Coasts. Instead, Jones Act carriers' resources are devoted almost entirely to the noncontiguous routes (Alaska, Hawaii, and Puerto Rico), where they face no competition from trucks or trains.

These exorbitantly high U.S. rates—in conjunction with a near-total absence of containerized waterborne transport along the coasts—encourage shippers to take their cargo out of the water and move it on highways or by rail or air. As a result, greater demand for trucks, trains, airplanes, and pipelines increases the rates of those modes for all businesses that move merchandise to retail outlets, inventory to warehouses, and intermediate goods to manufacturing facilities. In other words, because a shipper who would choose to move his cargo from Boston to Miami by coastal vessel is, under market conditions, compelled by the exorbitant rates (or the absence of service) to use trucks instead, that non-market demand serves to increase truck rates for all shippers, including those for whom trucking may be the *only* choice, such as those shipping from, say, Boston to Syracuse.

The dynamics described above—protected shipbuilders producing higher-priced ships for protected carriers, which beget higher waterborne shipping rates, which beget higher surface transportation rates—all contribute to higher U.S. transportation costs. Those inflated freight expenses increase the costs of production for U.S. manufacturers and the cost of living for U.S. families be-cause, inevitably, they are passed down the supply chain and reflected in higher input costs and higher retail prices.

According to calculations from data obtained from the Bureau of Transpor-tation Statistics, businesses, government, and households incurred $2.2 tril-lion of transportation services in 2017.[12] That intermediate input is needed to deliver raw materials and components to factories and finished products to warehouses, wholesalers, retailers, businesses, and residences. The Jones Act inflates those transportation costs and puts U.S. businesses at a disadvantage relative to foreign competitors, while reducing real household income. Conservatively, if the Jones Act explains a mere 1 percent of those costs, getting rid of the law would free up $22 billion to be deployed more efficiently elsewhere in the economy.

Meanwhile, the diversion of cargo from water to land and air generates other unavoidable costs.

Environmental Costs

Cargo transported on trucks, trains, and airplanes generates significantly more carbon and other greenhouse gases than does cargo transported on ships. As to emissions of other pollutants and particulate matter, trucks are dirtier—and trains slightly cleaner—than ships. However, because the impact of these kinds of emissions are localized—the adverse health effects depend on their proximity to where people live and work—voyages by ship are less environmentally damaging because large portions of the routes are out at sea and traverse populated areas less often than rail transport.

According to a 2011 Government Accountability Office analysis, trucks emit 229.8 tons of CO_2 equivalents[13] per million ton-miles, trains emit 28.96 tons per million ton-miles, and ships emit 17.48 tons per million ton-miles.[14] In other words, the average truck generates more than 13 times the amount of carbon emitted by ships, while trains produce about 66 percent more carbon than ships.

In addition to these greenhouse gases, trucks generate higher levels of particulate matter and other pollutants than do ships. Relative to ships, trucks emit 10.2 times more particulate matter and 6.4 times more nitrogen oxide, while trains generate 54 percent more particulate matter and 44 percent more nitrogen oxide.[15]

Furthermore, trucks burn far more fuel than trains or ships. On a ton-mile basis, due to their buoyancy, ships are far more efficient users of energy than trucks. And ships powered by natural gas—which technology and regulation promote but the Jones Act deters—consume no petroleum and emit much less air pollution. As scholar Timothy Fitzgerald explained in a March 2020 paper published by the Cato Institute:

> Different transport modes generate different sets of environmental costs. . . . Trucks are less energy efficient than ships, so they use more energy per ton-mile and generate more emissions. . . . The good news is that relative to the overall transportation sector, maritime transport is clean. Reallocating freight across modes has the potential to reduce GHG emissions.[16]

Unfortunately, moving freight by water in the United States has grown less popular over time, which is a trend attributable to maritime regulations, including the Jones Act, as well as to the fact that the relatively high environmental costs of trucking and rail are not captured in the rates charged by the carriers. If those external costs were reflected in the price of service, waterborne freight—with its environmental cost advantages—would be much more highly utilized.

Fitzgerald estimates that "intensive and extensive changes" to the Jones Act could reduce environmental costs by as much as $8 billion per year.[17]

Infrastructure and Repairs

With a growing percentage of America's freight being moved by land, there is greater demand for roads, bridges, and rail, and a greater need for upkeep and repair of existing infrastructure. That wear and tear—degraded pavement, potholes, decaying bridge tresses and supports—translates into external costs, some of which are attributable to the Jones Act for incentivizing the use of road and rail over water transportation. Greater use of surface transportation also means more tire blowouts, axle breaks, windshield damage, mechanical problems, traffic accidents, and train derailments.

Those costs are borne by businesses (maintenance and repair of truck and automobile fleets); households (maintenance and repair of personal vehicles); and taxpayers (taxes to pay for new roads, new rail, and upkeep and repair). The U.S. Bureau of Labor Statistics' Consumer Expenditure Survey, for example, estimates that consumers spent, on average, $890 on automobile maintenance and repairs in 2018.[18]

Freight trucks account for a disproportionate share of the wear and tear on roads and should be responsible for a commensurate share of the expenditures needed for highway upkeep and repair. A minimal reduction in the anticipated growth of trucks on highways can make a significant difference. For example, an oft-cited 1979 GAO report concluded:

> Although a five-axle tractor-trailer loaded to the current 80,000-pound federal weight limit weighs about the same as 20 automobiles, the impact of the tractor trailer is dramatically higher. Based on [American Association of State Highway and Transportation Officials] data, and confirmed by its officials, such a tractor-trailer has the same impact on an interstate highway as at least 9,600 automobiles. Increasing truck weight causes an ever increasing rate of pavement damage.[19]

Accordingly, although trucks account for about 10 percent of the vehicle miles traveled annually in the United States, they are estimated to be responsible for more than 75 percent of the Federal Highway Administration's pavement maintenance costs.[20]

Infrastructure costs are especially relevant today in light of the discussion in Washington about a possible infrastructure spending bill that could have a price tag in excess of President Trump's initial call for $1 trillion in spending.[21] Repairing, building, rebuilding, and maintaining roads, bridges, and rail are all components of U.S. infrastructure spending. So is the dredging of harbors and rivers to clear accumulating silt, widen channels, and deepen harbors for the larger containerships calling on U.S. ports, and for the construction of levies and dikes to mitigate the effects of climate change.

The Jones Act figures here, too, through its restriction on the transport of "valueless cargo," which includes silt from dredging operations, on non–Jones Act vessels.[22] That restriction makes it nearly impossible for U.S. port authorities and the U.S. Army Corps of Engineers to keep up with U.S. dredging demands, which continue to increase with the growth in international trade, the advent of larger international containerships, the effects of mother nature, and the fracking revolution that has thrust the United States to the top among the world's leading producers of oil and natural gas.

The widening of the Panama Canal to accommodate a new class of supersize containerships, which offer 2.5 times more cargo capacity than previous containerships and promise 15 to 20 percent lower shipping costs, was completed in 2016.[23] But of the 17 major container ports on the Gulf of Mexico and Atlantic coasts, just five have the channel depth to accommodate ships of at least 12,000 TEUs, although modern ships can be as large as 23,000 TEUs.[24] Among the reasons for inaction in the face of these infrastructure bottlenecks is the absence of legally qualified dredging and silt transportation vessels. The result is a domestic dredging industry that has very little competition, has limited incentive to invest in new equipment, and that cannot meet the growing demand for dredging projects.

According to a database of U.S. Army Corps of Engineers dredging projects, one company, Great Lakes Dredge and Dock, accounted for 25 percent of the value of all awarded contracts over the period from 1990 through 2018.[25] Four companies—Great Lakes, Weeks Marine, Manson Construction, and Dutra Dredging—accounted for more than half of the awarded contracts and controlled 98.3 percent of private sector hopper dredge capacity.[26] When more firms compete for dredging projects—which is to say, when there is more competition for public procurement dollars—the cost to U.S. taxpayers declines. A 2018 study published by the Center for Strategic and International Studies concluded that the cost of removing silt declined by 32 percent when there were two bidders, as opposed to only one, and it declined by 65 percent when there were four or more bidders.[27]

Reducing surface freight and easing supply restrictions on the ever-expanding demand for dredging would reduce U.S. infrastructure costs significantly.

Lost Wages and Lost Output

The diversion of freight onto our increasingly congested highways worsens an already bad traffic problem and imposes a significant drag on the U.S. economy. Traffic jams on major highways keep the equivalent of 425,533 truck drivers sitting idle for a year, according to a study by the American Transportation Research Institute. These delays added $74.5 billion in operating costs to the trucking industry in 2016.[28] The American Transportation Research Institute estimates that congestion-related delays increased the trucking industry's fuel consumption by 6.87 billion gallons in 2016, at an additional expense of $15.74 billion.[29]

According to U.S. transportation consultancy INRIX, in 2018 Americans lost an average of 97 hours to traffic congestion, costing them nearly $87 billion in lost wages—an average of $1,348 per driver.[30]

Those 18-wheelers clogging our highways account for an estimated 20 percent of the nation's traffic congestion—roughly $17.4 billion per year. Most of the congestion occurs in and around major metropolitan areas along interstates running parallel to the Atlantic Ocean (I-95), the Gulf Coast (I-10), and the Pacific Coast (I-5), where coastal transport via containership could prove a more efficient alternative, but for the Jones Act.

Congestion costs Americans billions of dollars each year, and the problem will only get worse as more freight is moved on our highways. The Department of Transportation forecasts that domestic freight tonnage will increase by 40 percent over the next three decades, and that truck tonnage will increase by 44 percent.[31] One solution—or a pathway to mitigation—is coastal shipping.

Foregone Domestic Sales

The Jones Act's adverse effects on U.S. transportation costs are so significant that they can lead to some very perverse commercial decisions. In the energy and agricultural sectors, especially, where the number of Jones Act–eligible oceangoing vessels is so limited, it is often the case that U.S. businesses are incentivized to purchase raw materials and intermediate goods from foreign suppliers, despite abundant sources of domestic supply. Likewise, U.S. producers of commodities and manufacturing inputs often favor exporting their products to downstream foreign firms rather than selling them to domestic customers on account of higher transport costs.

For agricultural commodities, where the domestic and import prices don't often diverge too significantly, the proximity, convenience, and predictability of domestic sourcing should tip the scale in favor of that option. But when the delivered price is made to reflect transportation expenses, which under normal circumstances typically would reinforce the domestic choice, the Jones Act can alter the calculation.

To be sure, if a foreign supplier can offer better sales terms than domestic suppliers, then it may make perfect sense to import. Likewise, if a foreign customer can purchase on terms more favorable than domestic customers, then exporting may be the optimal choice. But if artificially inflated domestic transportation costs tip the balance in favor of importing or exporting, then the foregone domestic transaction represents an opportunity cost. And those opportunity costs are attributable to the Jones Act.

Recent data from the U.S. Energy Information Administration indicate that roughly five times more Texas crude oil is shipped in foreign-flagged tankers to refineries in eastern Canada than is shipped in Jones Act tankers to refineries in the Northeast.[32] The oil shipments from Texas to Canada cost approximately $2 per barrel but can cost $5 to $6 when destined for the Northeast.[33] The cost difference for a 300,000-barrel tanker amounts to around $1 million, meaning that a Texas oil producer receives $1 million less for its oil when it ships to Northeast refineries than when shipping to Canadian refineries.

Meanwhile, refineries in the Northeast that struggle to maintain reliable supplies of U.S. crude must import their raw materials from as far away as Africa. As U.S. oil producers were reporting record amounts of exports in 2017 (some two million barrels per day), East Coast refineries were importing 900,000 barrels per day.[34]

There are other examples of U.S. suppliers and purchasers choosing foreign over domestic partners because of the effects of the Jones Act. Reportedly because of uncompetitive domestic shipping rates, poultry and hog producers in North Carolina have imported feed grains from Canada and Brazil rather than purchasing them from farmers in the Midwest. [35] Rather than purchase supplies of road salt from domestic sources, local and state governments have instead famously opted to contract with foreign sources. The same goes for natural gas, which is frequently shipped from foreign suppliers to Puerto Rico and the various New England states that suffer from limited pipeline capacity.

It is difficult to estimate the aggregate net opportunity cost of replacing what would otherwise be domestic transactions with imports and exports. But for every import and export transaction that occurred because the delivered domestic price was too high on account of artificially inflated U.S. transportation rates, there is a cost that could have been foregone, absent the Jones Act. Given the billions of domestic and cross-border transactions that take place daily, the aggregate number adds up quickly.

Foregone Export Revenues

The Jones Act is first and foremost a set of trade barriers, intended to protect U.S. shipbuilders, carriers, and mariners. Like all U.S. trade barriers, the Jones Act is a costly imposition on Americans. The denial of foreign competition ensures that domestic transportation costs are higher than they would be otherwise, leading to higher production costs for U.S. businesses, higher costs of living for American households, and a variety of additional costs described above.

But another specific set of victims are U.S. exporters. Because the U.S. government insists on keeping shipbuilding and maritime services officially off-limits in trade negotiations, foreign governments have limited the access of U.S. exporters to their agricultural, goods, and services markets. This foreclosure of potential export sales revenue is another significant opportunity cost of the Jones Act.

American trade negotiators have treated the Jones Act as sacrosanct for years. From the original negotiations of the General Agreement on Tariffs and Trade (GATT) in 1947, the United States insisted on carveouts for shipbuilding and maritime services. That insistence was carried through the Uruguay Round of negotiations, which established the World Trade Organization in 1995. In those negotiations, according to trade scholar Craig Van Grasstek in his 2013 history of the World Trade Organization, the United States

> insisted on retaining one such item that was for them the most sacrosanct of the sacred cows. [U.S. trade negotiator Andrew] Stoler was forced to spend an enormous amount of time and effort negotiating the preservation in the . . . exemption for American Jones Act restrictions, which Mr. Stoler would later refer to as "the ugly birthmark on the new-born baby."[36]

Van Grasstek notes how U.S. insistence on nonconforming measures for the Jones Act was both an irritant and an awful example to our major trading partners:

> The European Community and Japan both strongly opposed continuation of existing grandfather rights under the new institution, at least as a general principle, though that did not prevent them seeking special dispensation of their own. The Europeans placed a high priority on retaining the "voluntary" export restraints that restricted Japanese automotive exports to their market, for example.[37]

According to a European Union position paper, "[t]he prevailing situation, [the Jones Act status quo], has negative economic consequences for the EU's shipbuilding industry by closing the US market for ships, certain segments of which, for example passenger ferries, are of interest to EU shipbuilders."[38] Many countries with advanced shipbuilding and robust maritime services capabilities would like to have a chance to compete in the U.S. market. As noted, that competition would benefit the economy in myriad ways.

Jones Act restrictions preclude those opportunities and invite protectionist responses or excuse longstanding protectionist policies abroad. Speaking at a Heritage Foundation event a few years ago, economist and trade policy expert Gary Hufbauer of the Peterson Institute for International Economics hinted at the potential value of the foregone benefits to U.S. exporters, stating:

> With global free trade in services, we could increase our exports by about $300 billion. But as long as we have the Jones Act and these other sacred cows in place, it'll be really hard, if not impossible, to get other countries to liberalize to the extent we would like.[39]

Around the same period as Hufbauer's Heritage presentation, Rep. Charles Boustany (R-LA) asked then U.S. Trade Representative Michael Froman at a House Ways and Means Committee Hearing on President Barack Obama's trade policy:

> Every administration has resisted intense pressure from foreign nations to compromise our maritime programs, including the Jones Act, in international trade agreements, recognizing the potential adverse impacts on the national and economic security of this country. Can you assure me that you, as the U.S. Trade Representative, will continue these precedents established by prior administrations and ensure that the Jones Act will not be diluted in any trade agreements that are negotiated during your tenure?[40]

Froman, who champions trade liberalization and tried to dismantle other protectionist barriers, responded:

> This administration has continuously ensured that the application of the Jones Act is permitted under each of our trade agreements. As we continue to participate in discussions where this issue may arise, including trade agreement negotiations, we will continue to take this position.[41]

American trade negotiators realize that the Jones Act stands in the way of better access for U.S. businesses to foreign markets. Yet the Jones Act continues to be treated as untouchable.

Conclusion

Beyond the six broad categories outlined in this chapter, there are a host of other real costs of the Jones Act that are even more difficult to measure. What is the real cost of the Jones Act's failure to fulfill its main purpose of ensuring a fleet of reliable ships and a ready reserve of mariners? What is the cost of our reliance on foreign sealift capacity? What is the cost of delays in getting relief supplies to U.S. locations affected by natural disasters? What are the costs of the greater number of highway fatalities and train derailments that might have been avoided had cargo been transported on ships?

Various economic studies on the costs of the Jones Act have focused predominantly on the distribution of rents among the shipbuilders, the carriers, and the shippers. To be sure, protecting domestic shipbuilders from foreign competition raises the cost of ships to domestic carriers, and restricting shipping routes exclusively to domestic carriers who are compelled to use domestic labor raises the cost of transportation to domestic shippers.

But those are only the immediate costs of the Jones Act. Further research needs to be done so that policymakers and the public have a better idea of the burdens imposed on America by this 100-year-old law.

6. By Land or by Sea: Does the Jones Act Cause Land-Based Transport Congestion?

Thomas Grennes

The Jones Act has survived for a century, and it retains strong political support in Congress and among government regulators. Why has it lasted so long, despite most analytical studies indicating that it is not beneficial for the nation as a whole?[1] Strong political support is a bit of a paradox, because the U.S.-flagged fleet and the American shipbuilding industry have shrunk dramatically under the Jones Act's watch. A simple explanation for the act's durability is that its benefits are concentrated, but its costs are widely diffused. These costs have made U.S.-flagged ships uncompetitive relative to both foreign-flagged ships on international routes and uncompetitive with other transportation modes on domestic routes. The decline of international routes is easy to document. American businesses that export and import have abandoned U.S.-flagged ships almost completely: recently, those ships carried less than 2 percent of the country's exports and imports.[2]

On domestic routes, where the Jones Act is applicable, the decline has been less obvious and less extreme, but the share of domestic trade using waterborne transportation has dropped for many decades relative to land-based transportation modes. Cargo that could be carried by U.S.-flagged ships is instead being transported by trucks, railroads, pipelines, and airplanes. This chapter will concentrate on the diversion of transportation from water to land that has been described by Andrew Gibson, a former head of the U.S. Maritime Administration, and Arthur Donovan, currently a professor at the U.S. Merchant Marine Academy, as "the abandonment of the ocean."[3]

Cabotage in Other Countries and Transportation Modes

Do other countries have similar protectionist laws, and has there been a similar substitution of land transportation for water transportation abroad? Many countries have measures that protect domestic trade, but the Jones Act is one of the world's most extreme, as measured by the Organisation for Economic Co-operation and Development's Services Trade Restrictiveness Index.[4] Most other countries do not require that ships be domestically built to engage in domestic trade.[5] Domestic waterborne trade is a much more important mode of transport in many other countries.[6]

But are other transportation modes subject to the same kinds of rules as shipping in the United States? Simply put, no. While ships must be domestically built, trucks, planes, railroad equipment, and pipeline equipment can be imported.[7] American airline companies purchase aircraft from Airbus (Europe); Embraer (Brazil); and Bombardier (Canada).[8] American trucking companies buy trucks from Sweden, Germany, and Japan, among other countries. Differential regulation, such as the Jones Act's build requirement for U.S. ships, contributes to substituting land-based transportation for water-based transportation and to the abandonment of the ocean as a useful means of transportation.

Goals of the Jones Act

Has the Jones Act achieved its goals of strengthening U.S. shipbuilding and the U.S. Merchant Marine? Several pieces of evidence indicate no. American shipbuilding is shrinking, and the Jones Act fleet is in decline. Also, for domestic trade, there has been a major substitution of land-based transportation for ships. Essentially, Jones Act ships operate only where they face no serious competition from other modes of domestic transportation. Curiously, many supporters of the Jones Act acknowledge the decline of American shipbuilding and the U.S. Merchant Marine since the act has been in place, but they refuse to admit that it was a major cause of the contraction.[9] When Sen. Wesley Jones (R-WA) proposed the 1920 law that bears his name he justified it in terms of national security, but he also had a narrower goal in mind: he wanted to protect the maritime businesses of his Washington constituents from foreign competition. That narrow protectionist goal has been accomplished, but the country has suffered. For every dollar gained by protected businesses in Washington and other states, more than a dollar was lost by consumers and other businesses.[10]

The American shipbuilding industry is small and getting smaller. More than 90 percent of commercial ships recently constructed have been built in Japan,

South Korea, or China.[11] Almost no one buys American-built ships unless they are required to do so. They cost much more than foreign-built ships, and they cost more than land-based transportation with the same capacity. Few American builders of oceangoing commercial ships remain. One of the few survivors, Philly Shipyard, had no ships on its orderbook as of the fourth quarter of 2019.[12] Workers have been laid off, and there is doubt as to whether the shipyard will survive.[13]

World shipyards are struggling to survive a surplus of ships. The major Asian shipbuilders produce a large volume of ships that allows them to benefit from economies of scale; U.S. production is too small to benefit from economies of scale, and few Americans are trained to build ships. Americans have complained frequently about Asian shipbuilding subsidies. However, the Trump administration's preference for bilateral solutions to problems has prevented it from filing formal complaints with the World Trade Organization. Recently, Japan made a formal complaint against shipbuilding subsidies by South Korea, and the European Union announced its intention to support the complaint.

The U.S. Merchant Marine has shrunk to the point where it is a tiny share of the world fleet. As Rear Admiral Mark H. Buzby, administrator of the Maritime Administration stated, "It has been in steady decline since World War II as a result of decreasing demand and rising costs compared to international fleets."[14] The fleet is so small that in an emergency it is difficult to get access to a ship on short notice. The high cost of acquiring a new American-built ship results in the U.S. fleet being older and less safe than the foreign-flagged fleet.[15] Buzby warns about the shortage of trained American mariners, but the small and shrinking size of the fleet means that the shortage could get worse unless more foreign mariners are employed. Current rules require that at least 75 percent of the unlicensed mariners be Americans, but if that percentage could be lowered, there is a large supply of trained international seamen who could be hired. The potential labor supply includes all the mariners who are currently employed on foreign-flagged ships that carry U.S. exports and imports.

Although the Jones Act was intended to strengthen American shipbuilding and the U.S. Merchant Marine, both have suffered major declines during the century that the act has been in effect. In addition, the inflated costs of building and operating U.S.-flagged ships have caused domestic trade to be redirected from water to land. This detour of trade has caused the United States to lose the advantages of water as a marine highway.

How Does the Jones Act Raise Costs?

Ships are much more expensive to build in the United States than in major Asian shipyards. U.S.-built ships have been recently estimated to cost up to five times as much as those built overseas.[16] As a result, owners replace them less frequently, the U.S.-flagged fleet is older and less efficient, and the ships are less safe to operate.[17] American ships do use some foreign components, but the Maritime Administration requires that at least 50 percent of the tonnage of the components for vessels built with U.S. government financing must be transported on the more-expensive U.S.-flagged ships, which erases some of the cost advantages of using these imports.[18]

U.S.-flagged ships, including those in the Jones Act fleet, are required to have larger crews than their foreign-flagged rivals, which adds to labor costs. These crew-size requirements, however, are made without regard for advances in automation. More automated processes could be carried out while some mariners remain on board, and completely autonomous ships would be the extreme case of zero crew on board.[19] The Air Force is already using autonomous planes (e.g., drones), and naval officials are planning to use autonomous ships. Crew sizes on foreign-flagged ships represent a kind of free-market solution. Shippers choose ships and crews that deliver their cargo safely, on time, with minimum damage, at a competitive price. Crew sizes vary by country of registry, but the largest registries have safer records than the United States.[20]

Carriers of some products have found a way to circumvent certain rules that apply to ocean-going ships on some routes. They have switched to articulated barges that allow them to use crew sizes one-third the size of crews on larger ships.[21] Barges are used primarily to transport oil on coastal routes, without having to bear the higher costs of acquiring tankers and paying their larger crews. Given the Jones Act requirements, the barges provide some savings. However, they have the disadvantages of having to stay near the coast, they cannot be used in bad weather, and they sacrifice the economies of scale that tankers provide. The Jones Act has diverted some transportation from water to land, and from large ships to these less-efficient barges.

Requiring American crews raises costs, because wages of American mariners are higher than their foreign counterparts. The wages of these mariners are further inflated by the subsidies to cargo-preference ships that Jones Act ships must compete with for crew members. Higher labor costs make U.S.-flagged ships less competitive.

Jones Act supporters and American labor unions oppose using more foreign mariners, and they often mention potential security problems. This concern about citizenship appears to ignore the fact that American imports and exports are carried almost entirely by foreign-flagged ships that are manned by foreign crews that have operated out of American ports for many years. If there is a shortage of Americans with the requisite skills, why not increase the allowable percentage of foreigners to 100 percent? The relevant foreign mariners would probably have the same skills and loyalty as the foreign mariners who serve on nearly all the ships that carry U.S. exports and imports every day. These mariners must have work visas, and they are vetted by the relevant U.S. security authorities.

Congestion on Land

The U.S. economy recovered from the Great Recession (2007–2009) with an extraordinarily long expansion. As of January 2020, the economy has been expanding for nine years, and the unemployment rate has fallen to 3.6 percent—the lowest rate in 50 years. Prolonged growth has put strains on all domestic transportation modes. There have been widespread reports of shortages of trucks, truck drivers, railroad cars, and pipeline capacity. If pipelines do not exist in a region or are operating at capacity, they can become a barrier to trade that results in surpluses in some regions and shortages in others, resulting in large regional price differences. In August 2018, the absence of pipeline capacity resulted in a price discount of $23 per barrel of oil in the Permian Basin of Texas relative to the price of crude oil in Houston.[22]

Transportation congestion on land is a current problem, but the diversion of cargo from waterborne transportation to land transportation has been occurring for many decades since the Jones Act has been in effect. Since 1960, the volume of waterborne transportation in the United States has decreased by 50 percent, but the volume of rail transportation has increased by 50 percent, and the volume of cargo carried by trucks and other forms of land-based transportation has more than doubled.[23] Americans who had regularly used the Panama Canal to transport goods between the West Coast and East Coast rarely use it for domestic transportation anymore.[24]

This substitution of transportation modes is not part of a broader pattern that affects other countries. Waterborne transportation between the United States and Canada and Mexico has not decreased. Trade with those neighbors is not covered by the Jones Act, and foreign-flagged ships are used. Many of the land routes used by trucks, railroads, and pipelines run parallel to the alternative coastal water routes, but American businesses have systematically chosen to transport more of their cargo on land. Higher costs induced by the Jones Act are a major factor. An extreme example of diversion is trade in liquefied natural gas (LNG).[25] Shipping LNG by water requires special tankers, yet no such Jones Act–compliant ships exist today. Thus, the Jones Act has eliminated waterborne domestic trade in that commodity.

By inflating the costs of using ships, the Jones Act sacrifices some inherent advantages of water transportation. Ships can carry more cargo per trip, they do not bear the costs of maintaining rights-of-way, and they have fewer limitations on the dimensions and weight of cargo.[26] They also produce significantly fewer carbon emissions than other forms of transportation.[27] Revitalizing domestic shipping would substantially increase the capacity of the nation's freight network. It would effectively increase the nation's deteriorating infrastructure at a negligible cost.

The long-term trend toward moving cargo traffic from water to land has increased highway, railroad, pipeline, and port congestion. One writer has accused the Jones Act of causing traffic jams on land.[28] The problem of underutilizing water transportation was recognized by Congress as early as 2007 in the Marine Highway Initiative.[29] However, the high cost of loading and unloading cargo at ports remains an obstacle to the goal of moving traffic from trucks to water. Diverting cargo from water to land sacrifices some important advantages of water transportation, such as economies of scale.

Port issues are not addressed directly by the Jones Act. However, the Foreign Dredge Act of 1906 is a similarly protectionist law that reinforces the Jones Act by influencing the choice between water and land transportation.[30]

Port inefficiencies or blockages make it more difficult, and more costly, to connect water and land transportation. If there are port bottlenecks, shippers sending to domestic destinations will use land transportation exclusively. American ports are characterized by lower productivity relative to foreign ports.[31] There has been resistance to automation in U.S. ports, and in some cases, the hours per day when cargo can be transferred from ports to trucks are fewer than in foreign ports. The cost of transferring cargo at ports between land and water is the largest component of using water transportation. Because of the Foreign Dredge Act, foreign dredging companies are unable to offer their services to U.S. ports, making the process slower and more expensive. Unless port costs can be reduced, the goal of expanding the use of marine highways will be difficult to achieve.

Conclusion

An unintended consequence of U.S. marine policy has been to make U.S.-flagged ships uncompetitive with foreign-flagged ships in international transportation and uncompetitive with land-based transportation on domestic routes. This inward-looking maritime policy has been described by some as the "abandoned ocean."[32] American maritime policy has resisted automation in shipbuilding and in the operation of ships and ports. To become more competitive internationally, U.S.-flagged ships would have to be allowed to follow the standards of foreign-flagged ships. All four Jones Act requirements (U.S.-built, -owned, -crewed, and -flagged) make these ships less competitive. In domestic trade, efficient regulation would apply the same standards across all transportation modes. Applying the U.S.-build requirement to ships, but not to other modes, is a serious penalty that reduces the share of shipping in the transportation mix. A moderate reform would relax the build-American requirement, at least for the noncontiguous regions of Alaska, Hawaii, and Puerto Rico.[33] Ending all requirements of the Jones Act for ships on all routes would provide greater efficiency gains, but it would face powerful resistance. The greatest gains would come from relaxing restrictions on all transportation modes and allowing free domestic and international trade in the services of ships, trucks, railroads, planes, pipelines, and dredging.

7. The Environmental Case for Jones Act Reform

Timothy Fitzgerald

Environmental costs are a textbook example of external costs—air emissions, water contamination, and degradation of land resources—that fall on people other than those who created and caused them. The external costs of freight transport vary by mode, such as truck, rail, air, or water. Insofar as the Jones Act changes people's choices about how freight moves, the environmental effects are likely to change if and when provisions of the Jones Act are reformed. This chapter explores the environmental gains that could be realized as a result of Jones Act reform.

Advocates for domestic carriers assert that the Jones Act is central to protecting the domestic waterborne shipping industry and minimizing its impact on consumers. However, the private costs of transport do not capture all of the relevant costs. Because waterborne shipping has lower environmental costs than many other modes, protecting certain classes of carriers has an impact beyond the transport market. Reforming the Jones Act could help reduce the environmental costs of freight transport because shipping by water is cleaner than the alternatives.

Given full purview over the transport system, economists would seek to internalize environmental externalities so that private transport fees reflected the full social costs for every transport mode. This would raise the market cost of transport, and as a result, the total amount of transport would also decline. The modal shares of transport would be reallocated from relatively high to relatively low external costs, and the net effect for low external cost modes is ambiguous. While overall environmental costs would decline, using the relatively cleaner mode more often could increase the costs associated with that mode.

U.S. Freight Transport under the Jones Act

The Jones Act limits choice for domestic waterborne transport to qualified carriers. The industry that the cabotage restriction is intended to protect, however, faces difficult market conditions. The Jones Act–eligible merchant fleet has dwindled to 99 oceangoing ships, and marine transport is largely restricted to the noncontiguous states and territories of Alaska, Hawaii, and Puerto Rico, where there are no available substitutes. In addition, the Jones Act fleet is older than both the international fleet as well as the foreign-built U.S.-flagged fleet that is engaged in international trade. The lack of marine shipping traffic has made it difficult for carriers to justify ongoing investments at a pace to match other fleets.

Marine shipping is not competitive with alternative modes, with the natural advantages of marine transport likely undermined by higher operating expenses. Estimates of the higher operating costs vary from 13–170 percent.[1] In 2018, the Organisation for Economic Co-operation and Development (OECD) rated U.S. maritime freight as 60 percent more restrictive than the average OECD country.[2]

The net effect of making waterborne transport relatively more expensive is that less freight moves by ship and other vessels than would otherwise be moved, absent the Jones Act, and the effect persists year after year. In 2016, only 4.2 percent of U.S. domestic freight tonnage moved by water, compared to 65.7 percent by truck.[3] Further underscoring the disparity, waterborne freight transport moved only 1.8 percent of total freight value, which suggests that the tonnage that does move by water is disproportionately composed of low-value products. These tonnage shares reflect the direct costs of shipping, not external costs.

Including environmental costs would likely make water transport more attractive on net, because its external costs are small relative to alternative modes. Water transport has the lowest greenhouse gas (GHG) emissions of any mode: one-third lower than pipeline, 70 percent lower than rail, more than 80 percent lower than truck, and hundreds of times lower than air.[4] Including environmental costs increases the net distortion created by underutilizing marine shipping. Table 7.1 shows that in 2015, ships and boats accounted for only 0.9 percent of all freight GHG emissions, compared to more than 80 percent for trucks. Taking these emissions into account makes water transport relatively more attractive. Transportation is a key emitter of GHG, accounting for 28 percent of all 2016 U.S. emissions.[5] It accounts for rising greenhouse gas emissions, with an increase of 20 percent between 1990–1992 and 2014–2016.

Table 7.1 Tonnage and emissions shares of U.S. freight traffic, by mode, 2016

	Tonnage share	greenhouse gas share	Relative greenhouse gas emissions intensity
Truck	66.1	80.5	1.22
Rail	9.1	8.0	0.88
Water	3.4	0.9	0.26
Pipeline	19.1	7.4	0.39
Air	0.01	3.2	320

Source: "National Transportation Statistics, 2019," Bureau of Transportation Statistics, https://www.bts.dot.gov/topics/national-transportation-statistics; "Inventory of U.S. Greenhouse Gas Emissions and Sinks, 1990–2016," United States Environmental Protection Agency (EPA), https://www.epa.gov/ghgemissions/inventory-us-greenhouse-gas-emissions-and-sinks; and author's calculations.

Note: The tonnage shares exclude tonnage moved without a domestic mode or by "other."

The environmental benefits of shifting toward maritime transport would help the U.S. economy. In 2002, the United States International Trade Commission estimated that full liberalization of the Jones Act would increase U.S. economic welfare by $656 million (1999 dollars). Removing only the domestic shipbuilding requirement but keeping all other provisions of the Jones Act in place was estimated to deliver an increase of $261 million in economic welfare. Economists Gary Hufbauer and Kimberly Elliott found a similar topline welfare figure using a different methodology, estimating that a full liberalization would increase U.S. economic welfare by $556 million (1990 dollars), with gross consumer gains of $1.8 billion.[6] Economists Joseph Francois, Hugh Arce, Kenneth Reinert, and Joseph Flynn arrive at a higher estimate of $3 billion (1989 dollars) in welfare cost, but add to the consensus that the Jones Act protects a relatively small number of jobs and firms at a broadly dispersed cost.[7] None of these studies have attempted to enumerate the external costs, and so they potentially represent an underestimate by measuring only direct cost differences.

While the emissions intensity of transportation has fallen over recent decades, compositional differences remain between transport modes. Most significantly, integrated assessment modeling shows that emissions damages are highest for pollutants that are not prevalent from transport sources.[8] Furthermore, economists Nicholas Muller and Robert Mendelsohn show that water transportation has very localized damages. Whereas highway and railroads crisscross the country, the damages from marine emissions are concentrated in coastal areas. The economic costs of local air pollutants depend on the location of emission. Greenhouse gases, in contrast, are global stock pollutants, so the economic value of those emissions does not depend on the location of emission. The economic damages of water transport are therefore likely to depend largely on the value of these emissions and local air pollution damages in coastal areas.

Transporters do not explicitly consider environmental costs, although policy interventions can be used to provide them with incentives to do so. To illustrate how environmental costs trade off with other types of costs, consider the problem of moving cargo from Corpus Christi, Texas, to Tampa, Florida. According to the Geospatial Intermodal Freight Transport (GIFT) model, the shortest-distance trip is one that relies heavily on ship, shaving about 150 miles (12 percent) off the shortest land route.[9] That itinerary does not minimize the time spent traveling. While the ship delivers the cargo in a total travel time of 63 hours, the shortest-duration trip is about 21 hours with delivery by truck. Neither of these routes consider potential slowdowns, some of which might be predictable, such as traffic congestion or hours of service regulations for truckers, and some of which might not be predictable, such as weather.

Shipping rates take these differences into account. Shipping rates vary with the timeliness of delivery, and sometimes shippers are willing to pay more for speedy delivery; each day of transit time is equivalent to an ad valorem tariff between 0.6 and 2.1 percent.[10] So a trip from Corpus Christi to Tampa that takes three days instead of one might be expected to cost 1–4 percent less. The value of time is borne out in the lower costs of inventory that firms must hold with just-in-time delivery. Slower supply chains can be just-in-time as well, making the variance of delivery time more relevant to inventory costs.

Returning to the GIFT model between Corpus Christi and Tampa, the consideration of external costs due to transport mode choices can lead to still more variation. For example, to minimize CO_2 emissions on a per twenty-foot equivalent (TEU) basis, ship transport is far preferred, in part because less than one-third of the energy inputs are needed to move the cargo by sea as opposed to moving it by land. It is not surprising that moving the freight by ship generates about one-third the CO_2 emissions as transportation by land. But marine transport is not the optimal transport mode for all environmental criteria. Other types of emissions, including particulate matter and sulfur and nitrogen oxides, are minimized by truck transport.

The socially optimal transport choice is one that minimizes the total costs, including the monetary cost, the value of time, and the external costs. A key question is whether reducing the amount of marine transportation decreases or increases the net environmental costs. Because marine transportation creates external environmental costs, it is true that reducing the amount of waterborne transport helps reduce those particular external costs. However, because freight and people that might otherwise move by boat or ship instead tend to move by alternative means, the relative environmental cost depends on the relative environmental costs across transportation modes.

Environmental scientist Mark Delucchi and economist Donald R. McCubbin summarize a number of studies examining different types of external costs for both passenger and freight traffic.[11] In order to estimate external costs, the physical differences in emissions are valued based on the impact they have on humans. Although water transport has not been as closely studied as other modes of transport, research has generally concluded that water has lower external costs than alternative transport modes. The external costs are concentrated in GHG emissions, so the marginal value of those emissions figures prominently in the overall calculation. Table 7.2 summarizes those results, showing a range of economic damage estimates (in cents per ton-mile) that reflect differences across modes, differences in research methodologies, and different levels of scientific uncertainty about the magnitude of the external costs. For the external costs attributable to health effects from the Clean Air Act's criteria air pollutants, the range of estimates is substantial but largely consistent across modes. Rail emerges as the lowest external cost mode in this regard, followed by water, air, and road. Consistent with the data in Table 7.1, climate costs are lowest for water transport, thanks to lower fuel requirements due to buoyancy.

Rail is second, followed by low-end road estimates. The range for road costs are well behind the higher climate costs from air transport.

Expanding from just GHG to criteria air pollutants, the environmental costs of freight transport become more nuanced. While water transport has lower external climate costs thanks to lower emissions, it has higher criteria emissions than other modes, notably rail. Taking these two types of emissions together, it is clear that water transport has lower external costs than air or truck. Rail and water have overlapping ranges of estimates, with rail slightly lower.

Comparing Total Costs across Modes

External costs are an important part of the picture, but the differences in direct costs across modes also matter. The Bureau of Transportation Statistics reports average revenues per ton-mile across modes, which are also included in the first row of Table 7.2.[12] Over time, water transport revenue has been between one-eighth or one-ninth of the revenue from trucks. In contrast, the cost

Table 7.2 Estimated direct and external costs by freight transport mode, cents per ton-mile

	Truck	Rail	Water	Air
Market rate	16.5–18.7	4	2.4–2.9	120–127
Air health	0.1–22.3	0.01–0.42	0.1–2.03	0.0–2.3
Climate	0.02–7.04	0.01–0.56	0.0–0.27	0.54
All external	0.12–29.34	0.02–0.98	0.1–2.3	0.54–2.84
Percent increase from including external costs	0.6–178	0.5–24.5	3.4–95.8	0.4–2.4
Total costs (cents per ton-mile)	16.6–48	4–5	2.5–5.2	120–130

Notes: External costs represent 2018 cents per ton-mile of freight traffic, as updated from estimates published in Mark Delucchi and Donald McCubbin, "External Costs of Transport in the U.S.," Institute of Transportation Studies, UC Davis, Working Paper Series, 2010. Rate data are from "National Transportation Statistics, 2019," Bureau of Transportation Statistics, https://www.bts.dot.gov/topics/national-transportation-statistics.

difference between water and rail is much smaller, with barge rates as close as three-quarters of rail rates. However, water transport is often less timely, as the GIFT simulations suggest. The market rate reflects the demand for timely freight transport, so the slower mode might receive a discount, all else remaining equal.

Internalizing external costs potentially changes the ordering of modes by costs. The high end of the range of external costs reported in Table 7.2 suggests that the environmental costs of water transport are potentially as high as the private costs. Truck is the only other mode that has as large a level of external costs. David Austin, a principal analyst in the Microeconomic Studies Division of the Congressional Budget Office, conducted a comprehensive study of external costs for truck and rail and found a lower ratio of external costs to market rates for trucks than the figures in Table 7.2.[13] External costs have the least effect on air transport, in part because the market rates are already so high.

Forcing providers to pay external costs therefore has the largest relative impact on water transport and the smallest relative effect on air. However, with external costs taken into account, water transport has the lowest overall costs of any transport mode. This is clear from the last row of Table 7.2.

Environmental Benefits of Jones Act Reform

An important policy question is the degree to which today's situation is attributable to the Jones Act and how much is attributable to intramodal competition. That is, is marine transport disadvantaged naturally or because of the Jones Act? Enumerating environmental costs is not directly related to that question but does affect the net change in human welfare from a policy shift. A comparison of the current situation and a counterfactual with a different cabotage regime helps show the differences in environmental costs. Consider three counterfactuals. In the first, imagine a purely intensive change in which the U.S. domestic fleet upgraded to an international standard of emissions intensity, but without a change in the volume of freight carried. In the second, consider the effect of increasing maritime freight transport by 10 percent, displacing truck and rail transport in equal proportions. The third case includes both the intensive and extensive effects.

The first case drives at the relatively antiquated nature of the U.S. fleet as compared to international comparators. In 2017, nearly one-third of all U.S.-flagged vessels were more than 25 years old; excluding towboats and barges, the proportion was more than 53 percent.[14] Because modern vessels are likely to have lower external environmental costs as a function of technological progress, their adoption alone might offer scope for improvement. The scope of liberalizing marine cabotage, let alone its effects, are uncertain. Hufbauer and Elliott provide some of the only quantitative estimates of the gains from reducing such barriers; they estimate a 22 percent price reduction as a result of complete repeal.[15] The posited extensive effect is therefore something less than previous estimates of the effect of a full repeal. These scenarios provide short-run estimates of cost savings, even though the physical transitions might take some time.

Table 7.3 summarizes the effect on environmental costs from freight transport under three alternative counterfactuals that potentially correspond to Jones Act reforms. In the first case, upgrading the Jones Act–eligible fleet to an emissions profile comparable to water transport in Europe would avoid environmental costs that are mostly attributable to criteria pollutant emissions. In part because of scientific uncertainty about the magnitude of the environmental cost from these emissions, these avoided costs range from $118 million to $3.96 billion. This improvement is derived from the same amount of freight moving on cleaner vessels.

The second case contemplates more freight moving by ship and displacing truck and rail traffic. The relative cleanliness of water transport compared to truck and rail comes into play at this point. This is reflected in the larger share of avoided costs of GHG emissions due to switching freight to a more energy-efficient mode. In this case the higher profile of criteria air emissions for water transport suggests that there could be a slight increase in environmental costs, mostly as relatively cleaner train traffic is replaced by the potentially most environmentally costly part of the U.S. fleet. However, the net avoided costs range higher than in the first case as more freight is reallocated to ships. This represents a real gain for the marine shipping sector. And a shift of relatively more freight from trucks rather than rail would raise the estimates further.

The third case combines the first two cases, making both greater use of waterborne transport as well as newer, cleaner vessels. This produces potential

Table 7.3 Net annual avoided environmental costs, millions of dollars

	Air	Climate	Net
Case I			
Upgrade to international	115–3,533	3–431	118–3,963
Case II			
Increase water freight 10%	−13–2,680	4–1,516	−9–4,196
Case III			
Both	102–6,213	7–1,947	109–8,159

Source: Author's calculations, based on estimates in Mark Delucchi and Donald McCubbin, "External Costs of Transport in the U.S.," Institute of Transportation Studies, UC Davis, Working Paper Series, 2010; Rainer Friedrich and Emile Quinet, "External Costs of Transport in Europe," chap. 16, in *A Handbook of Transport Economics*, ed. André de Palma, Robin Lindsey, Emile Quinet, and Roger Vickerman (Northampton, MA: Edward Elgar Publishing, 2011); "GIFT—Geospatial Intermodal Freight Transport Model," Laboratory for Environmental Computing and Decision Making, http://clarke.main.ad.rit.edu/LECDM/Webgift/WebGIFT.htm; Nicholas Z. Muller and Robert Mendelsohn, "Measuring the Damages of Air Pollution in the United States," *Journal of Environmental Economics and Management* 54, no. 1 (2007): 1–14; and David Austin, "Pricing Freight Transport to Account for External Costs," Congressional Budget Office, Working Paper no. 2015-03, March 30, 2015.

avoided costs ranging from $102 million to $8.2 billion. To put the $8.2 billion into context, it is just over 40 percent of recent value-added from water transportation, or about 1 percent of total transportation contribution to GDP. Francois et al. estimated that removal of the Jones Act could increase economic welfare by $3 billion (1989 dollars). This suggests that the environmental benefits could substantially increase the gains from reform.

Conclusion

Changing the Jones Act offers the prospect of substantially reducing environmental costs created by freight transport. Using more marine transport would reduce the emissions from freight transport, especially for greenhouse gases. Criteria air emissions from water transport are slightly higher than those of rail, but lower than those of trucks. Both intensive and extensive changes to the prevailing regime could yield reduced external environmental costs by as much as $8 billion per year. These gains provide strong additional motivation for Jones Act reform. While previous studies have provided a range of welfare gains from changes to a less-restrictive policy environment, the environmental gains offer a substantial boost. Using the most conservative estimates of the gains from reform, the environmental benefits increase the net gains by 50 percent. Much larger gains are possible, increasing the benefits of reform by double or more.

8. A Shift Toward Murkiness: How Conflicting Transportation Policies Have Forced Unsupervised Oligopolies on Jones Act Trades in the Past 23 Years
Manuel Reyes

Government policies can affect market competition for good or for ill. In some instances, policies restricting competition are intentional—the result of business lobbying—while in other cases they may simply be the result of insufficient scrutiny at the policy design stage.[1] In the case of the Jones Act, it may be both. Although the Jones Act is 100 years old and is clearly a protectionist law meant to keep international carriers out of domestic water trades, until 1995 other federal statutes somewhat prevented market concentration abuse. Unfortunately, transportation deregulation meant to increase competition was incomplete and contradictory, causing the opposite effect on the Jones Act trades by inhibiting market competition and forcing the creation of even more concentrated unsupervised oligopolies that are prone to market power abuse.

The Jones Act

The Jones Act's initial objective was to guarantee the United States with a merchant marine in case of emergencies and war by limiting access of international competitors to the domestic water trade market. By definition it is a protectionist law. Furthermore, it has failed miserably in its objectives. After a century of the Jones Act and several other laws with similar purposes, the U.S. Merchant Marine is experiencing record low numbers. Commercial shipbuilding and employment have decreased even while trade has increased exponentially.

The main reason for this failure is that higher operating and ship construction costs make U.S.-flagged Jones Act vessels less competitive than carriers using international flags.[2] In fact, the U.S. carriers that forcefully defend this protectionist law founded most of the international ship registries, such as those of Panama, Liberia, and the Marshall Islands, because they do not want to sail under the U.S. flag unless they have guaranteed cargo or a closed market, as in the case of Alaska, Hawaii, and Puerto Rico.[3] But for those jurisdictions, the clear lack of the Jones Act fleet's competitiveness directly translates into their own economies' lack of competitiveness.

Consequence of Regulatory Changes: Unsupervised Market Concentration

In addition to higher operating and construction costs, the situation is worsened by extreme market concentration. Although the Jones Act has existed for 100 years, for most of those it was applied in tandem with transportation regulations that sought to prevent abuse and to protect shippers and consumers. The Interstate Commerce Commission and the Federal Maritime Commission (FMC) had regulatory oversight over both domestic and international carriers. Tariffs had to be public and "reasonable," assured by these agencies' authority for passing judgment, including through public hearings where carriers had to open their books. The system was imperfect and claims of abuse by carriers were often filed with both agencies.

But in 1995, a shift toward murkiness occurred. As part of the deregulation process of all transportation in the United States that began in the 1970s, this oversight was eliminated with the Interstate Commerce Commission Termination Act of 1995.[4] The basic premise was that competition was a better regulator than the government. Unfortunately, the deregulation process was incomplete. It kept the Jones Act intact, and instead of fostering competition and transparency, the changes created a scenario of mostly unsupervised oligopolies in the three main markets under the Jones Act.

Congress did create a new agency, the Surface Transportation Board (STB), to supplant the Interstate Commerce Commission. However, its main focus is railroad transportation, and it has little authority over ocean transportation. Congress also maintained the FMC to oversee international ocean carriers, but for reasons unknown, transferred its oversight of domestic offshore carriers to the STB.

In terms of specific oversight, regulations for international carriers under the FMC are now very different than those for domestic carriers under the STB.

Probably most important is that Jones Act carriers are not required to file any data on private-service contracts, which in the Puerto Rico trade accounts for almost all movements. This means there are no reliable public statistics on the actual costs of transportation from the U.S. mainland to Puerto Rico. This information is paramount to an island that depends on this traffic, and its absence is actually used by the pro–Jones Act carriers to make farfetched allegations based on "confidential data" they alone have access to. In contrast, the FMC regulation that still applies to international carriers does require the filing of service contracts for oversight purposes.[5] There is no reasonable explanation for this difference, considering that competition in the Jones Act trades has always been limited and thus more prone to abuse.

In any case, the conflicting policies and the potential for abuse were clear to Congress when they passed the Interstate Commerce Commission Termination Act in 1995. In an apparent premonition of the risks and contradictions of eliminating the federal supervision of such concentrated markets, Section 407 of the act established that:

> [T]he Secretary of Transportation shall transmit to the Committee on Commerce, Science, and Transportation of the Senate and the Committee on Transportation and Infrastructure of the House of Representatives a study that analyzes each of the noncontiguous domestic trades, including analyzing
>
> 1. carrier competition in both regulated and unregulated portions of those trades;
> 2. rate structures in those trades;
> 3. the impact of tariff filing on carrier pricing;
> 4. the problems of parallel pricing and its impact on competition in the domestic trades;
> 5. the impact on domestic cargo pricing of foreign cargo services;
> 6. whether additional protections are needed to *protect shippers from the abuse of market power* [emphasis added]; and
> 7. the extent to which statutory or regulatory changes should be made to further the transportation policy of section 13101 of title 49, United States Code.[6]

Such language leaves no doubt that Congress knew there were problems but assigned its evaluation to the Department of Transportation (DOT), a historical guardian of the Jones Act not focused on protecting shippers. In compliance with this mandate, DOT published a report in 1997 titled "Competition in the Noncontiguous Domestic Maritime Trades."[7] It relied on information submitted by interested parties, with little independent or government-produced data. In the area of competition, the report acknowledged that the markets were very concentrated, but it argued that the entry and exit of competitors in previous years meant that carriers could not unreasonably raise prices or else others would enter the market. The report's authors conceded that, even though shippers argued there was parallel pricing between carriers, they found no clear evidence of that practice. They concluded that, while the public comments provided suggestions for additional protection, no respondent provided clear evidence to justify further investigation by the DOT. As we will see, these conclusions were proven wrong by price-fixing cases that later emerged.

In 2006 the DOT, with the Maritime Administration (MARAD), published another report with the same title and similar conclusions. Surprisingly, it admitted that such powerful agencies didn't have data on the subject, so they instead relied on a study by a private firm, Reeves and Associates, which was prepared for the Maritime Cabotage Task Force (in 2011 this organization changed its name to American Maritime Partnership), a group that lobbies on behalf of the Jones Act carriers. This admission should have seriously undermined the report's credibility. But facts are difficult things to permanently hide.

The Results of Policy Contradictions for Puerto Rico

At the same time that DOT and MARAD were denying shippers' claims of abuse, the Jones Act carriers began fixing prices in the Puerto Rico trade (as would be expected in an oligopoly operating without oversight). They were convicted for antitrust violations committed between 2003 and 2008.[8] The criminal cases were followed by a private class-action suit and independent lawsuits that cost the Puerto Rico economy hundreds of millions of dollars during its economic recession.[9] Amazingly, due to the lack of transparency and oversight, it is unclear if prices were ever adjusted after these cases. What is known is that neither the Department of Transportation nor the Maritime Administration nor the Surface Transportation Board—as the agencies that should have overseen the market and had reported to Congress that there were no problems—have taken any specific actions or even acknowledged the situation.

This lack of transparency has been further deepened by the corporate movements of these carriers after the antitrust cases. Two of the carriers that were previously publicly traded became private, a move often done to avoid scrutiny by regulators. Adding to the problem, in 2015 the largest of the shipping lines, Horizon Lines, left the market. At the time it had 30 percent of the Jones Act service to Puerto Rico and was the only carrier operating ships from the three main ports connecting Puerto Rico to the mainland: Houston, Jacksonville, and Pennsauken, New Jersey. Just two companies, TOTE Maritime and Crowley, now have more than 80 percent of the Jones Act market serving Puerto Rico, both of which have engaged in antitrust violations.[10]

But the lack of reliable information, the antitrust convictions, and the occurrence of particular emergencies, such as the sinking of the ship *El Faro* in 2015 and more recently, Hurricane María, underscore the situation of an island that is dependent on two companies that have almost complete control of its ports—with no oversight and a proven history of market abuse. Shippers, as well as consumers, are defenseless. Antitrust laws that presume open markets are not enough if there is no permanent oversight or data-gathering that would provide the basis for criminal or civil claims. Additionally, in extremely concentrated markets, players can easily engage in tacit or implicit collusion, which would not necessarily be in violation of antitrust laws but would still hurt shippers and consumers. As it is, Puerto Rico and the federal government are deliberately blind to what is actually happening with this service. Even after the antitrust convictions, the Government Accountability Office (GAO) released a report in 2013 titled *Puerto Rico: Characteristics of the Island's Maritime Trade and Potential Effects of Modifying the Jones Act*, in which shippers echoed complaints made in the previous Department of Transportation studies. But the GAO also downplayed their claims, stating:

> Shippers doing business in Puerto Rico reported that freight rates for foreign carriers going to and from foreign ports are often—although not always—lower than rates they pay to ship similar cargo from the United States, despite longer distances. However, *data were not available to allow us to validate the examples given or verify the extent to which this occurred.* According to these shippers, lower rates, as well as limited availability of qualified vessels in some cases can lead companies to source products from foreign countries [emphasis added].[11]

In sum, after a century of the Jones Act, the situation has further deteriorated in the past two decades by the conceivably unintended actions of Congress and the possibly intentional lack of action of the Department of Transportation and the Surface Transportation Board.

Procompetitive Policy Options

Alternative approaches can be found to achieve a policy's purpose that avoid unnecessary restrictions on competition. But in this case the policies are contradictory, or at least unclear. Pro–Jones Act groups cannot have it both ways. Protectionism seems contrary to procompetitive policy reforms. Basic economic theory suggests that when an essential service, filled with public interest, is concentrated in this fashion, government needs to provide oversight, much as state governments do with public service commissions in energy and other sectors. For an island there is no greater public service than maritime transport, and yet Hawaii and Puerto Rico are powerless to protect themselves because there is federal preemption, even though the rest of the continental states are not nearly as dependent on this service. This is unacceptable.

A starting point would be to recognize the immense problem created by the policy contradictions previously explained. The concentration of these markets is the direct result of protectionist policies, so governments cannot pretend to ignore this reality and continue to act as if these are open competitive markets that can self-regulate. Regardless of past antitrust convictions or whether data exists to put a specific price tag on all of this, we cannot continue to presume that carriers with extreme market power simply do not wield it.

If the policy remains "to encourage the establishment and maintenance of reasonable rates for transportation, without unreasonable discrimination or unfair or destructive competitive practices . . . [and] to *encourage and promote service and price competition* [emphasis added] in the noncontiguous domestic trade," then Congress needs to act.[12] As it stands, the federal government simply doesn't have the necessary data to determine if the rates being charged are unreasonable, unfair, or destructive.

The simplest solution is a full repeal of the Jones Act, allowing the market to self-regulate. But if that is not politically viable, or as an interim measure,

Congress at least needs to acknowledge that DOT and STB are not adequate overseers of competition issues within the Jones Act market, as demonstrated by the fact that they have not taken any actions after the antitrust convictions and further market concentration. Neither is the GAO an adequate overseer.

There are examples of transportation regulations to deal with such a situation. The most obvious is the FMC requirement that every service contract between carriers and shippers be filed confidentially. This provides for the possibility of real oversight and basic statistics that would help shippers and consumers. Another approach is found in 49 U.S.C. § 10706 (1996) dealing with rate agreements and their exemptions from antitrust laws. It orders an evaluation of competition issues in transportation, but instead of DOT it delegates the task to the Federal Trade Commission and the Antitrust Division of the Justice Department. Specifically, it orders that:

> (e) (1) The Federal Trade Commission, in consultation with the Antitrust Division of the Department of Justice, shall prepare periodically an assessment of, and shall report to the Board on—
>
> (A) possible anticompetitive features of—
>
> > (i) agreements approved or submitted for approval under subsection (a) of this section; and
> >
> > (ii) an organization operating under those agreements; and
>
> (B) possible ways to alleviate or end an anticompetitive feature, effect, or aspect in a manner that will further the goals of this part and of the transportation policy of section 10101 of this title.[13]

Changing the current statute to assign the Federal Trade Commission and Justice Department the responsibility previously given to DOT to perform an accurate assessment of the anticompetitive features of the markets would produce a better independent analysis of the situation. It would need to be complemented with the mandatory filing of private-service contracts to provide any agency with the required data to actually fulfill its statutory goals. These findings and statistics should be published in order to create market transparency and allow shippers to better negotiate their rates, or even be able to defend themselves using private antitrust claims if those claims are supported by the published facts.

There are several other alternatives to protect shippers and consumers that could be considered if a truly open market is not politically viable, such as partial or temporary waivers. What cannot continue is ignoring the effects of policy contradictions that have recently magnified the negative effects of the Jones Act by forcing and strengthening unsupervised oligopolies on unsuspecting and ill-informed shippers and citizens.

9. The Jones Act: A Costly Failure
Steve Ellis

Part of the Jones Act's purpose is to have U.S.-built, U.S.-flagged, U.S.-owned, and U.S.-crewed vessels "carry the greater portion of [the nation's] commerce." By that measure it has failed. Even worse, it is costing taxpayers.[1]

The Decline of Coastal Shipping

According to the Bureau of Transportation Statistics,[2] of the roughly 18 billion tons of freight moved by the U.S. transportation system in 2014, only about 2.2 billion tons—roughly 12 percent—moved by water.[3] Of that amount, less than half was transported on coastwise or Jones Act vessels. Furthermore, most of that was comprised of low-value bulk products, not high-value container shipments.

In fact, with the exception of shipping on the Mississippi River system, the volume of domestic coastal and Great Lakes shipping has declined by nearly 45 percent since 1960, while at the same time railroads, pipelines, and trucking have all seen their numbers dramatically increased.[4] Furthermore, higher-value cargo has shifted to truck and rail. This should be a concern to everyone because coastwise shipping represents what would be an efficient way to move goods within the United States without adding congestion to roads and rails.

Decline of Coastal Shipping Is Partly Due to the Jones Act

Massive foreign-flagged containerships regularly enter U.S. ports from abroad. While they can offload foreign cargo and load domestic cargo all along the coast, these shipping lines typically make few port calls due to shipper demands and economies of scale.[5] The Jones Act prohibits them from transporting goods between U.S. ports. Thus they are effectively limited from providing any services beyond delivering their foreign goods to a few destinations and taking whatever goods they pick up to another country.

In a more rational system, the void left by foreign shipping would be filled by smaller U.S.-flagged feeder ships. Operating as part of a hub-and-spoke system, they would transport goods from larger ports to smaller ones. But even with the market tilted in favor of domestic carriers, the cost of constructing and operating such ships is prohibitive. In fact, a U.S.-built feeder ship is estimated to cost up to $250 million.[6] In 2019 it was estimated that such vessels can cost up to five times more than one constructed overseas.[7]

This burden is further compounded by the high cost of operating U.S.-flagged ships, which is estimated to be 2.7 times that of their foreign counterparts. These factors, along with reduced competition, drive up the cost of transport and have contributed to a dearth of domestic shipping along the U.S. coasts. Instead, Jones Act ships are more typically found plying routes to noncontiguous states and territories where other forms of transport, such as truck and rail, cannot compete.

Ports Race to Attract Foreign Shipping

Since there is little coastwise trade, port cities find themselves in a race to become a port of call from the large foreign deep-draft containerships arriving from abroad. But the ports are not racing with their own feet, or paying with their own funds. Typically, the financial burden of port-deepening projects is shared with federal taxpayers, who shoulder 75 percent of the cost (which increased from 50 percent in December of 2019).[8]

Despite significant federal involvement, there is no national port-planning strategy to identify which port is most likely to provide the greatest return on investment for federal taxpayers. Instead, each individual project is considered in isolation when bureaucrats undertake the task of determining a project's cost-effectiveness. The inevitable result is no acknowledgement or analysis of how one project will likely siphon traffic from another, and there is absolutely no system of prioritizing projects, either. This is why taxpayer-funded port-deepening projects are planned, under construction, or have been recently finished in Boston, New York City (Port of New York/New Jersey), Philadelphia, Norfolk, Charleston, Savannah, Jacksonville, Port Everglades, and Miami. But that is just the Eastern Seaboard. There are other projects along the Gulf and West Coasts, such as Portland.[9]

These port-deepening projects are creating an overcapacity that is costly to taxpayers.[10] For instance, the ports Savannah and Brunswick in Georgia envision handling 10 million TEUs (TEU is a twenty-foot equivalent unit of container capacity) within 10 years.[11] That would be more than the top two U.S. container ports (Los Angeles and Long Beach) handled in 2016 combined.[12] With roughly 75 percent of the cost of each of these projects borne by the federal taxpayer, the tab reaches into the billions of dollars. Foreign shipping lines, meanwhile, reap the economic rewards of taxpayer-subsidized overcapacity. Even as they construct vessels drafting 50 feet to take advantage of economies of scale and more-efficient transport, the number of ports competing for their business exceeds the needs of the shipping lines, especially since deeper draft vessels can reduce draft requirements depending on their load volume. Thus, they can play one port against another to achieve additional discounts.

Foreign Dredge Act Adds Another Costly Headache

Inefficiencies wrought by the Jones Act are compounded by another protectionist maritime law called the Foreign Dredge Act. Passed in 1906, the law effectively prohibits foreign companies from competing for U.S. dredging contracts.[13] While, as previously indicated, there is a glut of port-deepening projects, the Foreign Dredge Act increases taxpayer costs by contributing to a lack of dredging capacity and competition for these projects. As with the Jones Act, national security arguments in favor of the law are highly dubious. Dutch and Belgian companies dominate the worldwide dredging market.[14] These are companies based in North Atlantic Treaty Organization (NATO) ally countries, and it is absurd to think that they would not meet U.S. dredging needs during a national security crisis. (Although we do live in a world where steel and aluminum from such noted adversaries as Canada and the European Union are deemed a national security threat.)[15]

Dredges are also used for other purposes, most notably beach "replenishment" or "renourishment" projects. These are basically dredge and fill projects to place sand on eroding beaches for storm damage reduction purposes. These are federal projects that are typically authorized for 50 years. Federal taxpayers' share of initial construction costs is 65 percent and 50 percent of the cost of ongoing sand pumping during that period.[16] Depending on erosion rates and storm activity, a round of renourishment could last a decade or less than a year. Regardless of the dubious federal nature of these projects, allowing foreign dredges to compete for these contracts could dramatically reduce federal costs.

Conclusion

The Jones Act has found ardent support from domestic shipyards, U.S. carriers, and their elected representatives. But the nation as a whole—and taxpayers—would benefit from either the wholesale dismantling of the act or a significant reform of the act. Besides denying Americans access to the use of foreign ships for domestic transport, the law has effectively stymied the development of a more-efficient coastwise trade of feeder ships among ports. Adding insult to injury, it has encouraged ports to pursue taxpayer-subsidized competing port-deepening projects across the country for the benefit of foreign shipping lines. Meanwhile, for those dredging projects that are needed, allowing foreign competition could dramatically reduce taxpayer costs. Ultimately, the whole cadre of cabotage and protectionist maritime laws, including the Jones Act and the Foreign Dredge Act, should be repealed.

10. Reform the Foreign Dredge Act to Create American Jobs and Save Taxpayer Money

Howard Gutman and Andrew G. Durant

Imagine waking one morning to discover all the airlines—foreign and domestic—were suddenly flying brand-new planes. Gone overnight are the cramped 40-year-old gas guzzlers, replaced by state-of-the-art Dreamliners and A330s. A flight that used to carry 50 passengers and cost a small fortune can now carry 250 passengers at one-third the cost. Demand soars, as do profits. The roads are less clogged. It is a terrific breakthrough. A real win-win.

But also imagine that at the same time this is happening there is a critical shortage of construction equipment that prevents airports from expanding. No matter how much the airport authorities are willing to pay, it is impossible for them to find the right equipment to do the job. There is ample equipment and expertise outside the United States, and such companies would use U.S. labor to do the job, but an obscure law forbids it. As a result, it will take decades to modernize the airports. Imagine that, until that far-off day in the future, jets can only fly half-full because runways are too short. Parking lots and public transportation are not being expanded because business does not pick up. Everywhere else in the world, bigger planes are flying to bigger airports. Just not here.

This hypothetical example illustrates what is happening in another key transport industry—the maritime trade. A number of papers in this book have emphasized the need to deregulate the maritime transportation sector so that goods (including commodities, liquefied natural gas, and crude petroleum) can move more efficiently within the United States. As in the previous chapter, our focus here is on where those ships are going and on where those goods will be loaded and unloaded, and thus we also consider the Foreign Dredge Act of 1906. Executive or legislative changes that allow for the modernization of American ports would be a potential game-changer for the American economy.

U.S. Ports Are a Neglected Engine of Economic Growth

U.S. ports are responsible for $4.6 trillion in economic activity—about 25 percent of GDP. The movement of goods through ports supports 23 million American jobs and provides $321 billion in tax revenue to federal, state, and local governments.[1]

The completion of the Panama and Suez Canal expansion projects in 2016 allowed for the passage of significantly larger containerships and tankers that could cut ocean shipping costs in half.[2] At the same time international shipping infrastructure was being supersized, the fracking revolution triggered tremendous inward investments in liquefied natural gas (LNG) and petrochemicals in the United States. Much of this new capacity has been built along the Gulf Coast. The problem for the United States is that, while U.S. oil and gas are now more competitive worldwide, none of the Southeast or Gulf Coast ports are deep and wide enough to accommodate the larger, more-efficient cargo ships. There are supply gluts in some parts of the country and shortages in others. Only one of the world's 20 busiest ports is in the United States. While the private sector has proposed several new export terminals, they cannot be built so long as a 114-year old law keeps dredging capacity offshore. The Foreign Dredge Act of 1906 is a significant bottleneck to economic growth and should be repealed.

Antiquated restrictions emanating from the Foreign Dredge Act of 1906 prevent foreign dredging companies from investing in the U.S. dredging industry, hiring American workers, and bidding for work—even if they use American labor.[3] President Trump has broad legal authority to waive these restrictive provisions. Alternatively, certain provisions of the Foreign Dredge Act can be amended by Congress as part of an infrastructure bill or other legislation.

At least 10 major U.S. ports are in need and awaiting significant dredging projects to allow them to be widened and deepened to accommodate post-Panamax ships.[4] By itself, the U.S. industry is too small to carry out this task. And, because U.S. dredges are small and inefficient, the costs are prohibitive. Thus, the expectation is that 10 such critical projects will not be completed—if at all—for at least the next 15 years. Allowing foreign dredging companies to invest in the U.S. dredging market and bid competitively for U.S. dredging projects, while keeping the requirement to use American labor, would provide

sufficient capacity to simultaneously undertake all of the 10 major port projects. Opening the U.S. market would also cut costs by more than 40 percent,
thereby ensuring that sufficient funding existed to begin these projects and
to complete them all within the next four years. The repair work and ancillary
vessel work created by the dredging boom would boost struggling U.S. shipyards. Allowing foreign dredgers to invest and bid competitively for critical
dredging projects would also preserve existing American maritime jobs, create
new American jobs, and save taxpayer money. It is, in short, the single most
important economic policy initiative in America today.

Do Other Countries Restrict Dredging?

The United States and China are the only large economies that prohibit foreign dredging companies from operating on their soil. While many countries
have some restriction on maritime transportation, very few restrict maritime
construction.

The Transportation Institute—a research organization that exists solely to
promote the Jones Act—cites a dated U.S. Department of Transportation survey
that found 75 percent of the 47 countries surveyed had restrictions on domestic
shipping, but only 15 percent had restrictions on dredging.[5] Since that survey was
undertaken, the global trend has been toward greater market opening. In recent
years, for example, Canada and Vietnam have opened their dredging markets.[6]

The Bottleneck in Dredging America's Ports

Both the U.S. Army Corps of Engineers (USACE)[7] and the Government Accountability Office (GAO) have confirmed that the more than 15-year estimated
delay in dredging the 10 most important ports to post-Panamax depths is due
to lack of dredging capacity and high costs.[8] The few U.S.-based dredgers have a
woeful lack of dredging capacity: they have failed to modernize their fleets and
technology, which inflates the time needed to complete the dredging of any port,
and the exorbitant costs bid by this handful of available dredgers, who have had a
monopoly on such work, unduly exhausts the existing funding. These two major
bottlenecks can be eliminated by allowing foreign firms to bid, thereby increasing the number of capable bidders. This will have the effect of radically increasing
the available capacity, upgrading the available technology, and slashing prices.

Foreign companies—using the same U.S. labor—will then be able to invest in the United States and bid competitively for U.S. dredging projects.

Lack of Existing U.S. Dredging Capacity

Given the relative lack of investment in new dredges and technology in the United States in the previous two decades (likely caused by industry management deciding to focus on the protected U.S. market and not competing internationally), the U.S. fleet has far fewer, far smaller, and far older dredges than their foreign counterparts. From 2000 to 2019, just four Belgian and Dutch companies built 56 new hopper dredges (almost all in European yards, where labor and energy costs are significantly higher than in the United States).[9] In contrast, all American shipyards combined only built four new dredges.[10] As shown in Table 10.1, these companies have 10 times the hopper dredge capacity of the combined U.S. fleet.[11] One or more of the four Belgian and Dutch companies win more than 90 percent of the competitive bids worldwide, while U.S. companies are not nearly as competitive outside the protected U.S. market. Because they compete worldwide, the four Belgian and Dutch companies operate 25 dredges that are larger than *any* dredge in the United States.[12] The largest Belgian-Dutch dredge is three times the size of the largest U.S. dredge.

Table 10.1 Change in hopper and cutter capacity, Belgian-Dutch companies, compared to the largest U.S. dredging company, 2004–2017

Company	Nationality	Hoppers, cubic meters (m³), percent	Cutters, kilowatts (kW), percent
Jan De Nul	Belgian	106	140
Van Oord	Dutch	9	7
Boskalis	Dutch	8	−18
DEME	Belgian	48	52
Great Lakes	American	−9	−10

Source: Rabobank, "Dredging: Rising Impact Hurricanes Stimulates Dredging Markets," October 2017.

In 2003, 2008, and as recently as 2014, the GAO issued reports criticizing the lack of competition in the U.S. dredging market and the resulting failure of American-owned companies to invest in improving and enlarging the fleet. The 2003 study found no evidence that prices or performance were better with the private sector bidding on federal projects than it had been when the work was reserved for U.S. Army Corps of Engineers dredges.[13] In a 2014 report to Congress, the GAO criticized restrictions limiting the use of the small and old dredges that remained in the USACE fleet. Restrictions on these dredges

> imposed costs on the Corps' dredging program but had not resulted in proven benefits, such as increased industry competition or lower prices for hopper dredging. . . First, since 2003, the number of companies with hopper dredges in the United States has not changed, although the number of industry hopper dredges and the total size of these dredges have *decreased*. . .[and] the total number of industry vessels *decreased* from 16 to 13 and the total capacity of these vessels, as measured in cubic yards, *decreased* by 16 percent [emphasis added].[14]

In addition, the report "did not find evidence of increased competition based on the number of bidders and winning bid prices for Corps hopper dredging projects since 2003."[15]

This lack of U.S. investment and capacity and the radical differences between the four Belgian and Dutch companies and the entire U.S. fleet was further documented in an October 2017 report on the global dredging industry published by Rabobank industry analysts.[16] In the report, Rabobank revealed how the fleets of the four major Belgian and Dutch companies and the only U.S. company large enough to make its list (Great Lakes, by far the largest U.S. dredger) had changed between 2004 and 2017 (see Table 10.1).

Table 10.2 compares the current hopper dredge capacity of the Belgian and Dutch companies to American companies. Hopper capacity is measured by the amount of material that the dredge can hold. A comparison of the U.S. fleet to the European fleet shows that the four largest Belgian and Dutch dredging companies have eight times the capacity of the combined U.S. fleet.

Table 10.3 compares the current cutter dredge capacity of the Belgian and Dutch companies to American companies. Cutter suction dredges use a very powerful cutter head to chew through hard rocks and to get into the nooks and crannies that hopper dredges can't reach. Material is either deposited into a

Table 10.2 Trailing suction hopper dredge capacity, Belgian-Dutch companies, compared to the U.S. fleet, 2017

Company	Nationality	Capacity, cubic yards
Jan De Nul	Belgian	447,524
Van Oord	Dutch	331,790
Boskalis	Dutch	281,944
DEME	Belgian	272,470
Great Lakes	American	49,987
Manson	American	23,012
Weeks Marine	American	16,553
Dutra	American	14,728

Source: IHS Markit, *International Dredging Directory*, August 2018.

barge (which typically may require towing) or is sent by pipeline to an onshore placement area. Typically, the placement areas must be within three miles of where the cutter is working. This limited range can prove to be quite expensive because special placement areas must be created which can add hundreds of millions of dollars to a project's cost. Using large hopper dredges eliminates this cost. Cutter dredges were considered state-of-the-art technology 25 years ago but have been eclipsed for most work by the hopper dredge. Here again, the Low Countries' industry is significantly larger than the U.S. industry but only by a factor of three, owing to a historical U.S. reliance on cutter dredges.

High Costs Cause Shortages in U.S. Funding and Contribute to Delays

American dredging firms have argued on occasion that, although U.S. dredging capacity is not able to handle all the work that is now critically needed, the capacity exists to handle those projects that the government is able to fund if they are done one at a time rather than all at once. They essentially claim that the terribly destructive U.S. dredging bottleneck is caused primarily by the funding shortfall rather than by the lack of capacity and capability.

Table 10.3   Cutter suction dredge capacity, Belgian-Dutch companies, compared to the U.S. fleet, 2017

Company	Nationality	Capacity, horsepower (hp)
Jan De Nul	Belgian	323,225
DEME	Belgian	239,516
Van Oord	Dutch	137,398
Boskalis	Dutch	128,310
Great Lakes	American	107,851
Weeks Marine	American	101,284
Orion	American	79,596
Manson	American	20,009

Source: IHS Markit, *International Dredging Directory*, August 2018.

As a preliminary matter, given the lack of capacity, the USACE routinely needs to divert dredges from approved and ongoing projects to respond to emergencies and shoaling needs, thus considerably delaying even *funded* projects. But more fundamentally, blaming the massive backlog in tackling vital U.S. infrastructure needs on funding rather than on the lack of investment, capacity, and capability of the U.S. dredge fleet ignores that the paucity of U.S. dredging capacity and capability creates, or at least contributes mightily to, the U.S. funding shortfall. The relative lack of size, capacity, and capability—added to the lack of real competition among the handful of U.S. companies in the bidding process—has greatly and unduly increased the cost of past and existing projects, as well as the projected costs of future projects. The dearth of capacity and unduly high costs directly cause the funding shortfalls.

The USACE has needed, and still needs, to design projects in a manner that allows them to be undertaken by the smaller, older, and less-well-equipped dredges that are available in the U.S. fleet. For example, projects that could be done far more quickly and economically by relying on large, fast hopper dredges that can efficiently carry dredge spoils great distances to offshore deposit sites must be designed for, and performed by, far smaller cutter suction dredges that require the U.S. dredgers to build onshore placement areas to hold the dredge spoils, thus adding years of delay and tens or hundreds of millions of dollars to a given project (such as in Houston, which has a 53-mile channel). Forced to rely on far smaller and less-advanced dredges, U.S. companies must often build blasting platforms and undertake blasting operations that add significant costs and delays to a project, while needlessly destroying coral. This has already occurred in Miami, according to a report by the Department of Commerce's National Oceanic and Atmospheric Administration.[17]

Although supporters of the U.S. industry tout that there are more than 50 American dredging companies, only a handful of American companies have a dredge large enough to enable them to bid on and handle these major port projects. Indeed, the 2015 USACE Awards Database confirmed that a single company handled 42 percent of the U.S. work, including every project over $100 million.[18] A 2018 Center for Strategic and International Studies (CSIS) report further confirms USACE's explanation of the high costs for U.S. dredging projects. Reviewing contract bid data for fiscal years 1997–2015 for maintenance hopper dredging projects in the Gulf Coast, the study explains that

> controlling for the size of the job, we found that the actual cost per cubic yard of material removed was inversely related to the number of bidders. That is, the actual cost per cubic yard of material removed was lower for projects with a greater number of bidders . . . [T]he actual costs to the Corps of the removal of one cubic yard of material was $5.32 when there was only one bidder for the project. When there were two bidders, the actual costs fell by $1.71 to $3.61 per cubic yard; when there were three bidders, the project costs fell by $2.30, to $3.02 per cubic yards; and for four or more bidders, the project costs fell by $3.45 to $1.87 per cubic yard. . . These results confirm the value (to the Corps, and indirectly to the taxpayers) of introducing more bidders into hopper dredging auctions.[19]

Thus, if four companies bid on a project, the price is 65 percent lower than when there is only one bidder. Having four or more companies bid results in a 40 percent discount compared to the price if only three companies participate. As the CSIS study confirms, even ignoring the vast size and capability differences between the companies seeking entry into the U.S. market and the existing U.S. fleet (resulting from the decades of massive investment difference), just adding extra bidders for each project will produce massive savings for both the ports and taxpayers.

Foreign dredgers bid aggressively against each other all over the world, and the four Belgian and Dutch companies highlighted earlier have won more than 90 percent of all international competitive bid projects, including, for example, the Panama Canal; the Suez Canal; Singapore; the Palm Islands of Dubai; offshore drilling islands (such as the Satah al-Razboot in Abu Dhabi and Pluit City in Jakarta); and coastal defense projects (such as in North Holland, Jakarta, and Ghana), among others. They have not, of course, yet engaged in formal bidding for any of the projects that are detailed in Army Corps project documents, but there is no strong economic argument for their exclusion.

Coastal Defenses and the Beneficial Use of Dredged Material

The number of Americans living in high-density coastal areas that are vulnerable to sea level rise will continue to increase. The threats to urban populations, infrastructure, and capital will increase as sea levels rise and hurricanes become more powerful. The devastation to New Orleans, New Jersey, New York, and Houston shows that the danger of strong storms is very real. The *Wall Street Journal* reports that prices for houses close to the beach in Florida have declined drastically compared to prices for houses further inland.[20] There is further evidence that coastal defenses are becoming a real concern:

- Florida Governor Ron DeSantis (R-FL) signed an executive order to "[c]reate the Office of Resilience and Coastal Protection to help prepare Florida's coastal communities and habitats for impacts from sea level rise by providing funding, technical assistance and coordination among state, regional and local entities."[21]
- New York City Mayor de Blasio (D-NY) announced a $10 billion plan to protect Lower Manhattan from the storms that "are already inevitable." The plan calls for the creation of more land in lower Manhattan—home of the world's financial markets and the nexus for the subway system—at heights of 20 feet.[22] This appears similar to the defenses that were erected to protect Rotterdam. Twenty-two hopper dredges were used to build the Rotterdam defenses and to extend the port. In comparison, the six largest U.S. dredging firms only have 15 hopper dredges between them.

- The State of Louisiana has funded a $20 billion project to limit the subsidence of land in the Mississippi Delta, which threatens lifestyles and habitat from salt-water incursion and makes coastal cities more vulnerable to high-impact hurricanes.[23]
- Hurricane Harvey demonstrated that a direct hit to Houston would severely damage port and industry infrastructure.[24] In future storms, even if the infrastructure survives—and there is no environmental calamity—it would still be months before people could return to work.[25] Several ambitious coastal defense plans are under consideration[26] because another direct hit on Houston would be an economic calamity that would hit *every* American: 70 percent of the fuel used by U.S. airlines is refined in Houston, and as of 2017, 30 percent of the total U.S. refining capacity for gasoline is also located in Texas.[27]

While there is no single solution for these challenges, they all involve dredging and the use of dredged material, whether it be for the construction of barrier islands, storm surge barriers, restoration of natural wetlands, or other measures. For the same reasons that U.S. port projects are grossly overpriced, building out coastal defenses in the United States will take decades longer if the tiny U.S. dredging industry retains its monopoly protection.

Accomplishing the Task: National Security Waiver or Revision of the Foreign Dredge Act

There are two readily available means to open the U.S. dredging market to investment and competitive bidding by foreign dredgers. The first is to waive certain provisions of the Foreign Dredge Act of 1906, which would be a positive start in lifting the burden of this law on U.S. ports. The second would be for Congress to pass comprehensive legislative reform, but this is likely the second step in the reform process. Both of these actions would have no impact on the Jones Act but instead would allow critical shortfalls in U.S. dredging capacity to be addressed immediately.

President Trump can immediately waive certain provisions of the Foreign Dredge Act of 1906. One option is to keep the existing requirement to use at least 75 percent U.S. labor and clarify that the Jones Act does not regulate the movement of sand as part of construction. In its December 2017 *National Security Strategy* report, the administration stated that

> for the first time American strategy recognizes that economic security is national security . . . economic prosperity at home is absolutely necessary for American power and influence abroad . . . The United States will promote exports of our energy resources, technologies, and services, which helps our allies and partners diversify their energy sources and brings economic gains back home. We will expand our export capacity through the continued support of private sector development of coastal terminals, allowing increased market access and a greater competitive edge for U.S. industries.[28]

On October 29, 2018, the Carlyle Group and the Port of Corpus Christi announced that they would work together to develop a crude oil export terminal that they hope to begin operating in late 2020. This project squarely meets the White House National Security Strategy standards for national security waivers: indeed, the project *requires* such additional, cost-effective capacity to be made available. In July 2018, two U.S. dredging companies submitted a fixed-fee bid for the first phase of a much more modest dredging project in Corpus Christi. The lowest bid was 80 percent higher than the USACE project budget. Since then, the USACE has publicly questioned whether it would be necessary to waive the Jones Act to allow European dredgers to bid for work in the United States, given the clear need for more-competitive bids.

A similar national security challenge exists at the Port of Houston. The port has been severely compromised by the millions of tons of sediment that washed into the Houston Shipping Channel as a result of the unprecedented rainfall brought by Hurricane Harvey. The complete closure of the channel for five days caused a major disruption to refinery operations, resulting in an average 15-cent per gallon increase nationwide within a week.[29] It has been estimated that "[e]ach 10-cent rise in the price of gasoline is equivalent to a $10 billion tax on consumers."[30]

Draft restrictions for most of the petrochemical industry and container terminals lasted for eight months following Harvey, and restrictions still existed more than a year after the hurricane for the upper channel, a reach that had more than 1,200 deep-draft vessel calls in that period. After the hurricane, the ships calling at the upper channel were limited to a 25-foot draft—the same as

100 years ago. The draft restriction of the main channel resulted in both business uncertainty and economic losses.[31] This loss occurred even though up to five federal dredges worked on storm recovery. As a practical matter, therefore, the ships and tankers using the Port of Houston must carry significantly less cargo in the channel in order to navigate safely.

Given their small size and advanced age, hopper dredges operated by American dredgers can only operate efficiently within 5–10 miles of the Houston Shipping Channel entrance. After that distance, it becomes cheaper for American dredgers to use cutter suction dredges, which creates the problem of where to place the dredged material. If the port could use modern hopper dredges, it would not need to spend any of that money. Moreover, the cost to dredge a cubic yard of material using a modern hopper dredge can be less than half the cost of using a cutter suction dredger.

While some opponents of reform try to bolster the Jones Act by arguing in favor of national security, none of their arguments apply to a waiver of the Foreign Dredge Act. For instance, dredges have never been part of the defense forces of the United States. Opening the market to allow North Atlantic Treaty Organization (NATO) allies to dredge in the United States using U.S. labor is, in fact, vital to enhancing the national security of the United States. Such a waiver will allow ports to be dredged in a manner that will slash export costs and allow American oil and gas to be readily exported. Opening the dredging market will also enhance national security by protecting vulnerable East Coast cities. What we see now, however, is that by limiting U.S. energy exports, these restrictions are impairing national security as defined by the current administration.

The national security waiver or the necessary legislative change can be realized, and the dredging market opened to new investment and competitive bidding, by focusing virtually exclusively on the Foreign Dredge Act of 1906. While a presidential waiver would provide a test case to demonstrate the value to the American economy and taxpayer from allowing more and larger companies to bid for projects, it would fall to Congress to make the changes to the Foreign Dredge Act that would create a more sustainable economic environment. The best way to accomplish this is to let one or two projects move forward under a waiver. After that, Congress will clamor to act.

Reforming the Jones Act

11. Needed: A Cost-Benefit Analysis of the Jones Act

Ted Loch-Temzelides

Part of the Jones Act's stated purpose is to ensure the viability of the U.S. maritime and shipping industries. Clearly, the act is protectionist, as it prevents foreign-flagged and foreign-built ships from carrying cargo between two points in the United States. This reduced competition in both shipbuilding and in transporting goods inevitably leads to higher prices. For example, Jones Act ships can cost four to five times as much to build as those built in foreign shipyards.[1] Critics of the act argue that a large fraction of these costs is passed on to consumers, who have to pay higher prices for the transported goods, or for goods using high-cost inputs that are transported by Jones Act vessels. Places such as Hawaii and Puerto Rico are particularly affected because of their reliance on maritime transportation.

Proponents of the Jones Act argue that it helps the U.S. maritime industry and that it is vital to national security. While the national security argument has some merit, the high costs associated with the Jones Act have led consumers of transportation services to seek alternatives to maritime transportation within U.S. borders.

Despite the Jones Act's importance, there is little economics literature devoted to a rigorous evaluation of the costs and benefits that it generates for the U.S. economy. As the active debate on the act suggests, its consequences are at least partly *redistributive*: protectionism creates an economic rent in the form of increased profits for industry participants at the cost of reducing the surplus to other producers, consumers of transportation services, and final consumers.

To properly evaluate these costs and benefits, we need a comparison of the total consumer and producer surpluses. Starting with the status quo under the Jones Act, we would need to compare the current total surpluses to the corresponding ones absent the Jones Act, in which case competition resulting from the entry of foreign producers would bring prices to the world-price level. Most foreign-flagged vessels operate in competitive, largely unregulated markets, and are often subject to low compliance costs. As a result, and since foreign and domestic vessels are largely considered to be near-perfect substitutes in transportation, foreign competition would likely result in significant reductions in freight rates should the Jones Act be repealed.

Of course, the Jones Act has far-reaching implications for the entire U.S. transportation sector, which are impossible to capture in their entirety. As an example, the U.S. trucking and rail industries, as well as the ports, would be affected in complex ways if the Jones Act were to be repealed. Perhaps most importantly for our focus, the domestic maritime industry would, at least in the beginning, most likely be largely uncompetitive given its higher cost structure, leading to a decline in the size of the domestic fleet, as only the most efficient and low-cost domestic firms would be able to compete. For a complete cost-benefit analysis, such losses in domestic producer surplus need to be aggregated and compared with the total increase in consumer surplus. The resulting net effect will determine the desirability of a potential policy change.

There are very few studies by economists considering the implications of repealing the Jones Act.[2] Martin Stopford's classic *Maritime Economics* textbook provides a comprehensive treatment of several topics related to maritime economics.[3] In a rigorous academic study, Richard A. Smith documents the decline in U.S. Merchant Marine employment since the Jones Act was implemented.[4] None of these studies attempts to perform a full cost-benefit analysis of the Jones Act. Perhaps the closest to our proposed approach can be found in the study by Justin Lewis, which computes a low bound for the losses associated with the act.[5] However, his analysis is limited due to the lack of availability of actual price data for Jones Act vessels.

Importantly, even if rigorous analysis convincingly concludes that repealing the Jones Act would lead to overall welfare (surplus) gains, this would likely be far from sufficient to make progress toward repealing the act. Since any potential changes to the act will create big losers, as well as (even bigger) winners, a discussion is needed on how the winners might at least partially "compensate" the losers, at least in the short run. As we have been painfully witnessing over several decades, absent such compensation it will be difficult to create the consensus that is necessary to implement changes. Yet critics of the Jones Act seldom discuss the size and the form of the "carrot" that will be necessary to induce cooperation from the domestic shipping industry.

Welfare Analysis: Consumer and Producer Surplus

The qualitative aspects of the welfare analysis are summarized in Figure 11.1 Let us consider a single Jones Act market, for example, product tankers. First, consider economic equilibrium in the status quo; that is, in the presence of the Jones Act. The graph on the right represents the world equilibrium product tanker freight-rate, p_w, as determined by world supply and demand. This is lower than p_{us}, the resulting freight rate in the United States under the Jones Act (left graph). The equilibrium quantity of maritime transport services by Jones Act vessels is represented by the horizontal distance $\overline{OB}$. The total welfare created in the United States is then given by the sum of the consumer surplus (area 1) plus the producer surplus (areas 2 + 3).

What if the Jones Act was to be repealed? Once permitted, foreign vessels would find it attractive to enter the U.S. market and supply their capacity at the initially high rate, $p_{us} > p_w$. This would increase the supply of vessels in the United States, thus bidding the price down to the world price, p_w. The total

Figure 11.1
Economic surplus

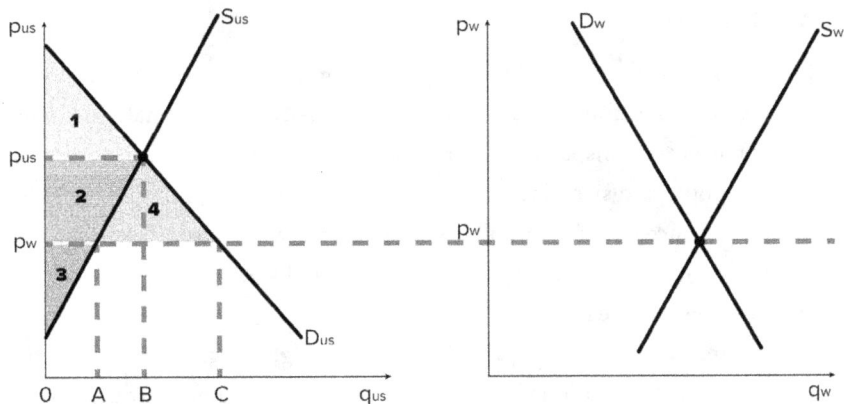

Source: Illustration by author; graph illustrates a theoretical proof of concept.

quantity of maritime transportation services in the United States extends all the way to $\overline{OC}$. However, notice that only interval $\overline{OA}$ is produced by U.S.-flagged vessels. These are the lowest-cost domestic vessels, which would compete with foreign providers. The remaining supply, as given by distance $\overline{AC}$, represents supply by foreign vessels.

The figure tells a robust qualitative story. While repealing the Jones Act would increase the total quantity of products transported across U.S. ports, the quantity transported by U.S.-flagged vessels is likely to *decrease*. The overall result is that U.S. consumer surplus would increase to areas 1 + 2 + 4 (from area 1 previously), while U.S. producer surplus would shrink to area 3 (from areas 2 + 3 previously). Thus, repealing the Jones Act would redistribute some existing surplus (area 2) from U.S. producers to U.S. consumers.

However, this is not all. Repealing the Jones Act would also add to overall efficiency by eliminating a deadweight loss (area 4). Determining the magnitude of these efficiency gains is a quantitative question. Notice, for example, that the relative size of the corresponding triangles depends on the elasticities of the corresponding supply and demand curves. To compute these magnitudes, we would need to econometrically estimate the corresponding supply and demand functions.[6] This, in turn, requires access to historical data on both domestic and international spot or charter rates. While data on international rates is available from various sources, it is difficult to obtain historical price rates for Jones Act vessels.

Conclusion

Repealing the Jones Act will inevitably lead to an economic surplus redistribution. Domestic consumers of transportation services, as well as final consumers of goods currently transported by Jones Act vessels, would gain (areas 2 + 4), while the profits and size of the current Jones Act fleet would decline (area 2). Since the presence of the act implies nonnegligible overall deadweight welfare losses (area 4), it is almost certain that there would be overall welfare gains should the Jones Act be repealed.

Two issues arise. First, the gains have to be weighed against the potential implications for U.S. national security, which are rather hard to quantify directly and have also been called into question.[7] In other words, we can compute a lower bound on how large the national security benefits of the act need to be in order to justify the welfare losses created by the act. Second, to go from theory to practice, in order to induce legislative change, the winners will need to compensate the losers in some way for the corresponding loss in surplus. The model presented here asserts that this should be possible, as market liberalization would be associated with an overall welfare gain. However, this will require the establishment of an active dialogue between critics of the act and representatives from the domestic shipping industry.

12. Time to Mobilize the Dispersed Costs of the Jones Act

Nicolas Loris

A drink is not just a drink when it reflects the history and flavor of a place.

So goes the slogan for Bob Gunter's Kōloa Rum Company on the island of Kauai.[1] Gunter takes pride in using local ingredients and bottled his first batch of Hawaiian rum in 2009 to share those unique flavors, history, and sense of place with the rest of the world.

Kōloa Rum uses Hawaiian cane sugar and mountain rainwater for its single-batch rum. The company purchases guava, passionfruit, and papayas from local farmers to produce its flavored varieties. Gunter partners with Kauai Coffee Company on the island to make a specialty brew for their coffee flavored rum. They even buy boxes from local island manufacturers.

But buying local does not always make financial sense for Gunter. And it is not always a choice. In fact, an antiquated, protectionist law *forces* Gunter to pay significantly more to use "local" shipping to send his rum to the mainland. Buying local means, because of the Jones Act, using U.S.-built, U.S.-owned, and U.S.-operated ships to send cargo rather than using cheaper, more efficient foreign-flagged carriers.

Advocates of the law maintain that the Jones Act is necessary to protect jobs and America's shipbuilding base, but the economic costs of the law far outweigh the benefits to protected special interests. Jones Act vessels are more expensive to build and have dramatically higher operating costs than other options available to shippers.[2] Jones Act vessels also have higher maintenance costs, as it is more costly to repair and maintain vessels in domestic shipyards compared to repairing and maintaining them in foreign ones.[3] Repair and maintenance work on U.S. tankers costs almost 70 percent more than comparable work on foreign tankers.[4]

Consequently, even though shipping cargo within the United States typically involves much shorter distances than international voyages, it is also much more expensive.[5]

For companies such as Kōloa Rum, the additional shipping costs are exorbitant. Gunter once shipped a container of rum to Sydney, Australia, but the product had to go to California first. In the past, there was no viable alternative to shipping to-and-from Hawaii and foreign destinations without first transiting through a U.S. mainland port.[6] Using a Jones Act vessel from Honolulu to Los Angeles, California—a distance of 2,618 miles—cost Gunter $6,900.[7] Using a foreign vessel from California to Sydney, a distance of approximately 7,500 miles, cost him $1,900.[8]

Every time Kōloa Rum ships its product to the mainland or Alaska using mandatory Jones Act vessels, the company's shipping cost more than triples.

Hawaii is already an expensive place to operate a business, and the Jones Act unnecessarily drives operating costs even higher. Ironically, international competitors find it cheaper to export rum to the United States than Gunter finds it to sell his product within his own country's borders.[9]

For some businesses, the steep price of the Jones Act was too much to overcome. O'Keefe & Sons Bread Bakers on the Big Island closed in 2008 after 13 years of operation.[10] Small business owner Jim O'Keefe laid off 50 workers and cited the more than six figures he spent on protectionist shipping costs as a major reason why the business shuttered its doors.[11]

Cumulatively, the premium American families and businesses pay because of Jones Act requirements conservatively reaches billions, if not tens of billions, of dollars every year.[12] Some businesses absorb the costs, which means less investment for a new piece of equipment or less money to hire a new employee. Other businesses pass the costs onto consumers, which suppresses demand and makes competing foreign products more economically attractive.

Entire Economy Affected

While America's noncontiguous states and territories suffer disproportionately, every single business that ships a product between U.S. points incurs those higher transportation prices. For instance, transporting energy—whether it is crude oil or refined products—from the Gulf Coast to the Northeast is more expensive than sending these products to a foreign destination.[13] For example, shipping crude oil from the Gulf Coast to Canadian refineries costs $2 to $3 per barrel, but thanks to the Jones Act it can cost between $5 and $6 to ship it to the East Coast.[14]

This not only adversely affects energy producers but also energy-consuming households and businesses. As the CEO of Gulf Oil pointed out in 2013: "If foreign-owned and flag ships were able to carry gasoline in U.S. waters, the price of gasoline in the North East and in Florida could be 20 to 30 cents lower."[15] Jones Act repeal would provide relief at the pump for drivers and also give U.S. businesses more of a competitive edge because their cost of business decreases with the decline in the price of gas.

Families in the Northeast, especially those dependent on home heating oil, would welcome more domestically produced crude and refined petroleum products transported by ship. This could be less expensive than imports or products transported by rail, where sufficient pipeline capacity is not available.

The opportunity costs are significant as well. Iowa and Ohio soybean growers miss out on opportunities to sell their product to North Carolina hog farmers, who choose to buy cheaper soybean meal from Brazil.[16] According to representatives of the Puerto Rican Farm Bureau, "[S]hipping feed from New Jersey by Jones Act carriers costs more per ton than shipping from Saint John, Canada, by a foreign carrier—even though Saint John is 500 miles further [sic] away."[17] But soybeans aren't the only casualty of the law. Other Puerto Rican food importers purchase corn, potatoes, and other agricultural products from foreign countries rather than U.S. farmers.[18]

The rock salt market is yet another market where the Jones Act disrupts open competition. The United States is the second-largest producer of rock salt in the world.[19] Ninety-five percent of the rock salt, which is used to salt roads during snow and ice storms, comes from seven states: Kansas, Louisiana, Michigan, New York, Ohio, Texas, and Utah.[20] These states and domestic rock salt producers lose when places such as Maryland and Virginia import their rock salt from Chile through the Panama Canal rather than purchase domestic rock salt shipped from the Port of South Louisiana.

The opportunity costs also extend beyond lost sales for American businesses. A few years ago, the Jones Act prevented New Jersey officials from using a foreign ship to transport salt from Maine in time to respond to a winter storm. James Simpson, the state's Department of Transportation Commissioner, stated, "I've got a shipload of salt, 400 miles from here. The only thing that we've been able to define as an American flag vessel would take us a month to get the salt here when I can have the salt here in a day and a half."[21]

New Jersey was forced to spend an additional $700,000 to use a Jones Act vessel to ship rock salt from Searsport, Maine, to Port Newark.[22] The state government could have spent that $700,000 elsewhere to the benefit of its citizens (or better yet, taxed them less!). Jones Act proponents called the New Jersey debacle a result of bad planning, but the real culprit is bad policy.

Illusory National Security Benefit

The national security benefits the Jones Act purportedly brings are similarly nonexistent. Supporters of the protectionist law argue that such benefits include a merchant fleet that the Department of Defense can use in times of crisis, and sustaining the industrial base for U.S. shipbuilding.

Neither argument has been borne out by actual experience.[23] Both the domestic fleet of ships and U.S. shipbuilding capabilities have atrophied significantly.[24] By 2000, the Jones Act–eligible fleet consisted of just 193 ships, and that number has now shrunk to 99, with 79 qualifying as militarily useful.[25]

Furthermore, the Department of Defense has frequently leased foreign vessels to execute missions that require additional sealift capacity. The Maritime Administration's Ready Reserve Force also proves that maritime security does not rely on the Jones Act.[26] This fleet, created for "transport of Army and Marine Corps unit equipment, combat support equipment, and initial resupply during the critical surge period before commercial ships can be marshaled," has supplied the military at the outset of both the Iraq and Afghanistan wars, as well as in past conflicts.[27]

Currently, 30 of the 46 Ready Reserve Force ships are foreign-built.[28] If the U.S. military is comfortable with using foreign vessels during wartime, the argument that they are less safe in commercial use makes little sense. Jones Act supporters often point out that Jones Act mariners would be available to crew reserve fleet ships in times of war. However, if more mariners are necessary for sustained periods of war, the Navy should address any strategic readiness shortfalls and mobilization needs it deems necessary using the defense appropriations process, which could include expanded training through the Navy Reserve. Providing the Navy's requirements through defense funding will allocate resources to what the Navy actually needs without the harmful economic distortions the Jones Act causes.

Even if there were a demonstrable national security benefit, the Jones Act is an incredibly inefficient way to maintain naval capabilities. Subjecting the entire U.S. economy and specific industries to the inefficiencies of a massive protectionist regime for the claimed security benefits is absurd, and it also has numerous distortionary impacts. If the U.S. military is not comfortable using foreign vessels, then it should simply purchase the ships it needs as part of the defense program and spread the costs to all American taxpayers as a public good.

Broad Repeal Coalition Needed

The difficulty in eliminating crony, preferential policies such as the Jones Act is the public-choice problem of concentrated benefits and dispersed costs. Entrenched interests have a strong incentive to maintain the status quo, which keeps them from having to compete for American customers—and their lobbying efforts reflect that. On the other hand, there is less incentive for an individual to bang on a member of Congress's door when the costs of the Jones Act are thinly spread across all consumers.

However, the costs are more substantial than simply tallying the aggregate cost to consumers. Small business bankruptcies because of the Jones Act, for example, are heartbreaking, and they tell a compelling personal story of the real costs of cronyism. In turn, they are a powerful weapon that can mobilize business communities, small and large, that are harmed by the Jones Act.

The states and territories of Alaska, Guam, Hawaii, and Puerto Rico have been carrying the mantle for Jones Act reform for decades because they incur the highest proportion of its costs. However, the preferential treatment for a select few also harms an eclectic mix of businesses on America's mainland. Small businesses, farmers, energy companies, and rock salt producers are just a handful of the industries negatively affected. There are many more businesses and communities out there. The revival of a repeal coalition could galvanize these businesses to unite against the common enemy that exists in the Jones Act.

The Case against the Jones Act

The late Sen. John McCain (R-AZ) was a unique champion for Jones Act repeal because he saw the policy for the protectionist nonsense that it is. His concern for U.S. national security was also beyond question. Sadly, however, few members of Congress have followed in his footsteps. If industries band together and collectively knock on doors, more members of Congress in Iowa, North Carolina, New Jersey, and other states will start to pay attention.

Strange bedfellows turn heads in Washington, and the case for Jones Act repeal should be one such instance. For instance, when a conservative and liberal think tank team up on an issue, or when Big Oil and Big Green form an influential alliance, people pay attention.

Many good economists have challenged the economic rationale for the Jones Act,[29] and many national security experts have pointed out the fallacies of the defense rationale.[30] True reform will come from unified, repetitive outcry from the "dispersed costs" coalition.

13. Reforming the Jones Act for American Energy Consumers

James W. Coleman

The shale revolution is steaming along, bringing the United States abundant energy, high-paying jobs, and new sway in global energy markets. But the Jones Act has cut many Americans off from these new resources, leaving them stranded in energy-starved markets. Congress should reform the Jones Act so these new riches can be shared with all Americans.

The Jones Act requires that shipments between two U.S. points be on U.S.-built, U.S.-manned, U.S.-flagged, and U.S.-owned vessels. But there are only 99 Jones Act–compliant large ships—including 57 tankers—which is not nearly enough to support the booming U.S. oil and natural gas industry.[1] In fact, there is not a single Jones Act–compliant ship that carries natural gas.[2] As a result, U.S. liquefied natural gas is being sent to China, Europe, and South America, while American consumers are cut off from their own country's resources.

The Jones Act has a long list of perverse consequences for American energy producers and consumers:

- Boston cannot have natural gas shipped from Louisiana, so it skirts U.S. sanctions to import gas from Russia.[3]
- Texas is constrained in its ability to send its flood of oil to Puerto Rico or the East Coast, so instead it ships the oil to Europe and China.[4]
- Forced to declare bankruptcy, the East Coast's largest refinery noted that it was actually "cheaper to transport crude oil from North Dakota to points in Western Europe than to transport the same crude oil to Philadelphia."[5]
- And Puerto Rico, forced to declare bankruptcy in 2017, and desperate for cheap oil and gas to maintain its power grid, must buy these commodities abroad at inflated prices.[6]

The U.S. energy boom is accelerating. To ensure that it benefits all Americans, the Jones Act must be reformed.

The American Energy Boom

Oil is the commodity that built the modern world. For more than a century, oil booms have built fortunes, nations, and legends. But in the history of the world, there has never been an oil boom like the one that is currently underway in the United States.

The biggest previous oil boom was in Saudi Arabia in the late 1960s, when it increased production by one million barrels of oil per day in a year. More recently, U.S. oil production has been up more than two million barrels per day, and more than half of that increase is in Texas. And in real terms, oil is worth more than twice what it was in the 1960s, so in monetary terms the current boom dwarfs any previous one.[7] Simply put, it is the biggest commodity boom the world has ever seen.

This is bringing countless benefits to the United States, especially in the oil producing regions of Texas, North Dakota, and New Mexico.[8] This flood of oil means cheap gasoline to drive the economy. And there has been a significant increase in natural gas production as well—giving the United States an affordable clean-burning fuel to power its electric grid.

This unprecedented boom, however, is straining transport networks, which are running at full capacity.[9] To keep the boom going, energy producers need to be able to send their oil and gas to new markets. Because of the Jones Act, American producers usually cannot ship this flood of oil and gas to U.S. ports—they have to send it abroad.

How the Jones Act Cuts Off American Consumers and Holds Back American Companies

The Jones Act is sometimes defended as an inducement for U.S. shipbuilding, but if that is the goal, it has been an abject failure: over the last century the number of U.S. oceangoing vessels has collapsed[10] and what remains of the American fleet is an aging remnant, far older than the international norm for shipping.[11]

As a result, it is generally impractical to ship American oil and gas to American ports. It costs up to three times more to ship oil from Texas to refineries on the East Coast than it costs to ship to Canada; even the cost of shipping from Saudi Arabia is less than half the price of shipping from a U.S. port.[12] Furthermore, shipping to Europe is just half the price of reaching a U.S. port.

But it gets worse. Even if producers were willing to pay these inflated prices, there is often simply no shipping available at any price. For example, large volumes of natural gas can only be transported overseas by cooling the gas until it becomes a liquid and then loading it onto a special refrigerated liquefied natural gas (LNG) carrier. There are no Jones Act–eligible LNG carriers, so the gas simply cannot be shipped to a U.S. port.[13]

Thanks to the shale revolution, the United States is now exporting LNG all over the globe—to Europe, Asia, and Latin America. These exports will ramp up in the coming years, making the United States one of the premier gas suppliers, providing clean fuel to the world and increased economic and geopolitical sway to America. But unless the Jones Act is changed, U.S. consumers will benefit little from this bounty.[14]

These perverse consequences for the LNG industry are just one example of a problem that the Jones Act creates for American companies every day: What can you do when you need a specialized product that is produced in the United States but cannot be transported by a Jones Act–compliant ship? Imagine that a U.S. producer needs a specialized rig for a new oil well: as the world's biggest oil and gas producer, the United States often has the needed equipment. But the antiquated Jones Act fleet often does not have vessels capable of transporting this kind of equipment. So the U.S. producer will have to find a foreign supplier to ship a replacement rig, increasing its expenses and costing American jobs.

Reforming the Jones Act

At a minimum, the Jones Act must be reformed so that it does not apply to goods such as liquefied natural gas that have no practical option for transport on Jones Act–compliant shipping. In these circumstances, no party benefits from the Jones Act: producers pay more to send their product to Asia, consumers pay more to import LNG from Russia, and this expensive and wasteful charade will ensure that no future Jones Act–eligible LNG carrier will ever be built in the United States.[15] That is simply not a realistic option because under the Jones Act the U.S. shipbuilding industry has withered away.

Currently, the Jones Act can only be waived when it is in the interest of national defense.[16] This waiver authority should be expanded in two ways. First, certain goods, such as LNG, should be categorically exempted from the Jones Act. If it is unlikely or impossible that the good will ever be transported by Jones Act–compliant shipping, there is no reason to hamstring American producers and cut off American consumers; the Jones Act should simply not apply to such products.[17]

Second, it should be broadened to include economically necessary waivers. Some studies indicate that in shipping-dependent locations such as Alaska, Hawaii, and Puerto Rico, the Jones Act costs consumers heavily.[18] A recent analysis published by the Organisation for Economic Co-operation and Development estimates that the law's repeal would increase U.S. economic output by up to $135 billion.[19] Congress should loosen the chains holding back these economies by providing waivers when it is economically necessary.

14. Why the Jones Act's U.S. Citizenship Quota Should Be Repealed

Daniel Griswold

The Jones Act has restricted competition in the domestic waterborne shipping business for a century. Much has been written about its requirements that ships must be U.S.-built, U.S.-owned, and U.S.-flagged, but the 75 percent U.S.-crewed mandate also impacts the U.S. economy and shipping industry. This requirement drives up the cost of U.S. shipping, especially to locations outside the continental United States. It also discriminates unfairly against U.S. residents who are noncitizens but who are otherwise authorized to work in the United States, while doing nothing to protect the security of the American homeland or enhance the capability of the U.S. military. Any conversation about reforming the Jones Act to better serve America's national interest must include a reasonable relaxation of the crew requirement.

Discriminating against Noncitizen U.S. Workers

The strongest argument against the U.S.-citizenship requirement for the crew is that it is needlessly discriminatory. There is no reason why noncitizens authorized to work in the United States should face discrimination when applying to work on a Jones Act ship.

Citizenship is a requirement for many jobs in the government, especially those requiring a security clearance and directly tied to national security. But in the private sector, citizenship is not typically required for employment. In fact, U.S. employment law specifically prohibits private employers from requiring U.S. citizenship as a condition of employment. The law requires all private-sector jobs to be open to all legally authorized U.S. workers, defined as not only citizens, but also permanent residents, asylees, and refugees. On its website, the Equal Employment Opportunity Commission declares, "Most employers should not ask whether or not a job applicant is a United States citizen before making an offer of employment."[1]

A citizenship requirement is not imposed on other forms of domestic transportation, such as trucking, passenger and freight rail, and domestic air travel. Like domestic waterborne shipping, U.S. commercial air service is subject to cabotage laws that forbid foreign-owned companies from competing on domestic routes. Yet unlike Jones Act carriers, U.S. airlines that operate between U.S. locations are not required to crew their flights with a certain quota of U.S. citizens. To work for an airline serving the domestic market, a potential cabin-crew member must have the right to work in the United States and possess a valid passport, whether U.S. or foreign. Potential employees are also subject to background screening by the Transportation Security Administration to obtain a security clearance pass, but they do not need to be a U.S. citizen.[2]

Security remains a major concern in an industry that suffered the catastrophe of the September 11, 2001, terrorist attacks. But imposing a quota of U.S. citizens on the hiring process has been wisely rejected in favor of more appropriate security steps. It's difficult to argue that the citizenship status of the crew of an airliner is less important from a national security perspective than the citizenship status of the crew of a coastal transport ship.

For shipping solely within American coastal waterways or interior waterborne routes, the government could maintain the requirement that all merchant marine personnel be legally authorized to work in the United States, but the 75 percent quota for U.S. citizens should be repealed.

Artificially Inflating the Cost of Waterborne Shipping

The 75 percent citizenship requirement for the crewing of Jones Act vessels is also costly for the shipping sector and the economy. This is especially true for shipping routes beyond the U.S. mainland—specifically those to Alaska, Hawaii, and Puerto Rico—that cross international waters where internationally competitive alternatives are widely available.

A number of studies have concluded that the U.S.-citizenship requirement adds substantially to the cost of domestic shipping. A 2002 analysis by the International Trade Commission concluded that, because of the Jones Act, the crew cost alone for a U.S.-flagged vessel was more than four times higher than for a typical oil tanker and more than six times higher for a containership compared to a foreign-flagged vessel. The trade commission further concluded that

"U.S. crew costs generally account for most of the differences in operating costs between U.S.- and foreign-flagged vessels. For example, manning costs account for over 50 percent of the operating cost differential for a typical oil tanker, and nearly 80 percent of the cost differential for a typical containership."[3]

A more recent study by the Alliance for Innovation and Infrastructure concluded that the average daily cost to crew a Jones Act tanker is $11,500—nearly six times the daily cost of $2,000 to crew a foreign-flagged vessel. "This six fold daily rate adds to the transportation cost, which is ultimately incorporated into the cost per barrel of the product," the study concluded.[4]

For ships serving points beyond the U.S. mainland, the entire Jones Act, including the crewing requirements, should be repealed and international shipping companies and international crews allowed to serve those destinations.

How the Jones Act Crew Requirement Weakens National Security

Advocates of the Jones Act argue that the crewing requirement makes America more secure by protecting us from potential intrusion by foreign-born terrorists and by maintaining a standing reserve of potential merchant marine seafarers should the nation need them in times of emergency.

As an article posted by the *National Interest* argued, "The requirement that all the officers and 75 percent of the crews engaged in cabotage be U.S. citizens goes a long way to reducing the risk that terrorists could get onboard or execute an attack on a U.S. target.[5] In effect, there is a system of self-policing that reduces the burden on law enforcement and homeland security organizations."[6]

This argument is made despite the lack of evidence that U.S. security has been compromised by the presence of noncitizen seafarers in U.S. waters. According to a 2011 report to Congress by the Government Accountability Office, seafarers—the overwhelming majority of whom are foreign—made about 5 million entries into American ports on commercial cargo and cruise ship vessels in fiscal year 2009. Yet according to the same report, "to date there have been no terrorist attacks involving seafarers on vessels transiting to U.S. ports and no definitive information to indicate that extremists have entered the United States as seafarer non-immigrant visa holders."[7]

The military does not require U.S. citizenship to serve in the enlisted ranks. According to the National Immigration Forum, about 24,000 noncitizens were on active duty in 2012, with 5,000 legal permanent residents joining the U.S. military each year.[8]

It's also worth noting that U.S. citizenship is no guarantee against terrorist intentions. Since 2014, more than half of the individuals charged with ISIS-related terrorist offences have been U.S. citizens, according to the Program on Extremism at George Washington University.[9]

Another national security argument from Jones Act supporters is that the U.S. military needs a reserve of trained merchant seafarers to transport troops and equipment during a national emergency. As Loren Thompson of the Lexington Institute noted in a 2017 column, 9 out of 10 trained mariners in the United States work on trade routes covered by the Jones Act. "In the absence of Jones Act protections, this workforce likely would not exist, forcing the Navy to rely on mariners who are not trained to a similar level of proficiency and/or are foreign nationals," he concludes.[10]

Yet the Jones Act has notably failed to maintain a viable fleet of ships and sufficient crew suitable to serve the military in times of need. The Jones Act fleet has been in long-term decline for decades because of its uncompetitive costs and the declining demand for waterborne transportation despite a growing economy. According to a recent report from the Grassroot Institute of Hawaii:

> Between 2006 and 2011, the Jones Act–eligible fleet shrank by just over 17 percent, with the number of each vessel type in that category falling, sometimes by a significant amount. If the Jones Act is intended to maintain the health of the commercial shipbuilding industry, then the shrinking U.S. merchant fleet demonstrates that the Act has been a failure in that regard.[11]

A shrinking fleet of Jones Act ships means a shrinking pool of qualified mariners for any future sealift operations. While the government does have a record of mariners who have received the required license, not all licensed mariners are still actively sailing, and others are deceased or unable to sail. According to a report for the U.S. Maritime Administration because "merchant mariner employment is voluntary, the number of people willing to sail in times of national need is unknown."[12]

Furthermore, the number of credentialed mariners the Jones Act is supposed to provide in times of need has been trending inexorably downward for decades. In recent testimony before Congress, a senior union official acknowledged that "the pool of licensed and unlicensed mariners has shrunk to a critical level" and, absent government action, "the military will no longer be able to rely on the all-volunteer U.S. Merchant Marine as our nation's fourth arm of defense."[13] The Maritime Administration report concluded:

> The demand for U.S.-flag commercial vessel services is not currently adequate to maintain the pool of qualified mariners necessary to meet [the U.S. Transportation Command and Military Sealift Command's] sealift activation and sustainment needs. The lack of demand is responsible for a corresponding decrease in U.S.-flag ships and, thus, mariner jobs.[14]

If the government foresees a need for merchant marine personnel to meet its future demands in times of emergency, it should develop a plan to meet that need that does not require the United States to maintain an aging, shrinking, and economically uncompetitive fleet of protected Jones Act ships. National security is important, but it should not be pursued in a way that unnecessarily discriminates against lawful U.S. residents and damages the economy and the long-term health of the domestic waterborne shipping industry.

15. Reforming the Jones Act: What the United States Can Learn from Canada

Taylor Jackson

While Jones Act supporters often cite the existence of cabotage restrictions in other countries as a reason for keeping the law in place, the extent of these practices elsewhere, as well as efforts to reform them, receive far less attention. In thinking about Jones Act reform, it is thus worthwhile to ask what maritime cabotage restrictions in other countries look like.

In this regard, the United States has a lot to learn from its neighbor to the north. Canada's more liberal maritime cabotage rules offer four examples of how the Jones Act could be reformed. [1] First, adopting Canada's use of a licensing and waiver system that is based on domestic need, and not national security, would expand service options for American consumers of shipping services in addition to yielding economic and environmental benefits. Second, a liberalized licensing system would also provide much-needed transparency to the U.S. shipping industry.

Third, in addition to actions the United States can take on its own, there is also an opportunity for Canada and the United States to expand upon their long history of mutually beneficial economic integration by extending it to the largely forgotten area of maritime transportation. Liberalization through trade agreements has already been tested through the Canada–European Union Economic and Trade Agreement (CETA), where Canada recently opened up limited parts of its cabotage services to European-flagged carriers. The trade agreement could thus serve as a model for cooperation between Canada and the United States.

Fourth, in contrast to the United States, government agencies in Canada have conducted reviews of the country's maritime cabotage regulations. While this process has created some reform, it has also produced a more-robust and open debate about cabotage restrictions, which is notably absent in the

United States. The United States should undertake a similar comprehensive review of the Jones Act.

The first section of this chapter will review the early history of maritime cabotage regulation in Canada and considerations for reform during the 1950s and 1970s.[2] The second section will describe the current system, which has been in place since 1992, and recent calls for reform. Finally, the third section will discuss four lessons that the United States can learn from Canada's regulation of maritime cabotage.

Canada's Maritime Cabotage History

The history of Canadian maritime cabotage restrictions predates Canada's 1867 confederation with a legacy in the policy choices of Great Britain.[3] With the end of the Seven Years' War and the conclusion of the 1763 Treaty of Paris, Great Britain was granted near-total control to regulate the shipping of its colonies.[4] Until 1849, shipping between two points in the United Kingdom and its North American colonies was restricted to British-flagged ships under the Navigation Acts.[5]

Following Canada's confederation, the Canadian parliament was given the authority to regulate navigation and shipping in its waters.[6] However, British law required that Canadian marine cabotage laws be consistent with those of the United Kingdom.[7] This would change in 1869, when the United Kingdom amended the law dealing with cabotage in overseas territories, thus prompting Canada to pass maritime cabotage laws of its own. But Canada's newly adopted rules left the British cabotage restrictions in place.[8] In principle, this meant that for a ship to be registered as a British ship and thus be eligible for Canadian marine cabotage operations, the vessel had to be owned by British subjects or British corporations that had their principle place of business in territories over which the British Crown had sovereignty.[9]

No substantive changes to the cabotage laws were made until 1931, when the Commonwealth countries, all of which were former British territories, ratified the British Commonwealth Merchant Shipping Agreement.[10] This agreement led to the adoption of uniform vessel registrations throughout the Commonwealth, including the mutual recognition of all ships registered in the Commonwealth as British ships. Through this action, Commonwealth members gained access to each other's protected shipping regimes.

The next major change to Canadian maritime cabotage rules came three years later with the passage of the 1934 Canada Shipping Act.[11] This legislation marked the first time that maritime cabotage, and shipping law in general, was wholly under Canadian jurisdiction. The regulatory regime that this law ushered in would largely remain intact until 1992.[12]

What did this law state? First, all coasting trade in Canada was restricted to British ships,[13] defined as one registered under a Commonwealth flag.[14] However, Section 661(1) still allowed foreign ships to obtain licenses from the Minister of National Revenue in order to participate in Canadian cabotage. This license would be granted if the foreign-built British ship paid a "duty of twenty-five per centum ad valorem on the fair market value of her hull, machinery, furniture and appurtenances."[15]

The granting of this license was mandatory upon the payment of what was effectively a tariff on foreign-built British ships. The logic behind the tariff was to provide protection for the Canadian shipbuilding industry, but such thinking was flawed. As maritime transportation experts J. R. F. Hodgson and Mary R. Brooks of Dalhousie University explain, the effectiveness of this tariff for building up the Canadian shipbuilding industry was highly questionable, given that it did not apply to ships built by Commonwealth members. In addition, Canadian shipbuilders were already receiving preferential customs and sales tax treatment and support under the Canadian Vessel Construction Assistance Act.[16]

It is worth noting that the cabotage provisions in the 1934 Canada Shipping Act did not introduce any restrictions on the nationality of the sailors employed on the British ships. This stands in stark contrast to the Jones Act, which places nationality requirements on vessel crews. It also provides an early example of Canada's maritime cabotage laws being more liberalized than those of the United States.[17]

Canada Evaluates Its Cabotage Laws

While Canada's maritime cabotage regulations, hampered by continued British influence, would not be substantively changed for almost 60 years, the decades following the 1934 Canada Shipping Act would see the law's effectiveness and necessity questioned in a number of government reports. In particular, these questioned whether relaxing cabotage restrictions would harm Canadian industry or whether restrictions should be expanded. In addition, these studies evaluated whether there was a national security rationale for maintaining these restrictive laws.

The first major governmental review of Canada's maritime cabotage polices was completed in 1957 with the delivery of the Royal Commission on Coasting Trade report under the supervision of the Honorable Justice W. F. Spence (hereafter the Spence Commission).[18] One of the study's primary aims was to analyze how maritime cabotage regulations affected Canadian shipping and shipbuilding, considering the existing restriction of Canadian cabotage to Canadian-flagged ships. It also examined the potential case for restricting cabotage to vessels that were both Canadian-flagged *and* Canadian-built.

As outlined in the Spence Commission report, the central argument for restricting maritime cabotage to Canadian-flagged ships was that such vessels were facing elimination from lower-cost ships in the UK registry, and that the public interest was best served by an "all-Canadian coasting fleet." However, the report recognized that the public interest also included low-cost service.[19] In its conclusion on this matter, the commission found that greater restrictions would cause a "substantial increase in transportation costs" and that "[r]estriction of the coasting trade to vessels registered in Canada would be detrimental to the public interest, whether the restriction applied generally or only to a particular part of Canada."[20] However, the commission did not recommend liberalizing maritime cabotage for all foreign vessels, instead finding that competition from the Commonwealth was sufficient to bring shipping rates in line with world prices.[21]

The commission's inquiry included public submissions from interested parties. Some of the submissions argued that maritime cabotage registry restrictions were necessary to ensure "a supply of vessels and crews to be needed in time[s] of war."[22] The commission rejected this line of reasoning, recognizing that reductions of commercial services would not likely be realized in times of war. The commission presumed that Canadian allies, primarily the United Kingdom, which already provided shipping services in Canada, would make those vessels available for "Canadian needs in the common cause."[23] In addition, the commission argued that even if the United Kingdom was involved in a conflict without Canada, thereby causing the withdrawal of UK ships from Canadian trade, "other neutral shipping could be made available by suspension of the coasting trade law if needed."[24]

Those supporting a Canadian-build requirement, such as the Canadian Shipbuilding and Ship Repairing Association, also relied on this shaky national security rationale.[25] It was argued that the Canadian shipbuilding industry, which was necessary for defense preparedness and national security, was on the verge of collapse. To ensure the industry's future, an assured volume of orders was needed, which could be achieved through the restriction of maritime cabotage to Canadian-built vessels.

The calls to add a build requirement to maritime cabotage restrictions was rejected by the Spence Commission and—notably—the majority of Canada provinces. Indeed, 8 out of 10 provincial governments, including those with shipbuilding industries, submitted briefs to the commission detailing their objections to such a restriction, expressing concerns about increased transportation costs.[26] These concerns were echoed by a number of users of shipping services and their associations, which prompted the commission to reject the proposal, stating that if the national security argument had any merit, it would be more effectively addressed through direct subsidization and not restrictions.[27]

The historical rejection of national security as an argument for maritime cabotage restrictions stands in stark contrast to the Jones Act and likely helps explain why Canada's maritime cabotage regulations have always been less restrictive. As evidenced in the Spence Commission report, lower-priced shipping services were of greater concern to both federal and provincial governments—in addition to different industry bodies—than restrictionist arguments based on national security.

Overall, the general conclusion of the Spence Commission was that Canada should maintain the existing maritime cabotage laws as they were. However, a little over a decade later, another government report came to a very different conclusion.

In 1970, the Canadian Transport Commission's Economic and Social Analysis Branch released "Report of Inquiry on the Coasting Trade of Canada and Related Marine Activity," authored by Canadian transport expert Howard Darling (hereafter the Darling Report).[28] Darling took an approach that was explicitly different than that of the Spence Commission. Instead of viewing maritime cabotage restrictions through the effect of transportation costs on the broader economy, he examined them as a matter of national economic policy aimed at building up specific Canadian industries. While the report did address whether cabotage restrictions should exist at all, or whether alternative measures that produced similar outcomes at lower economic costs could be achieved, Darling's focus remained on the degree to which maritime cabotage activities should be protected.[29]

This focus on protectionism led the Darling Report to recommend that Canada's maritime cabotage activities be restricted to Canadian-flagged ships. It further urged that activities falling under the maritime cabotage regime be expanded to include dredging, salvage, seismographic vessels, and supply and support ships, and that the cabotage laws' geographic scope be extended to the Canadian continental shelf.[30] The report also leveled criticism at the waiver licensing system that had long been a part of Canada's maritime cabotage regime. Specifically, it argued that the purpose of the waiver system should be directed toward replacing foreign vessels engaged in cabotage activities with Canadian ones, and as such the waiver fee should be increased to act as a deterrent.[31]

The Darling Report was not the last government study of Canada's maritime cabotage laws, nor did it produce any immediate changes to these laws. Its recommendations, however, would go on to form the basis of significant changes made to these laws in 1992 that continue to apply to this day.

Maritime Cabotage in Canada Today

In 1992, Canada enacted the first major change to its maritime cabotage laws since the 1930s through implementation of the Coasting Trade Act.[32] This law would embody many of the changes recommended in the Darling Report, such as giving Canadian-flagged ships, as opposed to British-flagged (Commonwealth) ships, exclusive access to maritime cabotage. Notably, the legislative changes to the maritime cabotage regime kept the licensing system and duty for foreign vessels in place.

Discussions surrounding the Coasting Trade Act in the House of Commons made it clear that the law's purpose was to prevent foreigners from competing against Canadian ship owners and operators. When Minister of Transportation Jean Corbeil, of the Progressive Conservative Party, introduced the initial bill, he stated that "[t]his act protects operators of Canadian-flag ships wishing to work within Canadian waters and on the Continental Shelf" from international competition.[33]

The Official Opposition, the Liberal Party, did not push back against added protectionism but instead argued that the legislation was not protectionist enough. Sergio Marchi, the Liberal Party's transport critic, stated:

> [t]hough the government may claim that this bill is its version of the American Jones Act, it does not even come close to the restrictive and prohibitory measures that the American shipping interests enjoy. . . . Canadian shippers in the marine industry are looking for leadership from this government to help our industry.[34]

Notably, however, national security continued to play little role in the justification of cabotage restrictions. Instead, Canadian legislators openly acknowledged that the purpose of these laws was to benefit Canadian shipping interests, even if this was to the detriment of Canadian consumers of those services.

Most of the 1992 act remains in place and serves as the legal basis for maritime cabotage in Canada. Article 3(1) of the Coasting Trade Act specifically prohibits any foreign ship from engaging in maritime cabotage.[35] Still, Canadian law is less restrictive than U.S. cabotage laws. For example, unlike the United States, there are no crew or build requirements for vessels, and Canada broadly permits foreign ships to receive temporary coasting trade licenses of no more than one year through an application process.[36]

The license is granted if the Canadian Transportation Agency has determined that "no Canadian or non-duty paid ship is suitable and available to provide the service or perform the service or perform the activity described in the application."[37] During this determination, the agency publicly posts the application, and objections can be registered in a given period. This fosters a degree of transparency within the cabotage system for all parties.[38] If Transport Canada deems the application to be valid, a license is granted, cabotage rights are extended, and the foreign vessel is allowed to carry out activities between Canadian destinations. The coasting trade license also allows foreign ships to receive temporary work permits for their crews. Use of this licensing system has been growing over the last decade. For example, in 2009 there were 72 license applications, compared to 106 in 2018, indicating a demand among Canadian businesses for the international fleet's services.[39]

The growing use of foreign vessels was also helped by the removal of the longstanding 25 percent duty on foreign-built cargo vessels, tankers, and ferry vessels (of more than 129 meters in length) in 2010, which reduced the cost of foreign ship procurement for Canadian carriers. The duty was lifted nearly a decade after a Canadian government review found that Canadian shipyards had no capacity to build vessels of this size, and that the duty was largely ineffective at spurring domestic shipbuilding.[40] Even here, Canada took a pragmatic approach to a clear problem in its shipbuilding industry.

Reforming Maritime Cabotage in Canada

While the Canadian cabotage regime is less restrictive than that of the United States, it is still more restrictive than other regimes, such as those of New Zealand and Australia (prior to 2012).[41] The negative impacts of existing cabotage restrictions were recently acknowledged by the Canadian government in early 2016 with Transport Canada's release of the review *Pathways: Connecting Canada's Transportation System to the World* (hereafter the Emerson Report), which included a review of Canada's maritime transportation network.[42] Regarding the economic effects of Canada's maritime cabotage restrictions, the Emerson Report stated that these restrictions

> are all protecting sectors that have not grown, or that no longer exist, from competition by cost-effective international operators interested in developing new services and markets. Some argue that this has worked to the detriment of the economy as a whole, and Canadians bear the cost for little apparent benefit.[43]

Beyond the economic costs stemming specifically from cabotage restrictions, the Emerson Report also recognized the environmental benefits that would come with a more broadly liberalized and expanded shipping regime, noting that

> [S]hort sea shipping—the movement of cargo by water without crossing an ocean—offers opportunities to move freight around congested land corridors such as on the Great Lakes and in the Lower Mainland of British Columbia, with lower emissions and

without the need for costly investment in new road and rail capacity. Marine is already the best way to move bulk and large break bulk freight. Many other countries also use short sea shipping for containers, and roll-on/roll-off (RO/RO) services for trucks especially in circumstances of congestion. These latter services are underdeveloped in Canada; for example, there are no domestic container services on the Great Lakes–St. Lawrence Seaway above Montréal, and RO/RO operations are generally limited to ferry services. While the feasibility of many initiatives has been explored and some new services attempted, the cost of operations for crews and vessels proved excessive; service providers and their sponsors could not sustain the losses.[44]

For example, the Detroit-Windsor border crossing saw almost 1.6 million truck crossings in 2018. The use of more environmentally friendly marine shipping options, with their lower emission and pollution levels, would help reduce such land-based traffic congestion. It is also a form of transportation less prone to accidents. However, such transportation options, according to the Emerson Report, remain underdeveloped.

The Emerson Report also recognized the regulatory burden of obtaining a license for a foreign vessel, which requires the investment of time and resources by Canadian firms that could ideally be better utilized elsewhere. Overall, while being a more relaxed licensing system than that of the United States, Canada's cabotage regime is not perfect. In fact, existing regulatory restrictions still curtail competition in the provision of marine shipping services, lead to the inefficient use of resources, and reduce mutually beneficial economic integration among regions and countries.[45] As political scientist Stephen Blank and economist Barry E. Prentice explain in the context of shipping on the Great Lakes:

> Canadian and American ships can only pick up or drop loads at ports in which either the origin or destination is their country. This means that two separate national fleets must be maintained, and that efficient "milk runs" or triangular routes cannot be developed.[46]

This ultimately produces higher marine transport costs and pushes shippers toward alternative transport modes, such as rail and truck services. Maritime cabotage liberalization would lower the cost of marine transport, offering particular benefits to shipping on the Great Lakes. Furthermore, Canadian and

American businesses would experience reduced costs for the transportation of goods in their supply chains.[47]

That maritime cabotage restrictions result in economic and environmental costs has been well documented. For example, the United States International Trade Commission has found, in a number of different studies, that removing Jones Act restrictions would result in welfare gains. Depending on the year of the study, the gains from liberalizing maritime cabotage were found to be between $656 million and $3.1 billion.[48] A study by economists at the Organisation for Economic Co-operation and Development also found that liberalization or removal of the Jones Act could increase industrial activity in the United States between $22 and $40 billion as a result of reduced water transportation costs.[49] Likewise, a recent study by economist William Olney found that the Jones Act has reduced internal trade and ultimately leads to higher consumer prices.[50]

Maritime cabotage restrictions also produce negative environmental impacts. Economist Timothy Fitzgerald has found that the Jones Act produces negative spillover effects by encouraging the substitution of marine transportation services for alternative modes that generate more greenhouse gas emissions and other pollutants.[51] Fitzgerald also found that U.S. cabotage restrictions encouraged the use of older and less-efficient vessels. This is concerning: a report by the United Nations Conference on Trade and Development finds that "younger vessels tend to be more efficient and less likely to break or cause environmental damage" compared to older vessels.[52] Like the United States, Canada's maritime cabotage policies surely lead to higher shipping costs compared to a fully liberalized system, thus producing similar deleterious economic and environmental consequences.

Overall, the Emerson Report noted that, while trade has become progressively liberalized between Canada and the United States since passage of the 1987 Canada-U.S. Free Trade Agreement, domestic transportation and marine shipping have remained relatively closed. It concluded:

> The current policy of prohibiting access to Canadian domestic operations by foreign-owned and registered vessels is restrictive and protectionist. The Review asked frequently for evidence of the negative impacts of liberalization, but none was forthcoming, apart from objections on the basis of the investments already in place. We believe

it is time to remove the impediments inherent in the Coasting Trade Act and to offer shippers an expedited process, based on market-oriented criteria, that responds to demand.[53]

From this, the Emerson Report made five recommendations on how to reform coasting trade in Canada "to increase the competitiveness of Canadian shipping and competition in the short sea shipping market," including:

- promoting short-sea shipping as a mechanism to alleviate congestion in urban areas and reduce Canada's growing greenhouse gas and air pollutant emission levels, especially through ports along the Great Lakes–St. Lawrence Seaway System;
- modernizing recruiting and training of Canadian seafarers and improving processes for attracting and certifying foreigner workers with the needed skill sets;
- phasing out the operating restrictions on the basis of reciprocity in the Coasting Trade Act, beginning immediately with container services and eliminating restrictions altogether within a transition period of no more than seven years;
- phasing out all remaining duties on imported vessels within a transition period of no more than seven years to respect Canadian ship-owners' recent investments in specialized vessels;
- aligning regulations governing Canadian-flagged ship operators to put them on a competitive basis with international operators who would be gaining access to Canada's domestic trades.[54]

One key component of the Emerson Report's recommendations is the notion that Canada should only liberalize its cabotage policies on the basis of reciprocity from other countries. Practically, this means that Canada would not liberalize its cabotage regulations until the United States was willing to make similar reforms to the Jones Act. However, the notion of needing reciprocity to liberalize misses the fact that Canadian consumers of shipping services would benefit even if Canada liberalized its cabotage regulations unilaterally.

However, in the wake of the report's release, reform has proved contentious. Indeed, the changes that have been made are minor and incremental, which is surprising given that the report found little evidence that could be provided for any negative impact of liberalization.[55]

Lessons for U.S. Reform

Ideally, the Jones Act would be repealed or, at the very least, reformed to eliminate the U.S.-build requirement and grant permanent exemptions to Alaska, Hawaii, and Puerto Rico. However, such reform remains unlikely in the near term because of the strength of maritime lobbying interests.[56] That said, Canada's maritime cabotage policies do offer examples of incremental reforms that the United States could learn from.

License and Waiver System

The first lesson from Canada would be to adopt a more liberalized waiver or licensing system for foreign vessels to conduct maritime cabotage within the United States. While the Canadian licensing system is imperfect, it has one major advantage. Currently, the Jones Act waiver regime is primarily centered around national security, whereas Canada's is based on economic need. A shift to Canada's approach would be a step in the right direction.

In the United States, there are two main tracks through which national security waivers can be granted. The first is through Customs and Border Protection (CBP) and the secretary of the Department of Homeland Security (DHS). Requests for waivers can be made to CBP, which then forwards the request to the Maritime Administration within the Department of Transportation to determine if any Jones Act–eligible vessels are available. After this evaluation, the DHS secretary then decides whether the proposed activity is in the interest of national defense.[57] Both agencies have set a high bar to meet this criterion, and they have stressed that such waivers should not "be issued for economic reasons such as commercial practicality or expediency."[58] As a result, few waivers have been granted, and these tend to involve fuel shortages or national emergencies, such as Hurricanes Katrina and María.[59]

The other track by which a Jones Act waiver can be granted is through the Department of Defense. In such cases, the defense department simply informs CBP when a waiver is needed and the waiver is automatically granted.[60] Congress also has the power to grant waivers, and has occasionally done so in cases where there are not any Jones Act–qualified operators with an interest in providing certain services or when there have been sudden increases in demand for services that Jones Act vessels cannot meet.[61] However, as the Congressional Research Service notes, in most cases it appears that the vessels that are granted waivers by Congress are "not commercially significant—for instance, that they are not large or even moderately sized cargo or passenger vessels."[62]

The national-security-centered Jones Act waiver system stands in contrast to the Canadian approach that is more focused on domestic need, including the economic reasons that Customs and Border Protection has indicated will not be considered. In the Canadian system, vessels are considered for licenses when no Canadian vessel is able to perform the service, whatever that service may be. As such, the vessel types applying for licenses in Canada are broad, including tankers, barges, cargo vessels, tugs, drill rigs, cable layers, and icebreakers, to name just a few. The broad range of vessels and services that can receive temporary cabotage licenses is beneficial for Canadian businesses and the economy as a whole. Absent licenses, these services would either have to be performed at a later time or not at all.

Expanded Transparency in Maritime Cabotage

The second lesson that the United States can learn from Canada is that a more liberalized licensing system would provide enhanced transparency. The Canadian licensing system is less onerous on those seeking licenses, involving only one government agency—the Canadian Transportation Agency—as opposed to the multiple agencies and government actors involved in granting waivers to the Jones Act. Moreover, the Canadian licensing process has transparency built into it, with all license applications posted online for Canadian vessel operators to raise objections to if they are available to carry out the service in question. This level of transparency could be an important component of a liberalized U.S. waiver system in order to obtain at least some buy-in from pro–Jones Act interests.

A more liberalized cabotage regime could also assist with removing some of the opacity that plagues the pricing of Jones Act carrier services. For instance, between 2003 and 2008, Jones Act carriers serving Puerto Rico began fixing their prices and were subsequently convicted of antitrust violations. The Jones Act's prohibition on foreign competition enabled these carriers to both demand higher rates and coordinate the setting of these rates. However, because of a lack of transparency under the Jones Act system and the associated pricing of service, it is unclear whether prices were adjusted after the antitrust cases.[63] It is possible that additional transparency, combined with increased competition under a more liberalized waiver system, could assist in making the comparative prices charged for shipping services more apparent. In particular, those wishing to use the waiver system could know what non–Jones Act vessels would charge for shipping services, and this could be used as a reference against Jones Act service providers.

Liberalization through Trade Agreements

The third lesson that the United States can learn from Canada's experience is that there is an opportunity to pursue liberalization through trade agreements. In 2014, Canada concluded the Canada–European Union Economic and Trade Agreement with the European Union. Chapter 14 of that agreement has opened up parts of Canada's cabotage regime to some competition from EU-flagged vessels.[64] These vessels can provide feeder services for cargo between the ports of Halifax and Montreal, as well as provide private and federally procured dredging services without a coasting trade license.[65]

The government of Justin Trudeau faced stiff opposition to these changes. In parliamentary debates on the CETA, some members of parliament argued that the "amendments to the Coasting Trade Act will . . . create unfair competition that no one ever asked for."[66] Some members used similar language that is often employed in support of the Jones Act,[67] stating that, "[i]t is already clear that good jobs will be lost here in Canada and that they will be replaced by cheap foreign labour." [68] Both claims are false. First, the Emerson Report did not find that liberalization would negatively impact Canada's cabotage market. Second, foreign seafarers can already work in Canada's maritime trade, and there is no evidence this has harmed Canadian workers.[69]

Like U.S. debates surrounding the Jones Act, the politics of maritime cabotage reform continue to prove contentious. Nevertheless, this has not stopped Canada from pursuing positive incremental reforms.

Canada and the United States could take an approach similar to that in the CETA and extend cabotage rights to each other in a reciprocal manner.

Granted, the preferential treatment of the EU in Canada's maritime cabotage regime through CETA was relatively minimal, but Canada and the United States are geographically linked and their economies much more integrated. Consequently, the two countries have much more to gain by extending cabotage rights to each other. Maritime transport remains particularly underdeveloped in the Great Lakes–St. Lawrence River area, despite its considerable potential benefits.[70] Expanded access to shipping goods by sea would add competition to transportation markets, lower transportation costs for businesses and consumers, reduce congestion at already busy ports of entry, increase the safety of transportation systems, and yield environmental benefits from lower emissions.[71] It would also provide the maritime shipping industry with new markets and opportunities.

Notably, integration of maritime shipping services has previously been sought in trade negotiations and proposed by agencies within the Canadian government. During the North American Free Trade Agreement (NAFTA) negotiations, Canada pushed for the United States to liberalize its maritime cabotage regulations. One hope was to see the United States adopt a Canadian-style waiver system and to remove U.S.-ownership requirements. However, the United States would not concede on this front and ultimately Canada, the United States, and Mexico all excluded their maritime cabotage industries from liberalization under NAFTA.[72] In addition, in its 2001 review of the Canada Transportation Act, the review panel recommended that the Canadian "government make clear to the government of the United States its preference for eliminating the restrictions on entry to domestic shipping in the Coasting Trade Act and offer to negotiate bilateral elimination of equivalent restrictions."[73] As the panel members saw it, the purpose of reciprocal liberalization was to encourage efficiency among shippers and thereby benefit users.[74]

To accomplish the goal of extending integration to maritime transportation, the United States–Mexico–Canada Agreement could be amended with a section granting each country's flagged vessels full cabotage rights. Alternatively, a side letter could be added to the agreement granting the same access for a trial period to evaluate the demand for such services.

Finally, it is worth pointing out that increasing the size of the fleet available for domestic shipping services would help buttress the Jones Act's stated purpose of ensuring that an adequate fleet of ships and merchant mariners are available in times of war or other national emergencies.[75] As Colin Grabow, Inu Manak, and Daniel J. Ikenson point out in chapter one, the Jones Act has not produced a robust fleet of vessels that could be used in times of national security crises. In fact, the number of vessels that meet Jones Act requirements is actually in decline. The size of the fleet of ships over 1,000 gross tons that can transport cargo and meet all Jones Act requirements has fallen from 193 in 2000 to 99 today, only 78 of which can be considered militarily useful.[76] The decline is even more precipitous over a longer time period, considering that in 1950 there were more than 400 Jones Act oceangoing ships.[77] In a time of emergency, mutual recognition of Canadian-flagged vessels for Jones Act service could allow Canadian ships or mariners to backfill domestic trade for the U.S. Jones Act ships or mariners that were pulled away for sealift purposes; could allow Canadian vessels or mariners to participate in a sealift capacity (since Canada is an ally and member of NATO, it is not a security threat and is already part of the U.S. defense industrial base);[78] and could allow Canadian ships to help deliver supplies during national emergencies, such as 2017's Hurricane María that devastated Puerto Rico. Such possibilities make Canada a natural partner for the United States in the liberalization of shipping services.

Reviewing Regulations

A final lesson for the United States is the relative proclivity of the Canadian government and its agencies to review their maritime cabotage rules, which has contributed to a more open and sustained debate on the topic. Most recently this tradition was continued with the 2016 release of the Emerson Review, which made a number of reform recommendations while also questioning Canada's cabotage restrictions at a more basic level.

These reviews do not always produce concrete regulatory changes, but they do allow for a more robust debate and objective analysis of positions taken by politicians and civil society groups. This experience stands in stark contrast to the United States, where the Jones Act is rarely called into question. At the very least, it is long past time for a modern and comprehensive study to evaluate the merits of the Jones Act.

Conclusion

For a century, the Jones Act has been an economic burden on the United States. Reform is long overdue. Here, Canada's maritime cabotage regime and efforts to reform it offer an example of what reform might look like. By adopting a more-liberal waiver system similar to that used in Canada, for instance, the United States could help ameliorate some of the Jones Act's negative consequences. In addition, the transparency such a system would add is also much needed. Finally, the United States and Canada could provide reciprocal recognition of each other's flagged vessels, thereby allowing expanded integration of their maritime transportation systems. The Canada–European Union Economic and Trade Agreement has laid the foundation for how this could be achieved, and it would be another step toward recognizing the long-standing benefits that have come from integrating cross-border supply chains. Either country could also grant such access unilaterally.

The United States and Canada have a long history of learning from one another to enhance our shared prosperity. Liberalization of the Jones Act waiver and the mutual recognition of Canadian and American vessels in maritime cabotage should be the next step in this storied tradition.

16. Updating the Jones Act for the 21st Century

Keliʻi Akina

In a perfect world, there would be no Jones Act.

Ships from any nation would be able to transport goods freely between American ports, and U.S. consumers would be able to enjoy an abundance of products from around the world at significantly lower prices.

Unfortunately, we don't live in a perfect world.

In our frustratingly imperfect existence, free trade is obstructed by protectionist cabotage laws, and the Jones Act is among the worst offenders. The restrictions imposed by the Jones Act cost the American economy billions of dollars.[1] The act itself is propped up by special interests and specious arguments.

As free-market advocates, we justifiably take pride in our pursuit of the perfect: a world without the Jones Act. The philosopher Plato might have commended our vision and reassured us that, somewhere in the great beyond, our conception of the perfect may exist. But he would also have urged us to recognize that we currently live in a dark cave of sorts, and the best we can attain is a reflection or limited version of the perfect. It would take Plato's student Aristotle to drive home the point that even in this imperfect existence we can still do good.

To keep our vision of the perfect from becoming the enemy of the good, we must immerse ourselves in the world at hand and engage with the way the public may react to pro–Jones Act arguments. That necessarily involves reframing the issue in a way that is sympathetic to their perspective. This is how we can position our reform proposals for practical success.

This means understanding the values that Jones Act supporters find reflected in the act, and looking for ways to address the motivations of Jones Act loyalists. Again and again, supporters of the act talk about American security and American jobs. We gain nothing by ignoring these strong, emotion-laden triggers.

Nor is it possible to argue them away, no matter how compelling our statistics and economic reasoning.

Words matter. To change public perception of the act and create an environment conducive to change, we need to think about how to discuss reform more effectively. This is where Hawaii's example may be instructive.

Because the Jones Act affects the noncontiguous territories in a more immediate and obvious way, Hawaii has been at the forefront of the Jones Act debate for years. Even in simple awareness, the average Hawaiian is likely to know more about what the Jones Act is—and why it matters—than most other Americans.

The good news is that education and awareness have led to a shift in popular opinion toward reform. For example, the state's largest daily newspaper, the *Honolulu Star-Advertiser*—hardly a crusader for free-market reform—has conducted two unscientific public online polls on the Jones Act in the past eight years. In 2012, it asked whether the Jones Act should be kept as is, repealed, or whether an exemption should be created for Hawaii; only 18 percent of newspaper subscribers voting in the poll wanted to keep the Jones Act.[2] The remainder were split between repeal, at 37 percent, and creating an exemption for Hawaii, at 45 percent. In 2017, opposition to the status quo was stronger.[3] When asked "What should be done about the maritime shipping law, the Jones Act?," 11 percent of readers wanted to keep the act as is, 35 percent wanted to modify some outdated provisions, and 50 percent chose the third option, "[d]itch; archaic in today's global marketplace."[4]

Keep in mind that Hawaii is effectively a one-party state, dominated by Democrats and strongly influenced by unions. On paper, Hawaii residents should be Jones Act defenders and apologists. But years of education and advocacy from the Grassroot Institute of Hawaii and other groups championing economic freedom have helped change the way the public sees the Jones Act. In the recent general election, we even saw both major party candidates for Hawaii's First Congressional District campaign in favor of Jones Act reform. Representative Ed Case, the Democrat who went on to win the election, has shown his willingness to break with the rest of the Hawaii delegation and support modernizing the Jones Act.

What can we learn from this? First, that states matter. Jones Act reform is usually seen as a federal issue, divorced from grassroots efforts in the states.

Jones Act lobbyists do not have to defend the act on a state-by-state basis. They rely on support at the federal level—from pro-military associations, shipbuilding companies, ocean cargo transport companies, and various unions—to persuade Congress that the act should be retained.

Reformers do not have the same luxury. The think tanks, activist groups, businesses, and private citizens who oppose the Jones Act have to change hearts and minds in every state. That is the only way to break the pro–Jones Act consensus in Congress that has frustrated reform for decades. We must drive the demand for change from the ground up, by persuading voters at the state level. This will require help from state groups and think tanks that understand local politics and know how to make the Jones Act a local issue.

From that comes the second important lesson: know what works and what does not.

Over the years, the Grassroot Institute of Hawaii has learned which messages resonate and which ones fall flat when it comes to the Jones Act. Ask Hawaii residents what's wrong with the act and they will tell you, "It raises the cost of living." They might add, "It's bad for business," or "It makes our groceries more expensive." What you will not hear are some of the points that we reformers are most fond of discussing, things like the dwindling number of ships in the Jones Act fleet, or the cost of the act to specific industries. As is the case with so many economic issues, the most persuasive argument comes down to the individual's own wallet.

Which leads us to the national security paradox.

Over and over, reformers have effectively demonstrated that the Jones Act has not helped our military readiness or national defense. Despite the fact that national security is its raison d'être, the Jones Act has proven to be ineffective in maintaining a strong merchant marine.

The problem is that, failure or not, the national defense argument so far has been sufficient to convince Congress to preserve the Jones Act. On paper, critics defeat the argument. But the sentiment behind the defense rationale is so strong, and the interests behind it are so influential, that we are unlikely to make any headway against the idea that the act is fundamental to our national security.

So what do we do? We practice the martial art of judo. We move out of the way of our opponent's strength and momentum and use it to achieve real progress toward a modernized Jones Act.

The two most politically powerful arguments put forth to defend the Jones Act are national security and jobs. We have invested untold time and energy confronting these arguments head-on, with little effect. While we have successfully proved that they are fallacious and unsupported by data, we have not broken their power to stymie repeal efforts.

Instead of pushing for total repeal or an ideal "pure" road toward eliminating the Jones Act and running headlong into our opponents' strength, we should step out of the way of those areas of strength and use the momentum of smaller reforms to our advantage. This means embracing a strategy that allows small successes to lead us to a meaningful victory.

Let us start with proposals that would sidestep the national defense and jobs rationales: for example, a modification of the build requirement, which would allow U.S. ocean transportation companies to buy ships from American allies, such as Japan and Korea. This would take much of the strength out of the national security argument—especially since the American crew requirement would remain. In fact, one could claim that this reform would strengthen military readiness and response. It also would fracture union opposition, as a change to the build requirement would not pose a threat to crews and dockworkers.

In short, by removing only the Jones Act's U.S.-build requirement, and not tampering with the U.S.-crewed, U.S.-flagged, and U.S.-owned provisions, we would leave intact the values of national defense and protection of most union jobs. This would allow many Jones Act loyalists to embrace a measure of reform—not abandoning the Jones Act, but updating it for the 21st century.

Supporters of the Jones Act have tried to downplay its impact on consumers by producing absurdities such as the notorious 2018 report sponsored by the American Maritime Partnership that claimed that on two days in March 2018, prices of 13 goods at a Walmart store in San Juan, Puerto Rico, happened to be less than those same goods at one of the retailer's stores in Jacksonville, Florida.[5] No explanation was provided for why these specific goods were chosen. That study was a futile attempt to negate the cost-of-living argument before it catches on beyond the shores of Hawaii and Puerto Rico.

Ultimately, the arguments for the Jones Act are based largely on jobs and national defense. We take those arguments away not by forcing their supporters to defend them, but by refusing to challenge them. This leaves Jones Act supporters with nowhere left to go.

The economic impact of moderate initial reforms will help us demonstrate the benefits of a complete overhaul of the act. In this way, we will continue to gain momentum and grow a grassroots movement that understands how removing the protectionist restrictions of the Jones Act will benefit Americans in a very tangible way.

In contrast, an approach that puts abolition of the Jones Act at the center of its rhetoric backs reformers into a corner. Again, words matter. When the late senator John McCain (R-AZ) attempted Jones Act reform, the focus of his proposed amendment was actually a modification of the build requirement, as suggested here. However, when he spoke about the proposal, he spoke about repealing the Jones Act. Given such all-or-nothing rhetoric, what could Jones Act supporters do but oppose reform of any kind? When no effort is made to respond to the values that Jones Act loyalists present as the rationale for the act, they have no motivation to cooperate with reformers.

This is the problem with a confrontational approach to a political problem. In other spheres, it would make sense to ask for everything and be prepared to compromise only after negotiations begin. However, when it comes to the Jones Act, supporters have no incentive to come to the negotiating table. If the only options are "repeal" or "keep unchanged," the Jones Act loyalists will become more entrenched in their position.

By making the case for modernization of the act, not repeal, we build a bridge that Jones Act supporters can cross. This approach provides a way for supporters to keep those things they really care about, such as subsidies, jobs, and security. We demonstrate an understanding that it's highly unlikely you can undo a hundred years of rules, regulations, and practice with the stroke of a pen—that there is more complexity to the Jones Act than many realize.

Jones Act supporters are not immune from seeing the problems in the act. They may be willing to take action that will reduce its negative economic impact—especially on other union-based American industries. The growing divide between union membership and union leadership presents an opportunity for Jones Act reformers, but we must demonstrate that we no longer view this as an all-or-nothing issue.

We need to offer a solution that brings Jones Act supporters to the negotiating table and creates the potential for a win-win scenario. Rhetoric about ending the Jones Act may excite reformers, but it can turn off Jones Act supporters. For decades, calls to eliminate the Jones Act have been ineffective, only persuading supporters to fight against change more fiercely. If we want a negotiation that results in modernizing the act, we have to demonstrate that there is something to negotiate.

To be clear, we must remain committed to the Platonic vision of a world without the Jones Act. It is still before us, just like the ideal of abolishing other barriers to free international trade. But we cannot achieve that goal in one leap. Instead, we must work within political reality and craft a strategy based on reforms that can achieve consensus. That means defusing the national security and jobs arguments by offering reforms that takes them off the table as a concern. And it means working with state organizations to educate voters on what the Jones Act is and why they should care about it.

In a perfect world, there would be no Jones Act. But we are not in a perfect world. So, let us embrace the Aristotelian approach and find the virtue within the merely good rather than frustrating ourselves with the elusiveness of the perfect. Instead of calling for repeal, let's rally together different interests that can all embrace updating the Jones Act for the 21st century.

17. Looking Back, Looking Forward: The Historical Lessons for Reform

Colin Grabow and Logan Kolas

One hundred years ago, the Merchant Marine Act of 1920 was signed into law. Among its provisions is Section 27, more commonly referred to as the Jones Act, which today serves as the basis for U.S. maritime cabotage restrictions. This 1920 law, however, was hardly the dawn of U.S. restrictions on domestic maritime transport. Such measures have been in place since colonial times. Properly viewed, the Jones Act is not merely a 100-year-old law, but the latest iteration of cabotage measures reaching back to before the republic's founding.

This chapter examines the history of cabotage laws in the United States, their resulting costs, and the context in which they evolved. A focus will be placed on the differing approaches taken by the United States and the United Kingdom toward cabotage in the 1800s, and the contrasting fortunes experienced by each as a result. Finally, the Jones Act will be placed under the historical microscope, revealing the story behind its passage and its protectionist origins. Today, the law stands as an archaic holdover and any belief that it benefits the U.S. maritime industry runs counter to historical experience.

Cabotage in Colonial Times

In 1651 England began passing a series of maritime laws which became known as the Navigation Acts. Motivated by a desire to stymie the strong trade position held by the Dutch and increase British maritime capabilities, these laws constituted a tangled web of subsidies, destination restrictions, competition exclusions, and other protectionist measures. Chief among these was the requirement that both foreign and domestic commerce be conducted with British-built, -owned, and -crewed ships.[1] England primarily viewed them as a means to increase colonial dependence and entrench a British shipping monopoly.

The Navigation Acts are often credited with sheltering the colonies' emerging maritime sector and creating preliminary conditions for its growth and expansion. But the colonies also enjoyed significant advantages that lent themselves to a vibrant maritime sector, including ample supplies of timber for shipbuilding as well as a deep pool of human capital.[2] Regarding the latter, author Winthrop L. Marvin wrote that "many of the most intelligent and ambitious of these shipbuilders of England and Holland came to seek their fortunes in the New World," so much so that English shipbuilders complained that New England had "drawn over so many working shipwrights that there are not enough left here [in London] to carry on the work."[3] This fusion of rich endowments in labor and raw materials helped to make the colonies renowned for their prowess in both shipping and shipbuilding.

Evidence of the colonies' competitiveness abounds. According to Marvin, before 1775 a white-oak vessel cost "perhaps $24 a ton in New England, and a live-oak ship about $38 a ton," while in Europe an oak vessel "could not be built for less than $50 a ton."[4] In his book *American Navigation*, meanwhile, Henry Hall says that American vessels were "cheaper than those of England, France, and Spain" and were "equally good models . . . sailed by better seamen."[5] Even before U.S. independence, the "building-art had so improved here as to make American ships respected everywhere for their speed, strength, and beauty, and to excite the liveliest anticipations as to the future of this republic in navigation."[6] Such factors help explain why, by 1776, ships built in the colonies comprised a full one-third of the British registry.[7]

As for the Navigation Acts, colonists often flouted them and abided by their strictures only when convenient.[8] Even so, many—tobacco farmers chief among them—began to resent British protectionism. As detailed by economist Douglas Irwin in his book *Clashing Over Commerce*:

> [A]bout 90 percent of the economic burden of the Navigation Acts is believed to have fallen upon the southern colonies, particularly tobacco planters in Maryland and Virginia, and might have reduced the region's income by as much as 2.5 percent in 1770. It was not a coincidence that these planters strongly supported independence.[9]

In light of that experience, it is curious that the United States, once having se-cured its independence, made the imposition of similar protectionist shipping measures one of its first orders of business.

Post-Revolutionary War Cabotage Policy

When Congress met in April 1789, its first act was to establish a tariff that in-cluded a 10 percent reduction in the duty charged for goods carried by U.S. ves-sels. The tariff bill also established a tonnage tax designed to further advantage U.S. ships.[10] The law placed a $0.50 per ton tax on foreign-built and foreign-owned ships, compared to $0.30 per ton for U.S.-built and foreign-owned ships, and only a modest $0.06 per ton tariff on U.S.-built and -owned ships.[11] Furthermore, U.S.-built ships in the coastal (i.e., domestic) trade only paid the tax annually, while foreign vessels were saddled with the tax at every port call.[12] Although nominally granting a mere preference to the U.S. Merchant Marine, for all intents and purposes the tonnage tax's high rates and application at each port call functioned as a prohibition of foreign ships in the coastal trade.

The motivations behind this early lurch toward maritime protectionism warrant scrutiny. One apparent consideration was a fear that goods traveling in non-U.S. ships would make the country's commerce vulnerable to foreign med-dling. In 1790, for example, George Washington used his second annual address to urge the promotion of U.S. shipping to make "commerce and agriculture less dependent on foreign bottoms" [a colloquial term for ships used to transport goods] which he warned could "fail us in the very moments most interesting to both of these great objects."[13] The next year, Secretary of State Thomas Jefferson sounded a similar note, stating that U.S. trade could be seriously injured if the country's transport was carried by ships of the same European powers the United States might find itself at war with.[14]

Also worth bearing in mind is the role played by U.S. merchant shipping during the recently concluded Revolutionary War. Unlike today, the addition of cannons could rapidly convert merchant ships into privateers that hunted enemy vessels. These privateers enjoyed considerable success, being credited with the capture or destruction of 600 British ships during the struggle for independence.[15] American merchant ships not only served commercial purposes, but also functioned as a de facto naval auxiliary.

Others, meanwhile, have ascribed more sinister motives to the early push for maritime protectionism. In *Our Merchant Marine,* engineer and economist David Wells says a deal was reached between Northeast maritime interests and Southern slaveholders by which protectionist navigation laws would be passed in exchange for extending the life of the slave trade.[16] Wells also attributes early support for such laws to a desire to retaliate against British laws targeting American shipping. He notes, for example, Britain's passage of a 1788 act "forbidding the importation of any American produce into any British colony, except in British bottoms."[17]

Whatever the cause for the early U.S. adoption of maritime protectionism, the American aptitude for maritime enterprise meant that the burden of such measures was minimal. Indeed, in *The Abandoned Ocean,* authors Andrew Gibson and Arthur Donovan go so far as to say that these early forms of protection cost the nation nothing given the highly competitive nature of U.S. shipping and shipbuilding.[18]

More maritime protectionism, however, was to follow. Almost three decades after its initial measures discriminating against foreign shipping, Congress passed the Navigation Act of 1817.[19] It is today regarded as the Jones Act's direct antecedent. The law was passed as a response to a Canadian attempt to capture a part of the U.S. shipping market by requiring gypsum—a major Canadian export—be given steep preference to be carried on Canadian ships.[20] The United States retaliated by passing the 1817 law, which included most restrictions found in the British Navigation Acts.[21] Among these included a complete ban on foreign vessels in coastwise trade.

The U.S. maritime industry continued to grow and would even thrive for about a 30-year period between 1830 and 1860. Dominated by wooden vessels, it became known as the golden age of U.S. shipping.[22] The country had abundant raw materials for shipbuilding, plenty of harbors, productive and well-trained shipbuilders (assisted by better education and better health), and, most importantly, well-managed and well-constructed shipyards.[23] American industry also had the advantage of feeble competition from the British, whose maritime industry was more interested in serving a captive market than evolving and competing in a changing economy.

These U.S. advantages would not last for long.

Repeal of the Navigation Acts

While the U.S. shipping and shipbuilding industries reached new heights, their British counterparts languished. This was not due to a lack of ability but rather incentives. Protected from U.S. and other foreign-built ships by the Navigation Acts, Gibson and Donovan note that British shipbuilders demurred from facing the Americans:

> The British were never able to duplicate the speed and reliability of the American packets. They certainly were capable of meeting the challenge head on, but they lacked the incentive to do so. Since the British Navigation Acts barred the purchase of American-built ships, British shipbuilders contented themselves with serving their protected market while ignoring the American price and quality challenge.[24]

Originally meant to bolster the British merchant marine, the Navigation Acts instead enervated it. Short-term profits gave way to long-term decline. This British abandonment of international shipbuilding enabled the U.S. shipbuilding sector to become the industry's premier player, while the British maritime sector found itself mired in an unsustainable status quo.

While the Navigation Acts' restrictions drew criticism from Britain's trading partners, many inside the country—where free-trade sentiment was ascendant, as evidenced by the 1846 repeal of the Corn Laws—also began to question their wisdom.[25] Parliament would hear complaints about the drop in British tonnage as compared to other countries, talk of a lower standard of living and reduced employment opportunities because the shipping industry was devoid of competition, and that shipbuilding capital was leaving Britain for greener pastures in Sweden and Russia.[26] In 1847, a drop in trade flows prompted the Navigation Acts' temporary suspension.[27]

The British maritime industry's dire straits prompted the launch of a formal inquiry by Parliament into the effects of the Navigation Acts. One of those who took part was John Lewis Ricardo, the nephew of political economist David Ricardo, who wrote about what he learned from the testimony provided in his book *The Anatomy of the Navigation Laws*. Among his observations were that the British merchant marine had flourished least where it had been protected, that monopoly status had produced inferiority, that the law produced retaliation from other countries, and that the law increased the cost of both transportation and goods purchased.[28]

The Navigation Acts had plainly become a liability to the very maritime industry whose fortunes it was meant to bolster, and members of the sector soon arrived in the halls of government in search of assistance. "So desperate was the case of the builders, owners, carpenters, seamen, and, in short, of all who sought to live by shipping," wrote Ricardo, "that they came to Parliament for a committee, to inquire whether anything could be done to save them from utter ruin."[29]

Predictably, these members of the British maritime industry did not beseech lawmakers to grant them the competition they so desperately needed, but rather to add further restrictions and increase government interventions. Indeed, liberalization was seen as the enemy, and supporters of the Navigation Acts warned that its repeal would spell the British maritime industry's doom.

Many of the arguments made against repeal of the navigation laws were on alleged national security grounds and are almost indistinguishable from the arguments made by supporters of the Jones Act today. In one such example, Admiral of the Fleet Sir Thomas Byam Martin testified before the House of Commons that allowing British shipowners to purchase their vessels from foreign sources would "inevitably diminish the shipwright class in this kingdom," a group upon which he said the "safety of England greatly depended." [30] Such claims that abandonment of the Navigation Acts would endanger national security was a recurring theme, with one member of Parliament warning that repeal would "imperil the safety of the country." [31]

Despite such apocalyptic warnings, free-trade forces carried the day, and on February 14, 1849, the House of Commons approved the repeal of the Navigation Acts. Evidence presented during debate over the bill may have contributed to the decision; that evidence included examples of higher transportation costs in comparison to foreign vessels and, in one particular episode, the inability to transport sugar from Mauritius—a British overseas possession—aboard foreign ships even though no British ships had been available. While 1849 marks the repeal of the Navigation Acts proper, British coastwise trade was not liberalized until 1854, with the five-year delay explained by a misplaced hope that the United States would reciprocate with the opening of its own domestic trade.[32] Although the United States was provided with an opportunity to liberalize its cabotage trade in similar fashion, it refused and instead sank deeper into protectionism.

The predictions of gloom and despair from supporters of the Navigation Acts, meanwhile, were never realized. Instead, the opposite occurred. Invigorated by the increased competition resulting from the country's embrace of free trade, Britain made innovative strides in shipbuilding. Capitalizing on the country's proficiency in the use of iron and steam that emerged during the Industrial Revolution, British shipbuilders were able to outpace American wooden-built ships with cheaper vessels offering larger carrying capacity at less weight.[33]

Liberalization's success extended to British shipping, which was finally able to buy quality ships at a competitive price. Notably, this extended to the coastal trade which, according to Wells, "immediately and largely increased under conditions of freedom." [34] Despite the entry of foreign ships into the trade, he notes that "the proportion of the total business transacted by British vessels was greater than ever before, and the superiority once established has never been impaired."[35]

Meanwhile, the U.S. maritime sector remained in retreat. Although the United States retained a sizeable coastwise shipping sector owing to the inability of railroads to reach certain destinations, overall the country found itself unable to compete in the iron age of shipping, where access to plentiful timber counted for much less. This is partly due to protections for the U.S. iron industry that drove up the metal's price and, along with it, the cost of domestic ship production.[36] But maritime protectionism also helps explain why the United States, hardly a bystander to industrialization, failed to keep pace in this new era. In his book *The Story of the American Merchant Marine,* author John Randolph Spears provides a revealing anecdote highlighting the complacency that U.S. protectionism engendered in its maritime industry:

> While the marine steam-engine has been perfected in Europe, it is worth noting by the way that the producer-gas engine, though yet in the experimental stage for ship use, has been brought to a higher state of perfection for land use in America than in Europe. Magazine articles by marine engineers have been published, urging American ship-owners to adopt this new method of propulsion, because it is to make a revolution almost as far-reaching as the iron screw steamer made in 1855. But the American ship-owner refuses to see his opportunity. *Having certain profits with old-style engines in the coasting trade, he is willing to let foreigners do the experimenting* [emphasis added].[37]

The contrast between newfound British maritime inventiveness and American indifference did not go unnoticed. Writing in the naval magazine *Proceedings* in 1882, Master C. G. Calkins of the United States Navy urged a similar embrace of liberalization to reinvigorate U.S. shipbuilding:

> With foreign competition will come increased inventive activity, and new motive-machinery and systems of construction may restore all the advantages we have lost by their adoption abroad in the past. With the natural advantages we enjoy, the time may soon come when our shipbuilders will be willing to compete with the world in turning out first-class vessels at moderate prices. When the British Navigation Act was repealed in 1849 our shipbuilders were the best in the world, but within a few years a new material and a new type of vessels were created which transformed the conditions of maritime progress.[38]

The advice of Calkins and other like-minded individuals, however, was not heeded. Instead of competing for preeminence in new shipping technology in the face of market-changing improvements, the United States Merchant Marine instead opted for the profits of a captive market.

As a result of this refusal to relent from protectionism, the U.S. maritime industry became steadily less competitive. By 1894 the state of U.S. shipbuilding would be sufficiently dire and the failure of protectionism so obvious that President Grover Cleveland would lament that the sector had been "protected to strangulation."[39]

Passage of the Jones Act

Despite the sharply differing fortunes of the U.S. and British maritime sectors following the repeal of the Navigation Acts, Congress refused to be dissuaded from its protectionist path. As the 1800s progressed, U.S. cabotage laws saw a general trend toward further tightening to eliminate creative legal means that emerged for evading such measures. In 1866, for example, Congress—with a likely eye toward the routing of goods through Canada—revised the 1817 Navigation Act to mandate the confiscation of merchandise transported between U.S. ports via a foreign port "on the northern, northeastern, or northwestern frontiers."[40]

Nonetheless, shippers persisted in their attempts to circumvent U.S. cabotage laws and their forced use of costly U.S. ships. Indeed, by the early 1890s such vessels were sufficiently uncompetitive that one shipper opted to send 250 kegs of nails from New York to Los Angeles via Antwerp, Belgium, in order to take advantage of cheaper foreign ships.[41] The shipment sparked a legal challenge from the U.S. government, but the court ruled in the shipper's favor as the journey did not involve direct transport between two domestic ports. As a result, in 1893 Congress voted to flatly prohibit "the transportation of merchandise in any such vessel or vessels from one port of the United States to another port of the United States *via any foreign port*" (emphasis added).[42] Further changes were made in 1898 to prohibit foreign ships from engaging in the domestic transport of goods, not only between ports, but "for any part of the voyage."[43]

Despite such measures, the door to foreign competition in domestic U.S. transport had not been entirely slammed shut. In 1913, U.S. Attorney General George W. Wickersham deemed the term "voyage" in the 1898 language to only apply to ocean transport. This interpretation allowed goods to be moved by rail from the United States to Vancouver, Canada, and then loaded aboard non-U.S. ships for transport to Alaska. Although this was no doubt a boon to residents of the territory, it raised the ire of Seattle-based shipping companies operating in the Alaska trade. In a bid to block this competition, the companies took their case to Washington, DC, where they found a powerful ally in a member of their state's congressional delegation, Sen. Wesley Livsey Jones (R-WA).

Hailing from North Yakima, Washington (present day Yakima), Jones was first elected to the Senate in 1908 and in March 1919 became chairman of the Senate Commerce Committee. He soon began to make his mark. That June—the same month that the Treaty of Versailles was signed—Jones presided over a series of hearings with an eye toward the disposal of ships built and acquired by the U.S. government during the recently concluded First World War, as well as the permanent establishment of a merchant marine.[44]

Seattle's shipping interests saw their opportunity. On February 20, 1920, one of Jones's constituents, William L. Clark of the Seattle-based Pacific Steamship Company, testified before the Senate Commerce Committee. Professing his deep interest in the development of a U.S. Merchant Marine, Clark said that realizing this goal must involve the elimination of certain "evils."[45] Among these, he claimed, were "vessels flying foreign flags in the carriage of our domestic commerce."[46] Clark was particularly exercised over what he described as subsidized foreign competition from Canada, out of whose ports operated "coastwise steamers . . . of a class and character calculated to take away from the United States water carriers the business of Alaska."[47]

To head off this competition, Clark proposed amending U.S. cabotage laws with the following language:

> No merchandise shall be transported by water, or by land and water, under penalty of forfeiture thereof, from one point in the United States to any other point in the United States, including any Territory, district, or possession thereof, either [through] or via a foreign port, or for any part of the transportation, in any other vessel than a vessel built and documented in the United States and owned by a United States citizen or citizens or by a United States corporation at least 75 per cent of the value of the securities of which are bona fide owned by a citizen or citizens of the United States.[48]

Clark and the Pacific Steamship Company would get their wish. Jones inserted Section 27—the Jones Act—into the Merchant Marine Act of 1920, revising existing U.S. cabotage laws. In a 2008 article, maritime lawyers Constantine G. Papavizas and Bryant E. Gardner provided a copy of the new cabotage language, with additions in italics and the deletions struck through:

> That no merchandise shall be transported by water, *or by land and water,* ~~under~~ penalty of forfeiture thereof *between points in the United States, including Districts, Territories, and possessions thereof embraced within the coastwise laws* ~~from one port of the United States to another port of the United States~~, either directly or via a foreign port, or for any part of the ~~voyage~~ *transportation,* in any other vessel than a vessel ~~of the United States~~ *built in and documented under the laws of the United States and owned by persons who are citizens of the United States, or vessels to which the privilege of engaging in the coastwise is extended by sections 18 or 22 of this Act.* ~~But this section shall not be construed to prohibit the sailing of any foreign vessel from one to another port of the United States: Provided, That no merchandise other than that imported in such vessel from some foreign port which shall not have been unladen shall be carried from one port or place in the United States to another.~~ [49]

Among the more notable features of the revised language are uses of "by land and water," discarding the term "ports" in favor of the broader "points," and a reference to vessels "built in" the United States. All of these are terms that were included in Clark's proposed amendment.[50]

The Merchant Marine Act of 1920, meanwhile, would be approved by Congress on June 4, 1920, and signed into law a day later. In his book *American Shipping Policy,* political scientist Paul Maxwell Zeis traces the bill's origins to legislation passed by the House of Representatives in November 1919 that was designed to end a crash shipbuilding program started by the government in 1916. That bill, Zeis says, was then rewritten by the Commerce Committee over which Jones presided at the behest of private shipping interests to also include the "reestablishment of discrimination against foreign shipping."[51] Of the bill's passage Zeis describes a process marked by haste, partisanship, and the triumph of special interests:

> This revised bill, one of the most important measures on shipping ever brought before Congress, received practically no debate in the Senate and passed without a record[ed] vote. Some opposition to the revised measure developed in the House but the rush for adjournment prevented any intelligent consideration of the bill by the lower chamber.
>
> A conference committee report which embodied most of the provisions of the Senate bill was adopted by a vote of 145 to 120. Most of the Representatives voted in blind support of the party leaders and it is extremely doubtful whether fifty members of the House appreciated the nature of the bill which they were making the law of the land. In this singular fashion was born the amazing Merchant Marine Act of 1920. Its real parents were not the Senate and the House of Representatives but rather the Senate Commerce Committee and the shipping lobby.[52]

Alaska, which did not become a state until 1959 and thus had no vote on the matter, soon felt the new law's impact. Two Canadian shipping companies were forced out of the market, leaving the territory's domestic waterborne transport in the hands of the Seattle-based duopoly of the Alaska Steamship and Pacific Steamship companies.[53]

The impact of this limited competition on shipping rates was disastrous. According to former Alaska governor Walter J. Hickel (R-AK), some shippers saw their cargo rates double, while the state's first governor, Ernest Gruening (D-AK), said that "several enterprises were immediately put out of business by the action of Congress in 1920."[54] Shipping to the state became so expensive, Gruening added, that handling costs for cargoes originating in Seattle and destined for Alaska were triple that of cargoes being shipped from Seattle to Asia.[55]

Decades later, a 1988 Government Accountability Office report placed the annual cost of the Jones Act's U.S.-build provision alone to be about 2 percent of the Alaska's total personal income.[56]

As for Clark and Jones, they would see their paths cross again. In August 1920 the two men would make a joint appearance at a public meeting in Tacoma meant to defend the Merchant Marine Act from criticism.[57] It was Jones's first discussion of the law in such an open format.

In the 1930s, Clark's Pacific Steamship company would be purchased by rival Alaska Steamship Company, which in turn would go out of business in 1971. Today goods transported by ship between Alaska and the U.S. mainland are handled by the Jones Act duopoly of Matson and TOTE Maritime.

The Jones Act, meanwhile, stands largely untouched despite the mounting evidence of its accumulated harms. Indeed, a 2019 Organisation for Economic Co-operation and Development study calculated that its repeal would produce economic gains of up to $64 billion.[58] Increasingly anachronistic, it was named by a 2013 World Economic Forum report as the world's most restrictive example of a maritime cabotage law.[59]

Nothing New under the Sun

The Jones Act is a modern-day incarnation of the Navigation Acts, with similar effects. As with under the Navigation Acts, the United States suffers from markedly higher transportation costs. As with under the Navigation Acts, Americans find themselves unable to transport goods from where they are produced to where they are in demand. As with under the Navigation Acts, a coddled U.S. maritime industry—once world-renowned—has become unable to keep pace with its international peers. And, as with under the Navigation Acts, any talk of repeal or reform inevitably brings ill-founded prophecies of doom.

The law is a fresh reminder that there is nothing new under the sun. Unlike the Navigation Acts, however, the United States has yet to rid itself of a measure that serves neither its broader economic interests nor those of the maritime sector whose fortunes it was ostensibly meant to promote. This can be largely explained by the existence of a committed lobby of shipbuilders, unions, and ship operators who are eager to maintain restrictions on competition. Capitalizing on the public's ignorance of the law and a fear of the unknown, such groups claim that reform or repeal would eliminate what's left of the U.S. maritime industry.

But history makes abundantly clear that the real danger lies in the protectionist status quo. What is eminently predictable is that clinging to the Jones Act will inflict further damage on the U.S. economy. What is known with complete certainty is that, under the suffocating embrace of the world's most restrictive cabotage regime, the U.S. maritime industry will continue to limp along in its current decayed state.

Perhaps the most powerful case for reform is from none other than Jones himself. At his August 1920 appearance in Tacoma, the senator vowed—in the words of one news report—that the Merchant Marine Act would only be changed if it "resulted in positive injury to American trade." Sen. Jones, the report added, said that he "did not want to drive foreign ships from our ports unless there are American ships to take their place."[60]

Plainly this has come to pass. Foreign ships have been barred from engaging in domestic trade and yet the small and costly U.S. fleet has proven incapable of replicating their diverse capabilities. As a result, it can be outright impossible to transport some products, including propane and natural gas, from one part of the United States to another due to a total lack of appropriate ships. In other cases, the expense of using U.S. ships makes it uneconomic. It is readily apparent that the 1920 Merchant Marine Act, and Section 27 in particular, has proven injurious to American trade.

The historical record, as well as current experience, makes abundantly clear that the Jones Act is a failed law whose fate was sealed at passage. An overhaul of the law, if not a full repeal, is of paramount importance if the United States is to reach its maritime potential.

Conclusion

Colin Grabow

The Jones Act is one of the U.S. economy's silent killers, frustrating the ability of Americans to do business with other Americans. Although higher transportation costs are its most obvious result, its consequences go far beyond this. It is why Puerto Rican electricity producers cannot buy U.S. natural gas in the midst of a domestic glut, and why Hawaii must turn to foreign sources of propane instead of the world's leading exporter of this product. It helps explain the lack of domestic shipping between the East Coast and West Coast, and the lack of domestic containerships along the congested I-95 corridor. It contributes to increased pollution, congested and crumbling highways, and reduced export opportunities with U.S. trading partners.

Each of these examples is another grain of sand in the economy's gears, causing it to grind ever slower. Individually nettlesome, their collective impact is intolerable.

That the law nonetheless persists can largely be attributed to the familiar phenomenon of dispersed costs and concentrated benefits. While Americans clearly suffer because of the law, the individual cost may be small, as the Jones Act's toll is spread across hundreds of millions of citizens. Most Americans do not know of the Jones Act's existence, much less its impact on their daily lives. There is not a single organization whose primary purpose is to highlight the Jones Act's costs and seek its repeal.

The law's beneficiaries have no such problem. Indeed, they regard the Jones Act as of existential importance and form numerous groups dedicated to its preservation, blanketing Capitol Hill with their talking points and campaign donations. As a result, the halls of government resemble less a true debating society than a pro–Jones Act echo chamber.

The law's beneficiaries win while the American people lose.

But "beneficiaries" is a term used with trepidation. Although maritime groups insist on the law's preservation it has become increasingly clear that it is doing them no favors. For decades the U.S. maritime industry has been in steady decline, whether measured in the number of ships, mariners to crew them, or shipyards to build them.

The Jones Act is no innocent bystander here. American shipbuilders, as is typical of sectors smothered by protectionist measures, have become so uncompetitive that their offerings are overwhelmingly destined for the small captive domestic market. Jones Act shipping firms, forced to buy U.S.-built vessels at vastly inflated prices, charge such high rates that their services are almost exclusively offered for routes where they do not face competition from other forms of transport. Coastal shipping, which should be a key means of transport among the contiguous states blessed with thousands of miles of coastline and home to many of the country's major cities, lies largely fallow, with its vast potential untapped.

The Jones Act then is best understood as a law which imposes considerable costs in exchange for few, if any, benefits. It is a policy failure that is not advancing the long-term interests of anyone.

Change is desperately needed.

This book aspires to help spark such change by raising awareness of the Jones Act's many costs and failed ambitions. Only when citizens and policymakers are confronted with the law's glaring shortcomings can the prevailing dynamic be altered, and a new course charted.

Possibilities for Reform

Pushing for the Jones Act's repeal is, at least conceptually, the most straightforward means of lifting its burden. Politically, however, it's among the tallest of orders. The United States seems unlikely to shift from featuring the world's most restrictive cabotage regime to having none at all, at least not in quick fashion.

Nonetheless, opportunities exist.

The upside of having a particularly onerous cabotage regime is that there is a plethora of means to provide relief and advance liberalization. The following are proposals that fall short of repeal but would nonetheless provide meaningful relief or at least lay the groundwork for reform.

Improved Transparency

Fundamental to good public policy is a sense of costs, benefits, and trade-offs between the two. But when it comes to the Jones Act, policymakers are often left fumbling in the dark. The Jones Act serves as the cornerstone of U.S. maritime policy and yet the U.S. government appears to have precious little sense of its economic impact. Not only is such information lacking, but the federal government, with its vast resources, is not attempting to study it.

In fact, the federal government has undertaken no study of the Jones Act's national economic impact since 2002. Furthermore, the 2002 effort was not a standalone study but rather a 13-page examination of the law's costs by the U.S. International Trade Commission issued as part of a much longer report on significant U.S. import restraints. No government study solely devoted to the Jones Act's cost and implications for the U.S. economy has ever been conducted.

There are other notable gaps in our knowledge about the law. The Government Accountability Office, for example, has not studied the Jones Act's impact on Alaska since 1988, while a government examination of the law's implications for Hawaii has never been undertaken.

This is unacceptable.

Equally frustrating is the lack of objective data, which, even when provided, is sporadic. From 2001–2004, for example, the Maritime Administration (MARAD) provided a series of reports surveying U.S. shipbuilding and repair facilities. These publications included useful information such as the number of production workers, a list of active shipbuilding yards by region, and profiles of many of the major yards. But no subsequent reports have been released (although MARAD did issue a 2015 report on the U.S. shipbuilding and repair industry's economic importance).

MARAD's website also features vessel inventory reports but it has none prior to 1990, and data are also absent from April 2000 through January 2014, making historical trends more difficult to establish. The agency's most recent summary of the cabotage practices of other countries, meanwhile, is so dated that some of the countries surveyed include Yugoslavia and the Union of Soviet Socialist Republics.

This dearth of information has worked to the advantage of pro–Jones Act groups, who fill the void with their own numbers and provide no means to replicate their data. Absent official statistics, these proprietary figures have largely formed the basis of discussion surrounding the Jones Act, and are widely referenced by both politicians and media organizations when the Jones Act is discussed. Academics and researchers are therefore faced with the task of gathering original data to study the impact of the law, which is no easy feat.

Sunlight is urgently needed to pierce the murk. Such illumination could perhaps be best provided by an independent agency of the federal government, which should undertake a comprehensive examination of the Jones Act. This report would seek to answer, or at least discuss, some of the following questions:

- What is the overall economic impact of the Jones Act?
- What is the geographical distribution of the law's costs?
- Which industries are most affected by the law?
- What benefits, if any, does the law provide? Could these benefits be provided in a more efficient manner?
- How has the maritime industry changed since the law was passed? How well does the law comport with modern maritime realities?
- Has the law realized its stated goals?

In addition, reports should be regularly provided by MARAD that include comprehensive vessel inventories, the number of licensed mariners, and periodic assessments of the U.S. shipbuilding and repair industry. This industry evaluation should include such information as the number of skilled workers, production statistics, number of shipyards, and cost competitiveness with foreign-built vessels across a range of categories.

Good, replicable information and increased transparency should be among the lowest of the reform fruit to be plucked, and something that all stakeholders in the Jones Act debate should be able to agree on. Indeed, this isn't even a reform of the Jones Act but simply a call for increased clarity and transparency around one of the country's most consequential transportation laws.

Institution of a Waiver System

One modest reform that could be implemented is the establishment of an updated waiver system for those instances when a Jones Act ship is not available to perform a needed task. The Jones Act fleet is both small and limited in its capabilities. More than 40 percent of the fleet is comprised of a single vessel type: medium-range product tankers. There are a mere two dry bulk ships and no liquefied natural gas carriers, liquefied petroleum gas carriers, asphalt carriers, cement carriers, livestock carriers, or heavy-lift ships. In other words, even when Americans are willing to incur the high cost of using a Jones Act vessel the appropriate ship may not be available—or even exist.

The burden that such situations present could be easily relieved through the granting of waivers. Currently, however, administrative waivers can only be granted in those cases deemed to be in the interest of national defense. Waivers sought on the basis of economic or commercial need alone will not be granted.

This is plainly absurd. In instances where a needed type of vessel is not available, Americans should be able to contract with a non–Jones Act ship. The logic in favor of such an arrangement is overwhelming. If no Jones Act ship is available to perform a specific task, then the U.S. maritime industry will incur no lost business or jobs, while the party requiring the ship's services will still have their needs fulfilled.

Under such a system, a standing waiver should exist for any vessel type not found in the Jones Act fleet. For those vessels that do exist, a more transparent and efficient process should be established to apply for waivers in those instances that the needed type of vessel is not available. In addition, declarations of major disasters should be automatically accompanied by Jones Act waivers to eliminate uncertainty and speed relief. In the 2017 case of Hurricane María, for example, a major disaster was declared on September 20 but a Jones Act waiver was not issued until September 28. In such cases, shippers should be able to count on a full array of options to speed relief to where it's needed.

Permanent Exemption for Noncontiguous States and Territories

While the Jones Act is a burden on the entire country, its impact is particularly onerous for the noncontiguous states and territories. Unlike the U.S. mainland, they are almost entirely dependent on ocean transport for many of the products they consume. Alternative means of transport such as rail, trucking, and pipelines simply are not an option. And so, with the exception of expensive air transport, residents of Alaska, Hawaii, and Puerto Rico must turn to Jones Act carriers in order to do business with the world's largest economy.

There aren't many to choose from. In both the Alaska and Hawaii trades there are just two Jones Act ocean carriers, while in Puerto Rico two Jones Act carriers have 85 percent of the container capacity. The inevitable result of this limited competition is higher shipping prices and fewer transport options.

The few carriers operating in these trades are not only expensive but also lacking in capabilities. Puerto Rico, for example, relies upon natural gas for nearly 40 percent of its electricity generation needs but cannot purchase it in bulk quantities from the U.S. mainland owing to a total lack of liquefied natural gas carriers. A similar absence of appropriate Jones Act ships effectively makes U.S. propane off-limits to Hawaii and Puerto Rico. In other words, doing business with the U.S. mainland is not only more expensive but can also be impossible.

The Jones Act is an unconscionable burden to the noncontiguous states and territories that should be lifted immediately via a permanent exemption. This would be a means of providing substantial economic relief, including to poverty-stricken Puerto Rico, that would not cost the federal government a dime. In addition, such an exemption would provide an opportunity to study the impact of the Jones Act's removal on the most afflicted cases, which could bolster the evidence for its outright repeal.

Eliminate the Domestic-Build Requirement

The World Economic Forum has labeled the Jones Act the world's most restrictive example of a cabotage law, a designation that is no doubt in large part due to the law's domestic-build requirement.[1] The United States is a notable outlier in its embrace of this provision, which is only found among a handful of countries.[2] The requirement is even an anomaly within broader U.S. transportation policy, where foreign-built vehicles, rolling stock, and aircraft are all permitted.

Mandating the U.S. construction of vessels engaged in domestic waterborne transport imposes massive costs. According to the Congressional Research Service, a U.S.-built tanker can cost up to four times more than one built abroad, while a U.S.-built containership can be up to five times more expensive. Even tugboats are said to have their purchase price doubled by the law.[3] Multiplied across the vessels of the Jones Act fleet, that amounts to many billions of dollars being unnecessarily spent, which must be recouped through higher fees charged to the consumers of waterborne transport.

But consumers aren't the only ones who suffer from this provision. Costly vessels mean a less-competitive waterborne transport sector and thus reduced demand for its services. This, in turn, means fewer jobs for those employed on Jones Act vessels.

Perhaps worst of all, the measure has been completely ineffectual in promoting a robust U.S. commercial shipbuilding industry. Isolated from international competition, the industry has become totally uncompetitive in the construction of large oceangoing commercial ships, where it accounts for less than 1 percent of global production.[4] Unlike other countries, which enjoy competitive advantages in the production of certain ship types—chemical tankers in the case of Japan[5], or work/repair vessels in the case of Norway[6]—U.S. shipbuilders have no such niche.

Nevertheless, the removal of this failed policy would be a heavy legislative lift. Fortunately, numerous possibilities exist for making its repeal more politically palatable. Ending the U.S.-build requirement could, for example, be limited to vessels over 10,000 gross tons, where only a mere two or three are built per year. In addition, the U.S.-build requirement could be replaced with a tariff that could steadily be reduced over several years. Such a measure would provide U.S. shipyards with an opportunity to ready themselves for the new competitive environment they would be entering. To further ease this transition, the federal government could also approve a spending bill to replace the aged vessels of the Ready Reserve Force sealift fleet, providing business for U.S. shipyards as they prepare to enter the altered landscape.

Limited Cabotage Movements

Yet another reform worthy of consideration is the allowance of cabotage movements under particular circumstances. One possibility would be allowing non–Jones Act vessels to transport goods either originating from abroad or whose final destination is outside the United States. For example, cargo arriving in Long Beach, California, from Asia aboard a large containership could then be placed on smaller non–Jones Act feeder ships for transport to its final destination in Portland, Oregon. Or the reverse could take place. Not only would such an option increase transportation flexibility and help relieve pressure on trucking and rail, it would not harm U.S. carriers because they do not offer such transshipment services.[7]

Another option would be to allow ships arriving in the United States to perform one cabotage movement before departing to a foreign port. Such a policy already exists in New Zealand,[8] where foreign ships can engage in cabotage, provided that:

- The vessels are passing through New Zealand waters while on a continuous journey from a foreign port to another foreign port;
- The vessels are stopping in New Zealand to load or unload international cargo; and
- The transport of coastal cargo is incidental to transport of the vessel's international cargo.

This liberalized approach has been in place since 1994 and is estimated to have produced 20–25 percent coastal freight rate reductions between 1994 and 2000. The relaxation of cabotage restrictions is estimated to have resulted in reductions of 50 percent in certain instances, as well as intensified competition for domestic cargo between various forms of transportation and prompted more frequent service between the major ports of New Zealand's South and North Islands.[9]

American ports and coastal waters are already filled with non–Jones Act ships delivering cargo from abroad or picking cargo up for international transport. They represent a conveyor belt along the country's coasts that Americans are currently prohibited from taking advantage of. Allowing at least limited cabotage would be a means of allowing them to utilize this latent resource.

No Excuse for Continued Inaction

These proposed reforms should not be viewed as an exhaustive list. Indeed, other measures which readily come to mind include relaxing the 75 percent U.S.-ownership requirement to encourage investment, waivers for vessels that meet particularly rigorous environmental standards, waivers for the transport of certain products, or expanded options for the employment of foreign citizens aboard U.S. vessels—there is plenty of room for creative thinking.

Whatever the approach, there is no excuse for doing nothing. The evidence of the Jones Act's costs to the U.S. economy and its failure to bolster the U.S. maritime sector are too overwhelming to stand idly by.

We at the Cato Institute will continue to do our part by researching and documenting the burden presented by the Jones Act and pressing the case for change. We invite others to do the same. Only by combining our resources and raising awareness of this misguided law can we ensure that it does not persist for another 100 years.

Notes

Introduction

1. "Pop Culture: 1920," United States Census Bureau, https://www.census.gov /history/www/through_the_decades/fast_facts/1920_fast_facts.html.

2. 46 U.S.C. §883 (1958), 46 U.S.C. § 50101 (2012).

3. "Cabotage," Merriam-Webster, https://www.merriam-webster.com/dictionary /cabotage.

4. Hull means the shell, or outer casing, and the internal structure below the main deck, which provide both the flotation envelope and structural integrity of the vessel in its normal operations. In the case of a submersible vessel, the term includes all structural members of the pressure envelope.

5. Superstructure means the main deck and any other structural part above the main deck.

6. 46 C.F.R. § 67.97.

7. Cato Institute, "The Jones Act: High Steaks," YouTube video, March 7, 2019, https://youtu.be/Oq4YQgxMquQ.

8. *Maritime Transportation: The Role of U.S. Ships and Mariners," Hearing Before the Subcommittee on Coast Guard and Maritime Transportation of the House of Representatives Transportation and Infrastructure Committee* (statement of John Porcari, Deputy Secretary Department of Transportation, et al.), May 21, 2013.

9. U.S. International Trade Commission, *Shipbuilding Trade Reform Act of 1992: Likely Economic Effects of Enactment*, USITC Publication 2495 (Washington: USITC, June 1992).

10. "Summary Tables: United States Flag Privately Owned Merchant Fleet, 2000–2016," U.S. Department of Transportation, Maritime Transportation, https://www.maritime.dot.gov/sites/marad.dot.gov/files/docs/outreach/data -statistics/7061/us-fleet-summary-table-2000-2016-1.pdf.

11. "United States Flag Privately Owned Merchant Fleet Report, as of January 15, 2020," U.S. Department of Transportation, Maritime Transportation,

https://www.maritime.dot.gov/sites/marad.dot.gov/files/oictures/DS_USFlag
-Fleet_20180101-REVISED.pdf.

12. U.S. Department of Transportation, Maritime Administration, *Maritime Workforce Working Group Report* (Washington: MARAD, September 29, 2017), pp. 1, 32.

13. Zoe Chance, "Episode 524: Me and Mr. Jones," transcript, National Public Radio, March 12, 2014, https://www.npr.org/templates/transcript/transcript
.php?storyId=289116345?storyId=289116345.

14. Karin Gourdon and Joaquim J. M. Guilhoto, *Local Content Requirements and their Economic Impact on Shipbuilding: A Quantitative Assessment*, Organisation for Economic Co-operation and Development Science, Technology and Industry Policy Papers no. 69 (Paris: OECD, 2019).

15. John Frittelli, "Shipping under the Jones Act: Legislative and Regulatory Background," Congressional Research Service, R45725, May 17, 2019.

16. Costas Paris, "Philadelphia Shipyard Fights Again for Its Life," *Wall Street Journal*, April 17, 2019.

17. Department of Justice, "Four Shipping Executives Agree to Plead Guilty to Conspiracy to Eliminate Competition and Raise Price for Moving Freight to and from the Continental U.S. and Puerto Rico," press release, October 1, 2008.

18. Jaison Abel et al., *Report on the Competitiveness of Puerto Rico's Economy* (New York: Federal Reserve Bank of New York, June 2012).

19. Paul Krugman, "America's Un-Greek Tragedies in Puerto Rico and Appalachia," *New York Times*, August 3, 2015.

20. U.S. International Trade Commission, *The Economic Effects of Significant U.S. Import Restraints, Phase III: Services*, Publication no. 2422 (Washington: USITC, 1991); U.S. International Trade Commission, *The Economic Effects of Significant U.S. Import Restraints: Second Update*, Publication no. 3201 (Washington: USITC, 1999); and U.S. International Trade Commission, *The Economic Effects of Significant U.S. Import Restraints: Third Update*, Publication 3519 (Washington: USITC, 2002).

21. U.S. Government Accountability Office, *Puerto Rico: Characteristics of the Island's Maritime Trade and Potential Effects of Modifying the Jones Act*, GAO-13-260 (Washington: GAO, 2013).

22. Steven Mufson, "Tanker Carrying Liquefied Natural Gas from Russia's Arctic Arrives in Boston," *Washington Post*, January 28, 2018.

23. U.S. General Accountability Office, *Alaskan North Slope Oil: Limited Effects of Lifting Export Ban on Oil and Shipping Industries and Consumers*, GAO/RCED-99-191 (Washington: GAO, 1999).

24. U.S. Government Accountability Office, *Maritime Security: Federal Agencies Have Taken Actions to Address Risks Posed by Seafarers, but Efforts Can Be Strengthened*, GAO-11-195 (Washington: GAO, 2011), p. 1.

25. U.S. Government Accountability Office, *Maritime Transportation: Implications of Using U.S. Liquefied-Natural-Gas Carriers for Exports*, GAO-16-104 (Washington: GAO, 2015), p. 30.

Chapter 1

1. The Jones Act is Section 27 of the Merchant Marine Act of 1920. However, the terms "Jones Act" and "Merchant Marine Act of 1920" are often incorrectly used interchangeably, including by the U.S. Maritime Administration (MARAD). See, for example, "The Maritime Administration's First 100 Years: 1916–2016," U.S. Maritime Administration, updated March 25, 2019.

2. United Nations Conference on Trade and Development, *Rethinking Maritime Cabotage for Improved Connectivity*, Transport and Trade Facilitation, Series No. 9 (Geneva: UNCTAD, 2017).

3. The other countries that fully exclude foreign-flagged ships from cabotage are Belgium, China, Colombia, Estonia, Greece, Indonesia, Italy, Lithuania, Sweden, and Turkey. See "Services Trade Restrictiveness Index Regulatory Database," Organisation for Economic Co-operation and Development.

4. World Economic Forum, *Enabling Trade: Valuing Growth Opportunities* (Geneva: World Economic Forum, 2013).

5. "How Protectionism Sank America's Entire Merchant Fleet," *The Economist*, October 5, 2017.

6. United Nations Conference on Trade and Development, *Rethinking Maritime Cabotage for Improved Connectivity*.

7. Robert Y. Cavana, "A Qualitative Analysis of Reintroducing Cabotage onto New Zealand's Coasts," *Maritime Policy Management* 31, no. 3 (2004): 179–98.

8. Thomas Grennes, *An Economic Analysis of the Jones Act* (Arlington: Mercatus Center, 2017).

9. "Summary Tables: United States Flag Privately Owned Merchant Fleet, 2000–2016," U.S. Department of Transportation, Maritime Administration, https://www.maritime.dot.gov/sites/marad.dot.gov/files/docs/outreach/data-statistics/7061/us-fleet-summary-table-2000-2016-1.pdf; and "United States Flag Privately Owned Merchant Fleet Report," U.S. Department of Transportation, Maritime Administration (as of January 15, 2020), https://www.maritime.dot.gov/sites/marad.dot.gov/files/oictures/DS_USFlag-Fleet_20200115_Bundle.pdf.

10. *U.S. Maritime and Shipbuilding Industries: Strategies to Improve Regulation, Economic Opportunities and Competitiveness, Before the United States Congress House Committee on Transportation and Infrastructure, Subcommittee on Coast Guard and Maritime Transportation* (statement of Mark H. Buzby, Administrator, Maritime Administration), March 6, 2019.

11. John Frittelli, "Revitalizing Coastal Shipping for Domestic Commerce," Congressional Research Service, R44831, May 2, 2017.

12. John Frittelli, "Shipping under the Jones Act: Legislative and Regulatory Background," Congressional Research Service, R45725, November 21, 2019.

13. Frittelli, "Revitalizing Coastal Shipping for Domestic Commerce."

14. "United States Flag Privately Owned Merchant Fleet Report," U.S. Department of Transportation, Maritime Administration, January 15, 2020, https://www.maritime.dot.gov/sites/marad.dot.gov/files/oictures/DS_USFlag-Fleet_20200115_Bundle_0.pdf.

15. The Oil Pollution Act of 1990 mandated that all oil tankers, which average 11 years of age, had to be double-hulled by 2015, which in turn encouraged the purchase of vessels much newer than the rest of the Jones Act fleet. "United States Flag Privately Owned Merchant Fleet Report," U.S. Department of Transportation, Maritime Administration, April 1, 2018, https://www.maritime.dot.gov/sites/marad.dot.gov/files/docs/outreach/data-statistics/6631/copy-dsusflag-fleet20180401-1.xlsx.

16. United Nations Conference on Trade and Development, *Review of Maritime Transport, 2019* (Geneva: UNCTAD, 2019).

17. Nickie Butt, David Johnson, Kate Pike, Nicola Pryce-Roberts, and Natalie Vigar, *15 Years of Shipping Accidents: A review for WWF Southampton Solent University* (London: Solent, 2014).

18. Thomas Grennes, "Does the Jones Act Endanger American Seamen?" *Regulation* 40, no. 3 (2017): 2–4.

19. U.S. Department of Transportation, Maritime Administration, *Report on Survey of U.S. Shipbuilding and Repair Facilities* (Washington: Office of Shipbuilding and Marine Technology, 2004).

20. U.S. Department of Transportation, Maritime Administration, *The Economic Importance of the U.S. Shipbuilding and Repairing Industry* (Washington: MARAD, November 2015).

21. Organisation for Economic Co-operation and Development, *Peer Review of the Japanese Shipbuilding Industry* (Paris: OECD, 2016); and Yin-Chung Tsai, "The Shipbuilding Industry in China," *OECD Journal: General Papers*, 2010, no. 3 (2011): 37–69, https://doi.org/10.1787/1995283x.

22. European Commission, *LeaderSHIP 2020: The Sea, New Opportunities for the Future* (Brussels: European Commission, February 20, 2013).

23. These numbers include seagoing propelled merchant ships of 100 gross tonnage (GT) and above, excluding inland waterway vessels, fishing vessels, military vessels, yachts, and offshore fixed and mobile platforms and barges (with the exception of floating production storage and offloading (FPSO) vessels and drillships).

24. Grennes, *An Economic Analysis of the Jones Act*, p. 12.

25. *Economic Importance of the U.S. Shipbuilding and Repairing Industry.*

26. "Ancient and Modern Mariners: The Romance of the High Seas in an Age of Quantification," *The Economist*, December 17, 2014.

27. "Ancient and Modern Mariners"; and National Research Council, *Crew Size and Maritime Safety* (Washington: National Academies Press, 1990), https://doi.org/10.17226/1620.

28. Ecorys Research and Consulting, *Study on Competitiveness of the European Shipbuilding Industry* (Rotterdam: Ecorys, 2009).

29. *Economic Importance of the U.S. Shipbuilding and Repairing Industry.*

30. James K. Matthews and Cora J. Holt, *So Many, So Much, So Far, So Fast* (Washington: United States Transportation Command, 1995).

31. Rob Quartel, "America's Welfare Queen Fleet: The Need for Maritime Policy Reform," *Regulation* 14, nos. 3–5 (Summer 1991): 58–67.

32. *On the State of Command, Before the United States Congress Senate Committee on Armed Services* (statement of General Darren W. McDew, United States Air Force Commander, United States Transportation Command), April 10, 2018.

33. Nicolas Loris, Brian Slattery, and Bryan Riley, "Sink the Jones Act: Restoring America's Competitive Advantage in Maritime-Related Industries," Heritage Foundation, May 22, 2014.

34. John Frittelli, "Cargo Preferences for U.S.-Flag Shipping," Congressional Research Service, R44254, October 29, 2015.

35. For more discussion, see Frittelli, "Cargo Preferences for U.S.-Flag Shipping."

36. The *New York Times* reported that in 2003 almost 500,000 troops were airlifted to Iraq on civilian aircraft via the Pentagon's Civil Reserve Air Fleet program. See Micheline Maynard, "Pentagon Gives Airlines a Lifeline With Payments for Moving Troops," *New York Times*, December 26, 2003.

37. Keith Hennessey, "How to Waive the Jones Act," June 18, 2010.

38. Josh Siegel, "Trump: Shipping Industry Doesn't Want Jones Act Lifted for Puerto Rico," *Washington Examiner*, September 27, 2017.

39. Lydia DePillis, "Relief Groups Hit Major Hurdles Getting Aid to Puerto Rico," *CNN Money*, October 23, 2017; and Ryan Schleeter, "Our Power, Our Future: Puerto Rico's Road to a #JustRecovery," *Greenpeace* (blog), October 19, 2017.

40. "Jones Act," Transportation Institute, https://transportationinstitute.org/jones-act/.

41. *The State of the U.S. Flag Maritime Industry, Before the United States Congress House Subcommittee on Coast Guard and Maritime Administration* (statement of Bill Van Loo, Secretary Treasurer, Marine Engineers' Beneficial Association), January 17, 2018.

42. *On the State of Command.*

43. Tim Colton, "Deliveries from U.S. Shipyards Since 1987," Shipbuildinghistory.com.

44. Frittelli, "Shipping under the Jones Act."

Chapter 2

1. Richard A. Smith, "The Jones Act: An Economic and Political Evaluation" (master's thesis, MIT Department of Ocean Engineering, June 2004), https://dspace.mit.edu/bitstream/handle/1721.1/33431/62868407-MIT.pdf.

2. Michael L. Grace, "History of the Alaska Steamship Company, Seattle, 1895-1971," *Cruising the Past* (blog), March 10, 2010.

3. Ernest Gruening, "Let Us Now End American Colonialism" (speech delivered to the delegates of the Alaska Constitutional Convention, November 9, 1955), https://www.alaska.edu/creatingalaska/constitutional-convention/speeches -to-the-conventio/opening-session-speeches/gruening/.

4. James K. Matthews and Cora J. Holt, *So Many, So Much, So Far, So Fast* (Washington: United States Transportation Command, 1995).

5. Keith Dominic, "Foreign Flag Shipping: A Weakness in the Sealift Trident," a paper submitted to the Faculty of the Naval War College in partial satisfaction of the requirements of the National Security Decision Making Department, May 4, 2009.

6. VISA is the Voluntary Intermodal Sealift Agreement. Begun in 1997, the program is meant to provide the military with access to commercial sealift and intermodal capabilities in times of conflict when there are insufficient ships available from other sources.

7. "Deliveries from U.S. Shipyards, 1947 to 1976," *Shipbuilding History*, June 7, 2010.

8. Victor Barnes et al., *Shipbuilding Industry, Final Report* (Washington: Industrial College of the Armed Forces, Spring 2009).

9. David E. Sanger, "On Second Thought, U.S. Decides Shipyard Subsidies Aren't So Bad," *New York Times*, October 3, 1996.

10. John Frittelli, "Revitalizing Coastal Shipping for Domestic Commerce," Congressional Research Service, R44831, May 2, 2017.

11. John Frittelli, "Shipping under the Jones Act: Legislative and Regulatory Background," Congressional Research Service, R45725, May 17, 2019.

12. Frittelli, "Shipping under the Jones Act."

13. "Summary Tables: United States Flag Privately Owned Merchant Fleet, 2000-2016," U.S. Department of Transportation, Maritime Administration, https://www.maritime.dot.gov/sites/marad.dot.gov/files/docs/outreach/data -statistics/7061/us-fleet-summary-table-2000-2016-1.pdf.

14. "United States Flag Privately Owned Merchant Fleet Report," U.S. Department of Transportation, Maritime Administration (as of February 4, 2019), https://www.maritime.dot.gov/sites/marad.dot.gov/files/oictures/DS_USFlag -Fleet_20190204_1.xlsx.

15. "Ship Inventory," U.S. Navy's Military Sealift Command.

16. Matthews and Holt, *So Many, So Much, So Far, So Fast*.

17. "Ancient and Modern Mariners: The Romance of the High Seas in an Age of Quantification," *The Economist*, December 17, 2014.

18. "The Jones Act is critical to the military strategy of the United States, which relies on the use of U.S. flag ships and crews and the availability of a shipyard industrial base to support national defense needs," Military to Maritime, https://militarytomaritime.org/about/the-jones-act/.

19. Bryan Clark, Timothy A. Walton, and Adam Lemon, *Strengthening the U.S. Defense Maritime Industrial Base: A Plan to Improve Maritime Industry's Contribution to National Security* (Washington: Center for Strategic and Budgetary Assessments, 2020).

20. "U.S. Maritime Industry," American Maritime Partnership, https://www.americanmaritimepartnership.com/u-s-maritime-industry/overview/.

21. *Maritime Transportation: Opportunities and Challenges, Before the Subcommittee on Surface Transportation and Merchant Marine Infrastructure, Safety and Security of the Senate Committee on Commerce, Science, and Transportation, United States Senate* (statement of Mark H. Buzby, Administrator Maritime Administration, U.S. Department of Transportation), April 24, 2018.

22. Colin Grabow, "The Jones Act: It's Worse than You Think," *Cato at Liberty* (blog), October 2, 2017.

Chapter 3

1. This was later made more explicit by the Merchant Marine Act of 1970, which, in its preamble, lists ensuring "efficient facilities for shipbuilding and ship repair" among its policy goals.

2. The U.S. Maritime Administration describes the Ready Reserve Force (RRF), which comprises nearly half of the government-owned surge sealift capacity, as a fleet that "primarily supports transport of Army and Marine Corps unit equipment, combat support equipment, and initial resupply during the critical surge period before commercial ships can be marshaled." See "The Ready Reserve Force (RRF)," United States Department of Transportation, Maritime Administration.

3. James K. Matthews and Cora J. Holt, *So Many, So Much, So Far, So Fast* (Washington: United States Transportation Command, 1995).

4. The eight vessels were the *Ponce* (RO/RO); *Strong Texan* (heavy lift); *Omi Champion* (tanker); *Overseas Vivian* (tanker); *Overseas Philadelphia* (tanker); *New York Sun* (tanker); *Solar* (tanker); and *St. Emilion* (tanker).

5. A. J. Herberger, Kenneth C. Gaulden, and Rolf Marshall, *Global Reach: Revolutionizing the Use of Commercial Vessels and Intermodal Systems for Military Sealift, 1990–2012* (Annapolis: Naval Institute Press, 2015), p. 106.

6. Matthews and Holt, *So Many, So Much, So Far, So Fast.*

7. The Military Sea Transportation Service was renamed the Military Sealift Command in 1970.

8. Lawson P. Ramage, "The Military Sea Transportation Service," *Naval War College Review* 22, no. 5 (1969): 4–11.

9. U.S. Department of Transportation, Maritime Administration, *Maritime Workforce Working Group Report* (Washington: Maritime Administration, 2017).

10. *Maritime Transportation: The Role of U.S. Ships and Mariners, Before the Subcommittee on Coast Guard and Maritime Transportation of the House of Representatives Transportation and Infrastructure Committee*, 113th Congress, 1st sess. (May 21, 2013).

11. Herberger, Gaulden, and Marshall, *Global Reach*, pg. 116.

12. Peter Navarro, "Buying American Can Help Keep the Philly Shipyard Afloat," *Philadelphia Inquirer*, June 29, 2018.

13. These four are Philly Shipyard in Philadelphia; General Dynamics-NASSCO in San Diego; VT Halter in Pascagoula, Mississippi; and Keppel AmFELS in Brownsville, Texas.

14. Philly Shipyard, *Q2 2019 and Half-Year 2019 Results* (Philadelphia: Philly Shipyard, Inc., July 15, 2019).

15. *On the State of Command, Before the Senate Armed Services Committee* (statement of General Darren W. McDew, United States Air Force Commander, United States Transportation Command), April 10, 2018.

16. National Advisory Committee on Oceans and Atmosphere, *Shipping, Shipyards, and Sealift: Issues of National Security and Federal Support* (Washington: NACOA, 1985).

17. *An Assessment of Maritime Trade and Technology* (Washington: U.S. Congress, Office of Technology Assessment, 1983).

18. U.S. International Trade Commission, *Analysis of the International Competitiveness of the U.S. Commercial Shipbuilding and Repair Industries* (Washington: USITC, April 1985).

19. Stephen Baker, Chris Degnan, Josh Gabriel, and John Tucker, *National Security Assessment of the U.S. Shipbuilding and Repair Industry* (Washington: Department of Commerce, 2001).

20. Victor Barnes et al., *Shipbuilding Industry: Final Report* (Washington: Industrial College of the Armed Forces, Spring 2009), https://es.ndu.edu/Portals/75/Documents/industry-study/reports/2009/icaf-is-report-shipbuilding-2009.pdf.

21. Deborah Broughton et al., *Shipbuilding Industry: Final Report* (Washington: Industrial College of the Armed Forces, Spring 2006).

22. Francisco Badiola et al., *Shipbuilding: Final Report* (Washington: Dwight D. Eisenhower School for National Security and Resource Strategy, Spring 2016).

23. *An Assessment of Maritime Trade and Technology*, p. 9.

24. John Frittelli, "Shipping under the Jones Act: Legislative and Regulatory Background," Congressional Research Service, R45725, May 17, 2019.

25. *An Assessment of Maritime Trade and Technology*, p. 86.

26. Jill Boward et al., *Shipbuilding Industry: Final Report* (Washington: Industrial College of the Armed Forces, Spring 2007).

27. Frittelli, "Shipping under the Jones Act."

28. "Navy Secretary Calls for Used-Ship Buy to Recapitalize Sealift Fleet," *Maritime Executive*, May 17, 2019.

29. U.S. House Armed Services Committee, "U.S. Transportation Command and Maritime Administration: State of the Mobility Enterprise," YouTube video, beginning at 1:40:20, March 7, 2019, https://youtu.be/-LOW6kH-sOY?t=6021.

30. Syamsul Bachri et al., *Shipbuilding Industry: Final Report* (Washington: Dwight D. Eisenhower School for National Security and Resource Strategy, Spring 2015).

31. The Maritime Security Program (MSP) provides an annual $5 million stipend to each of the 60 ships participating in the program. In exchange, operators of these vessels are required to make them available for charter upon request by the secretary of defense during times of war or national emergency. Although the ships participating in the MSP are U.S.-flagged and U.S.-crewed, they operate exclusively in the foreign trades because of their foreign construction.

32. International Organization of Motor Vehicle Manufacturers, "World Motor Vehicle Production," World Ranking of Manufacturers, Organisation

Internationale des Constructeurs d'Automobiles (OICA) Correspondents Survey, 2016–2017.

33. International Organization of Motor Vehicle Manufacturers, "World Motor Vehicle Production by Country and Type," Organisation Internationale des Constructeurs d'Automobiles (OICA) Correspondents Survey, 2016–2017.

34. Julie Johnsson, "Boeing Retains Crown as World's Largest Planemaker," *Bloomberg*, January 8, 2019.

35. Elwood Brehmer, "Rare Cargo Options Offered at Stevens Airport," *Alaska Journal of Commerce*, November 19, 2014.

36. Mary E. Chenoweth, *The Civil Reserve Air Fleet and Operation Desert Shield/ Desert Storm: Issues for the Future* (Santa Barbara: RAND Corporation, 1993).

37. Micheline Maynard, "Pentagon Gives Airlines a Lifeline With Payments for Moving Troops," *New York Times*, December, 26, 2003.

38. Duane H. Cassidy, "A Call to Action . . . Again," *Defense Transportation Journal* 45, no. 5 (1993): 50–52.

39. Clinton H. Whitehurst, *The U.S. Shipbuilding Industry: Past, Present, and Future* (Annapolis: Naval Institute Press, 1986), p. 26.

40. Frittelli, "Shipping under the Jones Act."

41. Frittelli, "Shipping under the Jones Act."

42. Comptroller General of the United States, *Maritime Subsidy Requirements Hinder U.S.-Flag Operators' Competitive Position* (Washington: GAO, 1981).

43. *Analysis of the International Competitiveness of the U.S. Commercial Shipbuilding and Repair Industries.*

44. Bruce Jones, Daniel B. Abel, Jennifer Carpenter, John Garamendi, and Todd Semonite, "Securing Maritime Commerce: The U.S. Strategic Outlook," panel at Brookings Institution, March 25, 2019, https://www.brookings.edu/wp-content /uploads/2019/03/fp_20190325_maritime_commerce_transcript.pdf.

45. Bryan Clark et al., *National Security Contributions of the U.S. Maritime Industry* (Washington: Center for Strategic and Budgetary Assessments, 2019).

46. Philly Shipyard, *2018 Annual Report* (Philadelphia: Philly Shipyard, Inc., 2018).

47. Philip Hoxie and Vincent H. Smith, *The Jones Act Does Not Add to Our Nation's Defenses* (Washington: American Enterprise Institute, May 2019).

48. U.S. Government Accountability Office, *Puerto Rico: Characteristics of the Island's Maritime Trade and Potential Effects of Modifying the Jones Act*, GAO-13-260 (Washington: GAO, 2013).

49. Baker et al., *National Security Assessment of the U.S. Shipbuilding and Repair Industry*.

50. Charlie Papavizas, "U.S. Coast Guard Issues Jones Act Build and Rebuilt Guidance," Winston & Strawn LLP, August 1, 2017, https://www.winston.com /en/maritime-fedwatch/u-s-coast-guard-issues-jones-act-build-and-rebuilt -guidance.html.

51. Charlie Papavizas, "U.S. Coast Guard Issues New Jones Act Build Guidance," *MaritimeFedWatch, Lexology* (blog).

52. Det Norske Veritas Group, "Daniel K. Inouye," vessel register, IMO no. 9719059, https://vesselregister.dnvgl.com/vesselregister/vesseldetails.html?vesselid =34847.

53. "U.S., Korean Shipyards Team Up to Build Jones Act Ships," *American Shipper*, April 4, 2006; and "Ship Design," General Dynamics NASSCO, https://nassco .com/products/design/.

54. General Dynamics NASSCO, "Matson Kanaloa Class (ConRo)," https:// nassco.com/wp-content/uploads/Matson-Kanaloa-Class-ConRo_Fact -Sheet-2016.pdf.

55. Philly Shipyard, *2018 Annual Report*.

56. In the 2008 court case *Philadelphia Metal Trades Council v. Allen et al.*, both the Aker Philadelphia Shipyard and General Dynamics NASSCO argued that a more limited ability to use foreign components in Jones Act shipbuilding would raise their price of these ships, thus leading to fewer such vessels operating in coastwise trades.

57. LTC Deborah Broughton et al., *Shipbuilding Industry: Final Report*.

58. "National Security Strategy of the United States of America," White House, December 2017.

59. Congressional Budget Office, *U.S. Shipping and Shipbuilding: Trends and Policy Choices* (Washington: CBO, 1984).

60. Francisco Badiola et al., *Shipbuilding: Final Report*.

61. John Frittelli, "Cargo Preferences for U.S.-Flag Shipping," Congressional Research Service, R44254, October 29, 2015.

62. Ronald O'Rourke, "DOD Leases of Foreign-Built Ships: Background for Congress," Congressional Research Service, RS22454, May 28, 2010.

63. Loren Thompson, "Aging Sealift Fleet Is Achilles Heel of Pentagon War Plans," *Forbes*, April 25, 2019.

Chapter 4

1. Peter Navarro, "Peter Navarro: Team Trump Is Protecting America's Vital Manufacturing, Defense Industrial Base from Big Risks," *Fox News*, October 10, 2018; "Presidential Executive Order on Buy American and Hire American," White House, April 18, 2017; and "Secretary Ross Releases Steel and Aluminum 232 Reports in Coordination with White House," U.S. Department of Commerce, February 16, 2018.

2. U.S. Customs and Border Protection, *What Every Member of the Trade Community Should Know About: Coastwise Trade: Merchandise* (Washington: CBP, January 2009).

3. *What Every Member of the Trade Community Should Know About.*

4. George Landrith, "The Jones Act Is a Tremendous Benefit to America," *The Hill*, October 22, 2018.

5. "Working in the United States," U.S. Citizenship and Immigration Services.

6. "Activities of U.S. Affiliates of Foreign Multinational Enterprises (MNEs)," U.S. Bureau of Economic Analysis.

7. Daniel Michaeli, "Foreign Investment Restrictions in Coastwise Shipping: A Maritime Mess," *New York University Law Review* 89, no. 3 (2014): 1047–87.

8. "The Committee on Foreign Investment in the United States (CFIUS)," U.S. Department of the Treasury.

9. Michaeli, "A Maritime Mess."

10. John Frittelli, "Shipping under the Jones Act: Legislative and Regulatory Background," Congressional Research Service, R45725, November 21, 2019.

11. Woodrow Wilson, "A Wilson Tariff Speech," in *The New Freedom* (New York: Doubleday, 1913), pp. 136–62.

12. Thomas Grennes, *An Economic Analysis of the Jones Act* (Washington: Mercatus Center, 2017).

13. "Bryan Cranston," Adam Carolla Show, ACP-190, October 27, 2009.

14. "Interactive Tariff and Trade DataWeb," U.S. International Trade Commission.

15. "Databases, Tables and Calculators by Subject," U.S. Bureau of Labor Statistics.

16. Andrew Wilford, "Keeping Up with the Jones Act," *American Spectator*, August 10, 2017.

17. "United States Flag Privately Owned Merchant Fleet Report," United States Department of Transportation, Maritime Administration, as of January 15, 2020, https://www.maritime.dot.gov/sites/marad.dot.gov/files/oictures/DS_USFlag -Fleet_20200115_Bundle.pdf; and "Summary Tables: United States Flag Privately Owned Merchant Fleet, 2000–2016," U.S. Department of Transportation, Maritime Administration, https://www.maritime.dot.gov/sites/marad.dot.gov/files/oictures /DS_USFlag-Fleet_20180101-REVISED.pdf.

18. "Interactive Tariff and Trade DataWeb."

19. Author's calculations from "Interactive Tariff and Trade DataWeb"; and "Industry Productivity and Costs, Value of Production (dollars)," Bureau of Labor Statistics, https://data.bls.gov/cgi-bin/dsrv?ip. The average tariff rate was calculated by dividing the duty revenue by the import value for each good.

20. "Interactive Tariff and Trade DataWeb"; and "United States Boating Industry Statistics," National Marine Manufacturers Association, https://www .nmma.org/statistics/publications/economic-impact-infographics.

21. Colin Grabow, "The Jones Act Makes Little Sense in a Globalized World," *Cato at Liberty* (blog), August 20, 2018.

22. "Ship Design," General Dynamics: NASSCO, https://nassco.com/products /design/.

23. Mike Schuler, "DSME Lands $120 Million Deal Out of Jones Act Ship Order," *gCaptain*, September 19, 2016.

24. C. Nichita, T. Nabergoj, and D. Sonechko, *The Ultimate Jones Act Dry Cargo Carrier: An Innovative LNG Fueled Container RO-RO Vessel*, Royal Institution of Naval Architects, May 21–22, 2014.

25. Karen Thomas, "Mitsui Engineering and Shipbuilding Buys TGE Marine," *LNG World Shipping*, October 3, 2015.

26. Svetlana Modeva, "Philly Shipyard Delivers Third Product Tanker to Kinder Morgan," *Vessel Finder*, July 27, 2017; and Philly Shipyard, "Philly Shipyard Delivers Fourth and Final Product Tanker to Kinder Morgan," press release, November 20, 2017.

27. "American Class Tankers," Kinder Morgan Terminals, https://www.kindermorgan.com/content/docs/american.pdf.

28. Andrew Wilford, "'America's Finest' Will Become another Country's Finest," *American Spectator*, May 7, 2018.

29. Colin Grabow, "The Jones Act Drives America's Finest into Exile," *Wall Street Journal*, April 29, 2018.

30. "Save Our Ship: A Coalition to Save a Ship and an Industry," Save Our Ship Coalition.

31. George F. Will, "George F. Will: No Bad Deed Unrewarded with Protectionism Rampant," *TribLIVE*, January 27, 2018.

32. Pavel A. Yakovlev, *Protectionism Will Not Improve National Security*, National Taxpayers Union Foundation, October 19, 2018.

33. "Open Letter to President Trump and Congress," National Taxpayers Union, May 3, 2018, https://www.ntu.org/library/doclib/embargoed-economists-letter-2018-1.pdf.

34. Gary Wollenhaupt, "American Shipbuilders Brace for Impact of Tariffs on Steel, Aluminum," *Professional Mariner*, September 27, 2018.

35. Michelle R. Smith, "American Boat Makers Feel the Crunch from Trump Tariffs," Associated Press, August 4, 2018.

36. Joseph Bonney, "US Ports Criticize Trump's Planned Steel, Aluminum Tariffs," *Journal of Commerce*, March 2, 2018.

37. Bill Decker, "Shipbuilding, LNG May Feel Sting from Trump Tariffs," *StMaryNow.com*, March 13, 2018.

38. Ken Hocke, "Barge Traffic Could Be Hurt by Trump Tariffs, Economist Says," *WorkBoat*, March 21, 2018.

39. "Trump's Steel Tariff Could Affect Defense Shipbuilders," *Maritime Executive*, March 2, 2018.

Chapter 5

1. Colin Grabow, Inu Manak, and Daniel J. Ikenson, "The Jones Act: A Burden America Can No Longer Bear," Cato Institute Policy Analysis no. 845, June 28, 2018.

2. John Frittelli, "Shipping under the Jones Act: Legislative and Regulatory Background," Congressional Research Service, R45725, May 17, 2019.

3. "Korean Shipbuilders Lose Large 9 Ultra Large Container Ship Deal to China," *The Medi Telegraph*, August 21, 2017.

4. "Hyundai Merchant Marine to Invest $2.8 bn on 20 Large Container Vessels," *Pulse*, September 30, 2018.

5. Philly Shipyard, "Matson Christens First Aloha Class Vessel 'Daniel K. Inouye' at Philly Shipyard," press release, July 2, 2018.

6. Costas Paris, "Philadelphia Shipyard Fights Again for Its Life," *Wall Street Journal*, April 17, 2019.

7. U.S. Government Accountability Office, *Maritime Transportation: Implications of Using U.S. Liquefied-Natural-Gas Carriers for Exports* (Washington: GAO, 2015), p. 16.

8. Frittelli, "Shipping under the Jones Act."

9. John Frittelli, "Revitalizing Coastal Shipping for Domestic Commerce," Congressional Research Service, R44831, May 2, 2017, p. 7.

10. Jaison Abel et al., *Report on the Competitiveness of Puerto Rico's Economy* (New York: Federal Reserve Bank of New York, June 2012), p. 13.

11. "Analysis of Issues Related to Maritime Transportation to Puerto Rico," Advantage Business Consulting, February 2019.

12. "Transportation Statistics Annual Report 2018," Bureau of Transportation Statistics, U.S. Department of Transportation, https://www.bts.gov/tsar.

13. According to the Eurostat website, a carbon dioxide (CO_2) equivalent is a "metric measure used to compare the emissions from various greenhouse gases on the basis of their global-warming potential (GWP)." See Eurostat, "Glossary: Carbon Dioxide Equivalent," https://ec.europa.eu/eurostat/statistics-explained/index.php/Glossary:Carbon_dioxide_equivalent.

14. "Table 4: Cross-Modal Comparisons of Externalities," in *Surface Freight Transportation: A Comparison of the Costs of Road, Rail, and Waterways Freight Shipments That Are Not Passed on to Consumers*, GAO-11-134 (Washington: GAO, January 2011). Based on 2007 emissions. Railroad emissions equal 28.96 tons per million ton-miles and waterways emissions equal 17.48 tons per million ton-miles.

15. "Table 4: Cross-Modal Comparisons of Externalities." Ship emissions comparisons for particulate matter and nitrogen oxide reflect inland waterway freight only.

16. Timothy Fitzgerald, "Environmental Costs of the Jones Act," Cato Institute Policy Analysis no. 886, March 2, 2020.

17. Fitzgerald, "Environmental Costs of the Jones Act."

18. "Consumer Expenditure Survey: Average Expenditure, Share, and Standard Error Tables," Bureau of Labor Statistics, 2018, https://www.bls.gov/cex/tables.htm.

19. *Excessive Truck Weight: A Burden We Can No Longer Support* (Washington: GAO, 1979).

20. Scott G. Borgerson, and Rockford Weitz, *America's Deep Blue Highway: How Coastal Shipping Could Reduce Traffic Congestion, Lower Pollution, and Bolster National Security* (Gloucester, MA: Institute for Global Maritime Studies, 2008).

21. Ashley Halsey III, "Congress and White House Agree to Spend $2 Trillion on Infrastructure," *Washington Post*, April 30, 2019.

22. Foreign dredges are also precluded from dredging in U.S. waters under the Foreign Dredge Act of 1906, which Howard Gutman and Andrew G. Durant discuss in chapter 10 of this volume.

23. *Proposal for the Expansion of the Panama Canal: Third Set of Locks Project*, Panama Canal Authority, April 24, 2006, p. 45, https://ufdc.ufl.edu/AA00010750/00001; and Grabow, Manak, and Ikenson, "The Jones Act: A Burden America Can No Longer Bear."

24. Ships of this size are referred to as Neo-Panamax (12,000 TEU) and Post-Panamax III (16,000 TEU). See Jean-Paul Rodrigue, "Channel Depth at Major North American Container Ports," Geography of Transport Systems.

25. "Dredging Statistics (Fiscal Years 1990–2019)" U.S. Army Corps of Engineers, Institute for Water Resources, https://publibrary.planusace.us/#/document/f8c3fd8b-3395-465e-fd59-9c7723c73010.

26. Ariel Collis and Robert N. Fenili, *Expanding Competition, Expanding Ports: Competition in U.S. Hopper Dredging* (Washington: Center for Strategic and International Studies, June 2018). (Statistics cited refer to the period 2006–2015.)

27. Collis and Fenili, *Expanding Competition, Expanding Ports.*

28. Alan Adler, "Traffic Jams Saddle Trucking with $74.5 Billion in Added Cost," *Trucks*, October 18, 2018.

29. "New ATRI Research Quantifies Impacts of Congestion on Fuel Consumption and Emissions," American Transportation Research Institute, press release,

March 5, 2019, https://truckingresearch.org/2019/03/01/new-atri-research-quantifies-impacts-of-congestion-on-fuel-consumption-and-emissions/.

30. "Congestion Costs Each American 97 Hours, $1,348 a Year," INRIX, February 11, 2019.

31. Frittelli,"Revitalizing Coastal Shipping for Domestic Commerce."

32. John Frittelli, Anthony Andrews, Paul W. Parfomak, Robert Pirog, Jonathan L. Ramseur, and Michael Ratner, "U.S. Rail Transportation of Crude Oil: Background and Issues for Congress," Congressional Research Service, R43390, December 4, 2014, p. 10.

33. Frittelli et al., "U.S. Rail Transportation of Crude Oil."

34. Gregory Meyer, "Why the US East Coast Imports Oil Despite Shale Boom," *Financial Times*, October 11, 2017.

35. U.S. Government Accountability Office, *Puerto Rico: Characteristics of the Island's Maritime Trade and Potential Effects of Modifying the Jones Act*, GAO-13-260 (Washington: GAO, 2013).

36. Craig VanGrasstek, *The History and Future of the World Trade Organization* (Geneva: WTO Publications, 2013), p. 66.

37. VanGrasstek, *The History and Future of the World Trade Organization*, p. 66.

38. "US Faces Grilling over Jones Act Exemption," *TMC News*, December 20, 2007.

39. Larry Luxner, "US Sen. McCain Sets Sights on Jones Act," *Journal of Commerce*, December 5, 2014.

40. "Questions for the Record for Committee on Ways and Means Full Committee Hearing on President's Trade Policy Agenda with Ambassador Michael Froman," July 18, 2013, http://big.assets.huffingtonpost.com/FromanWaysand MeansResponse.pdf.

41. "Questions for the Record."

Chapter 6

1. Thomas Grennes, *An Economic Analysis of the Jones Act* (Washington: Mercatus Center, 2017).

2. *State of the U.S. Flag Maritime Industry, Before the Committee on Transportation and Infrastructure, Subcommittee on Coast Guard and Maritime Transportation, U.S. House of Representatives* (statement of Mark H. Buzby, Administrator, Maritime Administration, U.S. Department of Transportation), January 17, 2018.

3. Andrew Gibson and Arthur Donovan, *The Abandoned Ocean: A History of United States Maritime Policy* (Columbia, SC: University of South Carolina Press, 2001).

4. "Services Trade Restrictiveness Index Regulatory Database," Organisation for Economic Co-operation and Development; Colin Grabow, "Another Jones Act Absurdity," *Cato at Liberty* (blog), September 21, 2018; and Mike Schuler, "New Report Details Cabotage Laws from Around the World," *gCaptain*, September 25, 2018.

5. John Frittelli, "Revitalizing Coastal Shipping for Domestic Commerce," Congressional Research Service, R44831, May 2, 2017.

6. Colin Grabow, Inu Manak, and Daniel J. Ikenson, "The Jones Act: A Burden America Can No Longer Bear," chap. 1, in *The Case against the Jones Act*, eds. Inu Manak and Colin Grabow (Washington: Cato Institute, 2020).

7. Frittelli, "Revitalizing Coastal Shipping for Domestic Commerce."

8. Andrew Tangel and Doug Cameron, "Boeing Boosts Financial Outlook," *Wall Street Journal*, October 24, 2018.

9. Mark H. Buzby, "Remarks to Northern Virginia Council of the Navy League" (speech at New York Harbor School Founders Luncheon, The Lighthouse at Chelsea Piers, New York, October 11, 2018).

10. Grennes, *An Economic Analysis of the Jones Act.*

11. Grennes, *An Economic Analysis of the Jones Act.*

12. Philly Shipyard, *Q4 2019 and Full Year 2019 Results* (Philadelphia: Philly Shipyard, Inc., February 11, 2020).

13. Costas Paris, "Philadelphia Shipyard Fights Again for Its Life," *Wall Street Journal*, April 17, 2019.

14. Buzby, "Remarks to Northern Virginia Council of the Navy League."

15. Thomas Grennes, "Does the Jones Act Endanger American Seamen?," *Regulation* 40, no. 3 (Fall 2017): 2–4.

16. John Frittelli, "Shipping under the Jones Act: Legislative and Regulatory Background," Congressional Research Service, R45725, November 21, 2019.

17. Grennes, *An Economic Analysis of the Jones Act.*

18. Frittelli, "Revitalizing Coastal Shipping for Domestic Commerce."

19. Maximo Q. Mejia Jr., "Developing a Regulatory Framework for Autonomous Shipping," *Baltic Rim Economies* 3 (October 2018): 36.

20. Grennes, "Does the Jones Act Endanger American Seamen?"

21. Frittelli, "Revitalizing Coastal Shipping for Domestic Commerce."

22. "Who Wins as Oil Price Differentials Widen in the Permian Basin?," Yahoo Finance, June 18, 2018.

23. Frittelli, "Revitalizing Coastal Shipping for Domestic Commerce."

24. Frittelli, "Revitalizing Coastal Shipping for Domestic Commerce."

25. Thomas Grennes, "World Trade in Liquefied Natural Gas: Opportunities and Obstacles for the United States," working paper, September 5, 2018; and Thomas Grennes, "A Jones Act Restriction with High Costs and No Benefits," *The Bridge* (blog), November 28, 2018.

26. Frittelli, "Revitalizing Coastal Shipping for Domestic Commerce."

27. "Carbon Emissions," World Shipping Council.

28. Erik Olsen, "An Arcane American Law Protected by Powerful Interests Is Causing Insane Traffic Jams," *Quartz*, August 7, 2017.

29. Scott G. Borgerson and Rockford Weitz, *America's Deep Blue Highway: How Coastal Shipping Could Reduce Traffic Congestion, Lower Pollution, and Bolster National Security* (Gloucester, MA: Institute for Global Maritime Studies, 2008); and John Curtis Perry, Scott Borgerson, and Rockford Weitz, "The Deep Blue Highway," *New York Times*, January 2, 2007.

30. Nancy McLernon, "Protecting U.S. Dredgers Kills Jobs," *Wall Street Journal*, April 16, 2018.

31. Frittelli, "Revitalizing Coastal Shipping for Domestic Commerce."

32. Gibson and Donovan, *The Abandoned Ocean.*

33. Michael Hansen, "Hawaii Shippers Council Outlines Jones Act Reform Proposal," *Hawaii Free Press*, April 13, 2012.

Chapter 7

1. U.S. International Trade Commission, *The Economic Effects of Significant U.S. Import Restraints: Second Update*, Publication no. 3201 (Washington: USITC, 1999); *The Economic Effects of Significant U.S. Import Restraints: Third Update*, Publication no. 3519 (Washington: USITC, 2002); United States Department of Transportation Maritime Administration, *Comparison of U.S. and Foreign-Flag Operating Costs* (Washington: MARAD, September 2011).

2. "Services Trade Restrictiveness Index Regulatory Database," Organisation for Economic Co-operation and Development, https://qdd.oecd.org/subject .aspx?Subject=063bee63-475f-427c-8b50-c19bffa7392d.

3. "National Transportation Statistics, 2019," Bureau of Transportation Statistics, https://www.bts.dot.gov/topics/national-transportation-statistics.

4. "Inventory of U.S. Greenhouse Gas Emissions and Sinks, 1990–2016," United States Environmental Protection Agency (EPA), https://www.epa.gov/ghgemissions/inventory-us-greenhouse-gas-emissions-and-sinks.

5. "Inventory of U.S. Greenhouse Gas Emissions and Sinks, 1990–2016."

6. Gary Clyde Hufbauer and Kimberly Ann Elliott, *Measuring the Costs of Protection in the United States* (Washington: Peterson Institute for International Economics, 1994).

7. Joseph Francois, Hugh M. Arce, Kenneth A. Reinart, and Joseph E. Flynn, "Commercial Policy and the Domestic Carrying Trade," *Canadian Journal of Economics* 29, no. 1 (1996): 181–98.

8. Nicholas Z. Muller and Robert Mendelsohn, "Measuring the Damages of Air Pollution in the United States," *Journal of Environmental Economics and Management* 54, no. 1 (2007): 1–14.

9. "GIFT—Geospatial Intermodal Freight Transport Model," Laboratory for Environmental Computing and Decision Making, http://clarke.main.ad.rit.edu/LECDM/Webgift/WebGIFT.htm.

10. David L. Hummels and Georg Schaur, "Time as a Trade Barrier," *American Economic Review* 103, no. 7 (2013): 2935–59.

11. Mark Delucchi and Donald McCubbin, "External Costs of Transport in the U.S.," Institute of Transportation Studies, UC Davis, Working Paper Series, 2010.

12 . "National Transportation Statistics, 2019."

13. David Austin, "Pricing Freight Transport to Account for External Costs," Congressional Budget Office, Working Paper no. 2015-03, March 30, 2015.

14. "National Transportation Statistics, 2019."

15. Hufbauer and Elliott, *Measuring the Costs of Protection in the United States*, p. 85.

Chapter 8

1. "Pro-competitive Policy Reforms," Organisation for Economic Co-operation and Development.

2. U.S. Department of Transportation, Maritime Administration, *Comparison of U.S. and Foreign-Flag Operating Costs* (Washington: MARAD, September 2011).

3. "Flag of Convenience," Wikipedia.

4. ICC Termination Act of 1995, Pub. L. No. 104–88, Stat. 803 (1995).

5. "How to File Service Contracts," Federal Maritime Commission.

6. ICC Termination Act of 1995, Pub. L. No. 104–88, Stat. 803 (1995).

7. U.S. Department of Transportation, *Competition in the Noncontiguous Domestic Maritime Trades* (Washington: DOT, March 1997).

8. "Four Shipping Executives Agree to Plead Guilty to Conspiracy to Eliminate Competition and Raise Prices for Moving Freight to and from the Continental U.S. and Puerto Rico," U.S. Department of Justice, press release, October 1 2008.

9. In re Puerto Rican Cabotage Antitrust Litigation, 815 F. Supp. 2d 448 (D.P.R. 2011); plea agreements as recent as 2012, USDCPR – Case No. 3:11-cr-00511-DRD and 3:12-cr-00590-DRD.

10. Reeve and Associates and Estudios Técnicos, Inc., *Impact of the U.S. Jones Act on Puerto Rico* (Ogden, UT: Reeve, 2018).

11. U.S. Government Accountability Office, *Puerto Rico: Characteristics of the Island's Maritime Trade and Potential Effects of Modifying the Jones Act*, GAO-13-260 (Washington: GAO, 2013).

12. 49 U.S.C. § 13101 (1996).

13. 49 U.S.C. § 10706 (1996).

Chapter 9

1. "Shipping," 46 U.S.C., https://www.law.cornell.edu/uscode/text/46.

2. "Table 1-56M: Waterborne Freight," Bureau of Transportation Statistics.

3. "Chapter 2: Freight Moved in Domestic and International Trade," Bureau of Transportation Statistics.

4. John Frittelli, "Revitalizing Coastal Shipping for Domestic Commerce," Congressional Research Service, R44831, May 2, 2017.

5. Bureau of Transportation Statistics, *Port Performance Freight Statistics Program: Annual Report to Congress* (Washington: BTS, 2017).

6. Frittelli, "Revitalizing Coastal Shipping for Domestic Commerce."

7. John Frittelli, "Shipping under the Jones Act: Legislative and Regulatory Background," Congressional Research Service, R45725, May 17, 2019.

8. Richard Shelby, "Shelby: Army Corps of Engineers Allocates $274.3 Million to Complete Port of Mobile Project," news release, February 10, 2020.

9. Alyssa Meyers, "$350m Boston Harbor Dredging Project Underway," *Boston Globe*, September 16, 2017; "Fact Sheet—New York and New Jersey Harbor Deepening," U.S. Army Corps of Engineers, February 1, 2019; "Main Channel Deepening Project," Port of Philadelphia (Philaport); "Port of Virginia's Harbor Deepening Project Gets Final Federal Approval," *gCaptain*, July 3, 2018; "Harbor Deepening," South Carolina Ports Authority; Russ Bynum, "$973M Deepening of Savannah Harbor Nearing Halfway Point," *U.S. News & World Report*, February 28, 2018; "Harbor Deepening," Jacksonville Port Authority; U.S. Army Corps of Engineers, "Port Everglades Harbor Deepening FL," March 2019; U.S. Army Corps of Engineers, "Miami Harbor Channel FL (Deepening)," March 2019."

10. Patrick Burnson, "Top 20 U.S. Ports: Competition Heats Up for Discretionary Cargo," *Logistics Management*, May 1, 2015.

11. J. Scott Trubey, "Georgia Ports Want to More than Double Container Capacity by 2028," *Atlantic Journal-Constitution*, February 5, 2018.

12. Patrick Burnson, "Top 30 U.S. Ports 2017: Preparing for the Uncertain," *Logistics Management*, May 2, 2017.

13. Ariel Collis and Robert N. Fenili, *Expanding Competition, Expanding Ports: Competition in U.S. Hopper Dredging* (Washington: Center for Strategic & International Studies, June 2018).

14. Rahul Karunakar and Hari Kishan, "Bull Run Finale for Global Stocks Not Far Off Now: Reuters Poll," Reuters, November 28, 2018.

15. Citing national security concerns, in 2018 the Trump administration imposed tariffs on imports of steel and aluminum, including from countries with which the United States has signed mutual defense treaties, such as Canada and numerous members of the European Union.

16. Nicole T. Carter and Charles V. Stern, "Army Corps of Engineers: Water Resource Authorizations, Appropriations, and Activities," Congressional Research Service, R41243, July 1, 2014.

Chapter 10

1. American Society of Civil Engineers, *2017 Infrastructure Report Card* (Reston, VA: ASCE, 2017), https://www.infrastructurereportcard.org/wp-content/uploads/2017/01/Ports-Final.pdf.

2. Jean-Paul Rodrigue, Claude Comtois, and Brian Slack, *The Geography of Transport Systems* (New York: Routledge, 2016).

3. At least three of the four foreign dredging companies we represent who want to invest in the United States already operate in U.S. offshore wind installation and environmental remediation projects.

4. The 10 major port projects are Boston, Charleston, Port Everglades, Sabine-Neches, Freeport, Brazos Islands/Brownsville, Jacksonville, Corpus Christi, Savannah and Brunswick, and Houston.

5. "Jones Act: Critical to Economic and National Security," Transportation Institute, https://transportationinstitute.org/jones-act/.

6. "Dredging Services in Canada's Coasting Trade," Transport Canada, December 10, 2018; and Delegation of the European Union to Vietnam, *Guide to the EU-Vietnam Free Trade Agreement* (Brussels: EU, March 2019).

7. For example, in 2017 the U.S. Army Corps stated that "the [U.S.] dredging industry has limited resources and equipment" and reiterated long-standing policy that dredges will be pulled from capital improvement projects when flooding reduces navigation in existing shipping channels. U.S. Army Corps of Engineers, *Savannah Harbor Expansion Project: Frequently Asked Questions* (Washington: USACE, April 7, 2017).

8. Government Accountability Office, *Army Corps of Engineers: Effects of Restrictions on Corps' Hopper Dredges Should Be Comprehensively Analyzed*, GAO-03-382 (Washington: GAO, March 2003); and United States Government Accountability Office, *Army Corps of Engineers: Actions Needed to Further Improve Management of Hopper Dredging*, GAO-14-290 (Washington: GAO, April 2014).

9. These four companies are: Jan De Nul, DEME, Van Oord, and Boskalis. "Trailing Suction Hopper Dredger," Jan de Nul Group, https://www.jandenul.com/fleet/trailing-suction-hopper-dredger; "Technology," DEME, https://www.deme-group.com/technology-0?f%5B0%5D=main_equipment%3A24&f%5B1%5D=secondary_equipment%3A27; "Trailing Suction Hopper Dredger," Van Oord, https://www.vanoord.com/activities/trailing-suction-hopper-dredger; "Equipment," Dredgepoint, https://www.dredgepoint.org/dredging-database/equipment?title=&tid=982&field_scrap_value_many_to_one=All; and "Fleet

and Equipment," Boskalis, https://boskalis.com/about-us/fleet-and-equipment
.html#view/grid/dredgerType/Trailing%20suction%20hopper%20dredger
/fleet/Dredgers/page/1.

10. "Trailing Suction Hopper Dredges," Great Lakes Dredge and Dock Company,
LLC, https://www.gldd.com/gldd-equipment-trailing-suction-hopper-dredges/;
"Dredges," Weeks, https://www.weeksmarine.com/equipment-division/dredges;
"Fleet," Manson, https://www.mansonconstruction.com/what-we-do/fleet
#Hopper%20Dredges/827155; "Fleet," Dutra, http://www.dutragroup.com
/equipment-aggregates-dredging-marine-construction.html?id=39; and
"Vessels Database," MarineTraffic, https://www.marinetraffic.com/en/ais/home
/centerx:-12.0/centery:25.0/zoom:4.

11. Hopper dredges are state-of-the-art and are used whenever possible.
A hopper dredge uses powerful drag arms to simultaneously chew up and
vacuum sediment, clay, and some rocks into its hold. When the hold is full,
the hopper dredge sails to the deposit site, opens its hold to release the con-
tents, and then returns empty to the worksite to repeat the cycle. Large hopper
dredges provide highly significant time and cost savings because they can col-
lect more material with each pass than a smaller dredge. And, because they
are sailing while they vacuum material, the hopper dredges do not disrupt
ongoing port traffic.

12. "Trailing Suction Hopper Dredger," Jan De Nul; "Trailing Suction Hopper
Dredger," Van Oord; "Fleet and Equipment"; and "Technology."

13. "Effects of Restrictions on Corps' Hopper Dredges."

14. "Actions Needed to Further Improve Management of Hopper Dredging,"
pp. 4, 22.

15. "Actions Needed to Further Improve Management of Hopper Dredging,"
p. 23.

16. Rabobank, "Dredging: Rising Impact Hurricanes Stimulates Dredging
Markets," October 2017.

17. Lizette Alvarez, "Dredging of Miami Port Badly Damaged Coral Reef, Study
Finds," *New York Times,* May 1, 2016.

18. "System for Award Management," U.S. General Services Administration,
https://www.sam.gov/SAM/.

19. Ariel Collis and Robert N. Fenili, *Expanding Competition, Expanding Ports: Competition in Hopper Dredging* (Washington: Center for Strategic and International Studies, June 2018).

20. Sarah Krouse, Laura Kusisto, and Tom McGinty, "Mounting Climate Worries Push 'Location, Location, Location' Off the Beach," *Wall Street Journal*, October 31, 2018.

21. "Governor Ron DeSantis Announces Major Water Policy Reforms," news release, January 10, 2019.

22. Joseph Spector, "NY Mayor Bill de Blasio Wants to Extend Manhattan's Shoreline to Protect against Flooding," *USA Today*, March 14, 2019.

23. "Loss of Louisiana Coastal Land Is an Ongoing Emergency," *Times-Picayune* editorial board, Nola.com, April 23, 2017, https://www.nola.com/opinions/article_b33e3cf8-08bf-51b9-928b-5d125835fded.html.

24. Joseph Bonney and William B. Cassidy, "Impact of Harvey Flooding Ripples through Logistics Networks," *Journal of Commerce*, August 29, 2017.

25. For computer simulations to help you understand the magnitude of concerns, see "Hell and High Water: Preparing Houston for the Next Big Storm," ProPublica, March 3, 2016.

26. The more ambitious Ike Dike would seek to protect the outlying Port of Galveston and the surrounding communities, while the Coastal Spine is a less-ambitious plan that would seek to protect the Houston Shipping Channel from a storm surge. Both the Ike Dike and the Coastal Spine would copy features from other storm protection systems, notably Rotterdam, which includes a massive gate to block storm surges.

27. "Texas: State Profile and Energy Estimates," U.S. Energy Information Administration, https://www.eia.gov/state/?sid=TX.

28. "National Security Strategy of the United States of America," White House, December 2017.

29. Clifford Krauss, "Texas Energy Industry Recovering From Hurricane's Disruption," *New York Times*, September 8, 2017.

30. Conor Dougherty and Nelson D. Schwartz, "Hurricane to Cost Tens of Billions, but a Quick Recovery Is Expected," *New York Times*, August 28, 2017.

31. Andrea Leinfelder, "Ports Ready to Ease Shipping Backlog after Harvey," *Houston Chronicle*, September 2, 2017.

Chapter 11

1. See, for example, John Frittelli, "Shipping under the Jones Act: Legislative and Regulatory Background," Congressional Research Service, R45725, May 17, 2019; and R. Kevin Adams et al., *Shipbuilding Industry: Final Report* (Washington: Dwight D. Eisenhower School for National Security and Resource Strategy, Spring 2014).

2. For a summary of the literature, as well as a discussion of the costs associated with the Jones Act, see Colin Grabow, Inu Manak, and Daniel J. Ikenson, "The Jones Act: A Burden America Can No Longer Bear," chap. 1, in *The Case against the Jones Act* (Washington: Cato Institute, 2020).

3. Martin Stopford, *Maritime Economics*, 2nd ed. (London: Routledge, Taylor & Francis, 1997).

4. Richard A. Smith, "The Jones Act: An Economic and Political Evaluation" (master's thesis, MIT Department of Ocean Engineering, 2004), https://dspace.mit.edu /bitstream/handle/1721.1/33431/62868407-MIT.pdf?sequence=2&isAllowed=y.

5. Justin Lewis, "Veiled Waters: Examining the Jones Act's Consumer Welfare Effect," *Issues in Political Economy* 22 (2013): 77–107.

6. T. Loch-Temzelides, K. Medlock, and A. Mikulska, "A Cost-Benefit Analysis of the Jones Act" (work in progress, 2015).

7. See, for example, "The Jones Act: Critical to Economic and National Security," Transportation Institute, https://transportationinstitute.org/jones-act/; and Colin Grabow, "Rust Buckets: How the Jones Act Undermines U.S. Shipbuilding and National Security," chap. 3, in *The Case against the Jones Act* (Washington: Cato Institute, 2020).

Chapter 12

1. Kōloa Rum Company (website), https://koloarum.com/.

2. Thomas Grennes, *An Economic Analysis of the Jones Act* (Arlington: Mercatus Center, 2017).

3. Colin Grabow, Inu Manak, and Daniel J. Ikenson, "The Jones Act: A Burden America Can No Longer Bear," chap. 1, in *The Case against the Jones Act* (Washington: Cato Institute, 2020).

4. United States International Trade Commission, *The Economic Effects of Significant U.S. Import Restraints: Fifth Update,"* Publication no. 3906 (Washington: USITC, 2007).

5. Jaison Abel et al., *Report on the Competitiveness of Puerto Rico's Economy* (New York: Federal Reserve Bank of New York, June 29, 2012).

6. Shipping options from Honolulu to foreign ports are available but have not always been an option for Gunter.

7. Maria Kanai, "Making Local Make Sense: Why Four Hawaii Companies Use Locally-Sourced Ingredients," *Hawaii Magazine*, February 17, 2017.

8. Kanai, "Making Local Make Sense."

9. Abel et. al., *Report on the Competitiveness of Puerto Rico's Economy*.

10. Malia Zimmerman, "Businesses Hit Hard by Costly Jones Act Regulations— Part 2 in a Series," *Hawaii Reporter*, March 18, 2010.

11. Zimmerman, "Businesses Hit Hard by Costly Jones Act Regulations—Part 2."

12. Grabow, Manak, and Ikenson, "The Jones Act: A Burden America Can No Longer Bear."

13. Grennes, *An Economic Analysis of the Jones Act.*

14. Matthew Philips, "U.S. Law Restricting Foreign Ships Leads to Higher Gas Prices," *Bloomberg Businessweek*, December 16, 2013.

15. Lori Ann LaRocco, "How Can Gas Prices Be Slashed? Repeal This Act," CNBC.com, July 24, 2013.

16. Grennes, *An Economic Analysis of the Jones Act.*

17. U.S. Government Accountability Office, *Puerto Rico: Characteristics of the Island's Maritime Trade and Potential Effects of Modifying the Jones Act*, GAO-13-260 (Washington: GAO, 2013).

18. *Puerto Rico: Characteristics of the Island's Maritime Trade.*

19. Dennis S. Kostick, "Mineral Resource of the Month: Salt," *Earth Magazine*, April 14, 2010.

20. Emily Ethridge, "Salt Encompasses Billion-Dollar Industry in U.S.," *Roll Call*, June 21, 2013.

21. Michael Tennant, "Federal Shipping Law Exacerbates Northeasterners' Winter Woes," *New American*, March 1, 2014.

22. MaryAnn Spoto and Mike Frassinelli, "Salt Shipment to NJ Costs $700,000 More by Barge than by Ship, Transportation Chief Says," nj.com, February 24, 2014.

23. Brian Slattery, Bryan Riley, and Nicolas D. Loris, "Sink the Jones Act: Restoring America's Competitive Advantage in Maritime-Related Industries," Heritage Foundation Backgrounder no. 2886, May 22, 2014.

24. Russ Kashian, Jeff Pagel, and Ike Brannon, *The Jones Act in Perspective: A Survey of Costs and Effects of the 1920 Merchant Marine Act* (Honolulu: Grassroot Institute of Hawaii, 2017).

25. "Summary Tables: United States Flag Privately-Owned Merchant Fleet, 2000–2016," U.S. Department of Transportation, Maritime Administration, https://www .maritime.dot.gov/sites/marad.dot.gov/files/docs/outreach/data-statistics/7061 /us-fleet-summary-table-2000-2016-1.pdf; and "United States Flag Privately-Owned Merchant Fleet Report, as of January 15, 2020," United States Department of Transportation, Maritime Administration, https://www.maritime.dot.gov/sites /marad.dot.gov/files/oictures/DS_USFlag-Fleet_20200115_Bundle.pdf.

26. Slattery, Riley, and Loris, "Sink the Jones Act."

27. "Ready Reserve Force, Maritime Administration Fact Sheet," U.S. Department of Transportation, Maritime Administration, 2017, https://www.maritime.dot .gov/sites/marad.dot.gov/files/docs/resources/newsroom/fact-sheets/3551/fact -sheet-rrf-2017-3.pdf.

28. U.S. Department of Transportation, Maritime Administration, *National Defense Reserve Fleet Inventory for the Month Ending September 30, 2018* (Washington: MARAD, 2018).

29. Grabow, Manak, and Ikenson, "The Jones Act: A Burden America Can No Longer Bear"; and Grennes, *An Economic Analysis of the Jones Act*.

30. Slattery, Riley, and Loris, "Sink the Jones Act"; and James Jay Carafano, Walter Lohman, Steven P. Bucci, and Nile Gardiner, "The Challenge for the Next President: Reversing the Decline in U.S. Power," Heritage Foundation Backgrounder no. 3050, October 20, 2015.

Chapter 13

1. "United States Flag Privately-Owned Merchant Fleet Report," U.S. Department of Transportation, Maritime Administration, August 2019, https://www .maritime.dot.gov/sites/marad.dot.gov/files/oictures/DS_USFlag-Fleet _20190815_Bundle_0.pdf.

2. Thomas Grennes, "A Jones Act Restriction with High Costs and No Benefits," *The Bridge* (blog), Mercatus Center, November 28, 2018.

3. Ben Lefebvre, "Russian Gas Defies U.S. Sanctions to Reach New England," *Politico,* January 26, 2018.

4. James W. Coleman, *Repeal the Jones Act for American Energy* (Washington: Regulatory Transparency Project, September 28, 2017).

5. Jarrett Renshaw, "Refiner Goes Belly-up after Big Payouts to Carlyle Group," Reuters, February 20, 2018. ("The refinery remained largely cut off from the cheap crude it needed to survive.")

6. James W. Coleman, "Repeal the Jones Act to Speed Puerto Rico Recovery," *Fox News*, October 11, 2017.

7. James W. Coleman, "The Third Age of Oil and Gas Law," *Indiana Law Journal* 95, no. 2 (2020): 389–430.

8. James W. Coleman, "Importing Energy, Exporting Regulation," *Fordham Law Review* 83, no. 3 (2014): 1357.

9. James W. Coleman, "Pipelines and Power-lines: Building the Energy Transport Future," *Ohio State Law Journal* 80, no. 2 (2019): 263–307.

10. Thomas Grennes, *An Economic Analysis of the Jones Act* (Arlington: Mercatus Center, 2017); and Steve Ellis, "The Jones Act: A Costly Failure," chap. 9, in *The Case against the Jones Act* (Washington: Cato Institute, 2020).

11. Thomas Grennes, "Does the Jones Act Endanger American Seamen?," *Regulation* 40, no. 3 (Fall 2017): 2.

12. John Frittelli, "Shipping U.S. Crude Oil by Water: Vessel Flag Requirements and Safety Issues," Congressional Research Service, R43563, July 21, 2014.

13. Greg LaRose, "Report Chills Idea to Link LNG Exports to U.S.-Built Ships," *Times Picayune*, December 4, 2015. There is a narrow exception to the U.S.-build requirement for LNG transport to Puerto Rico for vessels built before 1996, but there are only a few aging and inefficient vessels that could even theoretically qualify for this exception and many of these are already under long-term contract. U.S. Government Accountability Office, *Puerto Rico: Characteristics of the Island's Maritime Trade and Potential Effects of Modifying the Jones Act*, GAO-13-260 (Washington: GAO, March 2013).

14. See Nicolas Loris, "Time to Mobilize the Dispersed Costs of the Jones Act," chap. 12, in *The Case against the Jones Act* (Washington: Cato Institute, 2020).

15. U.S. Government Accountability Office, *Maritime Transportation: Implications of Using U.S. Liquefied- Natural-Gas Carriers for Exports*, GAO-16-104 (Washington: GAO, December 2015). ("Higher shipping rates likely associated

with U.S.-built-and-flagged carriers would decrease the competitiveness of U.S. LNG, but the extent to which this would occur and its effects are uncertain. As we have noted, world supply and demand conditions determine the extent to which there is a market for U.S. LNG exports, and those conditions would be affected by higher shipping costs for U.S. LNG exports.") Only 3 of 11 shipyards even expressed interest in building a ship, while only 2 had facilities large enough to build a LNG ship. None have any of the expertise necessary to build these ships (some have built LNG-powered ships, but the LNG engine is imported). The shipyards said they thought they could produce the first ship within about eight years, but they only have facilities to build one ship at a time, so it would take half a century to build a fleet. Fundamentally, there is no reason to build such specific ships when you could just ship to China, Europe, and Asia. The GAO is very clear that the LNG industry is crucially dependent on transport costs and would likely be destroyed by a U.S.-build requirement.

16. Waiver of Navigation and Vessel-inspection Laws, 46 U.S.C. § 501.

17. In other words, the Jones Act only imposes deadweight loss in these situations. See Ted Loch-Temzelides, "Needed: A Cost-Benefit Analysis of the Jones Act," chap. 11, in *The Case against the Jones Act* (Washington: Cato Institute, 2020).

18. Jeffry Valentin-Mari and José I. Alameda-Lozada, "Economic Impact of the Jones Act on Puerto Rico's Economy" (working paper presented to U.S. General Accountability Office, April 26, 2012), https://docplayer.net/494027-Economic -impact-of-jones-act-on-puerto-rico-s-economy.html; Simat, Helliesen, and Eichner, Inc., *The Jones Act and Its Impact on the State of Alaska*, vol. II, final report (New York: Simat, Helliesen, and Eichner, July 1982); U.S. Government Accountability Office, *The Jones Act: Impact on Alaska Transportation and U.S. Military Sealift Capability*, GAO-88-107 (Washington: GAO, September 1988); and Mike Hansen and Colin Grabow, "Column: Jones Act Expensive, Benefits Questionable," *Star Advertiser*, May 21, 2019.

19. Karin Gourdon and Jaoquim J. M. Guilhoto, *Local Content Requirements and Their Economic Effect on Shipbuilding: A Quantitative Assessment*, Organisation for Economic Co-operation and Development Science, Technology, and Industry Policy Papers no. 69 (Paris: OECD, April 2019), p. 21.

Chapter 14

1. "Pre-Employment Inquiries and Citizenship," U.S. Equal Opportunity Employment Commission.

2. "American Airlines Flight Attendant Requirements," Cabin Crew HQ; and "The Essential Guide to Becoming a Flight Attendant," FAQ's, https://www.flightattendantcareer.com/faq-s.

3. U.S. International Trade Commission, *The Economic Effects of Significant U.S. Import Restraints: Third Update,*" Publication no. 332–325 (Washington: USITC, June 2002), p. 121.

4. Alliance for Innovation and Infrastructure, *The Jones Act: Protectionism v Global Trade* (Arlington: AII, January 2016).

5. "Cabotage" is defined as the right to operate sea, air, or other transport services within a particular territory. Cabotage laws, such as the Jones Act, restrict the provision of such services within a particular country to that country's own transport services.

6. Dan Goure, "The Jones Act Is Needed Now More than Ever," *National Interest,* March 6, 2018.

7. U.S. Government Accountability Office, *Maritime Security: Federal Agencies Have Taken Actions to Address Risks Posed by Seafarers, but Efforts Can Be Strengthened,* GAO-11-195 (Washington: GAO, January 14, 2011), p. 12.

8. "New Americans in the U.S. Armed Forces Fact Sheet," National Immigration Forum, November 22, 2016.

9. Quoted in Uri Friedman, "Where America's Terrorists Actually Come From," *The Atlantic,* January 30, 2017.

10. Loren Thompson, "Why Repealing the Jones Act Could Be a Disaster for the U.S.," Forbes, October 17, 2017.

11. Russ Kashian, Jeff Pagel, and Ike Brannon, *The Jones Act in Perspective: A Survey of the Costs and Effects of the 1920 Merchant Marine Act* (Honolulu: Grassroot Institute of Hawaii, April 9, 2017).

12. U.S. Department of Transportation, *Maritime Administration, Maritime Workforce Working Group Report* (Washington: MARAD, September 29, 2017), p. 38.

13. Quoted in Colin Grabow, Inu Manak, and Daniel J. Ikenson, "The Jones Act: A Burden America Can No Longer Bear," chap. 1, in *The Case against the Jones Act* (Washington: Cato Institute, 2020).

14. Lewis Crenshaw, Mortimer Downey III, Beverly Godwin, William Kenwell, and Marvin Phaup, *Maritime Administration: Defining Its Mission, Aligning Its Programs, and Meeting Its Objectives* (Washington: National Academy of Public Administration, November 8, 2017).

Chapter 15

1. The Organisation for Economic Co-operation and Development's Services Trade Restrictiveness Index includes a measure of how restrictive maritime transport services are to foreign entry. Canada is one of the least restrictive countries for foreign entry into maritime transportation services. See "Services Trade Restrictiveness Index Regulatory Database," Organisation for Economic Co-operation and Development.

2. Maritime cabotage is referred to as "coasting trade" in Canada and it covers the movement of goods or persons between two points in Canada. For example, a trip between the two ports of Vancouver and Montreal via the Panama Canal is considered a domestic move.

3. Confederation is the process by which the British colonies of the Province of Canada, Nova Scotia, and New Brunswick were united into one federation on July 1, 1867.

4. Canada, Privy Council, *Report of the Royal Commission on Coasting Trade* (Ottawa: Privy Council, 1957), p. 2, http://publications.gc.ca/site/eng/9.818347 /publication.html. For an extensive overview of Canada's history with coasting trade regulation, see J. R. F. Hodgson and Mary R. Brooks, *Canada's Maritime Cabotage Policy: A Report for Transport Canada* (Halifax: Dalhousie University, 2004).

5. These acts were repealed in 1849, and in 1854 cabotage restrictions between ports in the United Kingdom and ports in the colonies were removed. However, the restrictions on cabotage within the colonies, including Canada, remained, subject to possible exemptions by Order in Council at Westminster. See *Report of the Royal Commission on Coasting Trade*, p. 7.

6. The Constitution Act, 1867, 30 & 31 Vict., c. 3 (UK).

7. Colonial Laws Validity Act, 1865, 28 & 29 Vict., c. 63 (UK).

8. *Report of the Royal Commission on Coasting Trade*, p. 8.

9. *Report of the Royal Commission on Coasting Trade*, p. 8.

10. "British Commonwealth Merchant Shipping Agreement," signed in London, December 10, 1931, https://discovery.nationalarchives.gov.uk/details/r/C3529795. This agreement can also be viewed in Appendix VIII of *Report of the Royal Commission on Coasting Trade*.

11. Canada Shipping Act, Prefix to Statues, 1934, 24 & 25 Geo. 5, Seventeenth Parliament, 517–1010.

12. Canada Shipping Act, Part XIII, governed coasting trade.

13. To be registered as a British ship under the Canada Shipping Act 1934, the ship had to be wholly owned by qualified persons, who were either natural-born British subjects or persons recognized as being such throughout British dominions; naturalized British subjects throughout the dominions; persons made denizens by letters of denization; and corporate bodies established under law and located in British dominions. Ships meeting these criteria could then be registered by the chief officers of customs at any port in the Dominion of Canada. See Canada Shipping Act, pp. 529–30.

14. Canada Shipping Act, Part XIII, Section 663 (1).

15. Canada Shipping Act, Part XIII, Section 662.

16. Hodgson and Brooks, *Canada's Maritime Cabotage Policy*, p. 27.

17. Hodgson and Brooks, *Canada's Maritime Cabotage Policy*, p. 27.

18. The Spence Commission was established on March 1, 1955, against the backdrop of construction that had begun on the opening up of the St. Lawrence Seaway, which would increase maritime traffic there and in the Great Lakes. There were 173 briefs filed and 200 witness appearances that, in total, generated more than 6000 pages of transcripts. See *Report of the Royal Commission on Coasting Trade*, pp. 5–6.

19. *Report of the Royal Commission on Coasting Trade*, p. 109.

20. *Report of the Royal Commission on Coasting Trade*, p. 139.

21. *Report of the Royal Commission on Coasting Trade*, p. 140.

22. *Report of the Royal Commission on Coasting Trade*, p. 136.

23. *Report of the Royal Commission on Coasting Trade*, p. 140

24. *Report of the Royal Commission on Coasting Trade*, p. 137.

25. *Report of the Royal Commission on Coasting Trade*, p. 157.

26. The governments of Ontario and Quebec did not register opinions. See *Report of the Royal Commission on Coasting Trade*, pp. 157–59.

27. As discussed above, Canadian shipbuilders were already receiving various forms of assistance from the Canadian government. See *Report of the Royal Commission on Coasting Trade*, p. 178.

28. Howard J. Darling, "Report of Inquiry on the Coasting Trade of Canada and Related Marine Activity," 1970, quoted in Hodgson and Brooks, *Canada's Maritime Cabotage Policy*, pp. 40–43.

29. Hodgson and Brooks, *Canada's Maritime Cabotage Policy*, p. 41.

30. Hodgson and Brooks, *Canada's Maritime Cabotage Policy*, p. 29.

31. Hodgson and Brooks, *Canada's Maritime Cabotage Policy*, p. 42.

32. Coasting Trade Act, S.C. 1992, c. 31, https://laws-lois.justice.gc.ca/PDF/C-33.3.pdf.

33. House of Commons Debates, October 9, 1991, Thirty-fourth Parliament, (Hon. Corbeil, PC), http://parl.canadiana.ca/view/oop.debates_HOC3403_03/1?r=0&s=1.

34. House of Commons Debates, October 9, 1991, Thirty-fourth Parliament (Mr. Marchi, LPC).

35. Foreign ships are all those that are not registered as Canadian ships, as defined in Part 2 of the Canada Shipping Act of 2001. In order to register a vessel in Canada, the vessel must be wholly owned by a "qualified person" and not registered in a foreign state. In general, qualified persons are defined as Canadian citizens or permanent residents and corporations that are incorporated under Canadian or provincial laws. See Canada Shipping Act, S.C. 2001, c. 26, https://laws-lois.justice.gc.ca/PDF/C-10.15.pdf.

36. Applications must be made by a resident of Canada or on their behalf by an authorized agent. See "Coasting Trade in Canada," Government of Canada, http://www.tc.gc.ca/eng/policy/acf-acfs-menu-2215.htm for details on requirements for applying for the license.

37. Coasting Trade Act, S.C. 1992, c. 31 Art. 4(1)(a).

38. See applications at "Marine Notices," Canadian Transportation Agency, https://portail-portal.otc-cta.gc.ca/en/marine-notices.

39. "Marine Notices," Canadian Transportation Agency.

40. The panel appointed by the government to review the Canada Transportation Act in 2001 called for the elimination of this duty, citing its impediments to the efficiency of Canadian carriers and their ability to acquire specialized fleets,

in addition to the fact that it distorts competition between transportation modes. See J. R. F Hodgson and Mary R. Brooks, "Towards a North American Cabotage Regime: A Canadian Perspective," *Canadian Journal of Transportation* 1, no. 1 (March 2007): 19–35; and *Vision and Balance: Report of the Canada Transportation Act Review Panel* (Ottawa: Government of Canada, 2001), http://publications.gc.ca/site/eng/9.695762/publication.html.

41. For an overview of maritime cabotage regulations in Australia and New Zealand, see Mary R. Brooks, *Intermodal Transport and Supply Chains: Liberalization in Maritime Transport* (Paris: OECD, 2009). On the changes in Australian legislation and the contrast with the previous, more-liberalized cabotage regime, see Maurice Thompson and Joel Cockerell, "Cabotage Reform in Australia—the 2012 'Reforms' and the Need for Further Reform," Clyde & Co., February 16, 2015.

42. Transport Canada, *Pathways: Connecting Canada's Transportation System to the World*, vol. 1 (Ottawa: Department of Transport, 2016), https://www.tc.gc.ca/eng/ctareview2014/CTAR_Vol1_EN.pdf.

43. Transport Canada, *Pathways: Connecting Canada's Transportation System to the World*, p. 218.

44. Transport Canada, *Pathways: Connecting Canada's Transportation System to the World*.

45. Stephen Blank and Barry E. Prentice, "NAFTA at 20: Time to Open the Internal Borders of North America to Cabotage," *Research in Transportation Business and Management* 16 (September 2015): 5.

46. Triangular routes refer to the fact that, for instance, an American ship on the Great Lakes could not pick up some cargo in Thunder Bay and then load additional cargo in Sault Ste. Marie before delivering everything to Milwaukee, thus forming a triangle. Due to cabotage rules, that base of the triangle has to always be in the home country of the vessel, which produces inefficient shipping routes. See Blank and Prentice, "NAFTA at 20," p. 7

47. Blank and Prentice, "NAFTA at 20."

48. U.S. International Trade Commission, *The Economic Effects of Significant U.S. Import Restraints: Third Update*, Publication no. 332-325 (Washington: USITC, June 2002); U.S. International Trade Commission, *The Economic Effects of Significant U.S. Import Restraints: Second Update*, Publication no. 3201

(Washington: USITC, 1999; and U.S. International Trade Commission, *The Economic Effects of Significant U.S. Import Restraints* (Washington: USITC, 1993).

49. Karin Gourdon and Joaquim J. M. Guilhoto, *Local Content Requirements and Their Economic Effect on Shipbuilding: A Quantitative Assessment*, Organisation for Economic Co-operation and Development, Science, Technology and Industry Policy Papers no. 69 (Paris: OECD, 2019), p. 6.

50. William W. Olney, *Cabotage Sabotage? The Curious Case of the Jones Act*, Department of Economics Working Papers 2019-03, Department of Economics, Williams College, October 9, 2019.

51. Timothy Fitzgerald, "The Environmental Case for Jones Act Reform," chap. 7, in *The Case against the Jones Act* (Washington: Cato Institute, 2020).

52. United Nations Conference on Trade and Development, *Review of Maritime Transport, 2019* (Geneva: UNCTAD, 2019), p. 30.

53. Transport Canada, *Pathways: Connecting Canada's Transportation System to the World*, p. 229.

54. Transport Canada, *Pathways: Connecting Canada's Transportation System to the World*, p. 230.

55. For example, as of December 10, 2018, owners of shipping containers can use vessels of any nationality without a coasting trade license to reposition their containers between Canadian ports. See "Coasting Trade in Canada," Government of Canada, http://www.tc.gc.ca/eng/policy/acf-acfs-menu -2215.htm.

56. See, Colin Grabow, Inu Manak, and Daniel J. Ikenson, "The Jones Act: A Burden America Can No Longer Bear," chap. 1, in *The Case against the Jones Act* (Washington: Cato Institute, 2020).

57. Jonathon Waldron, "How Difficult Is it to Obtain a Jones Act Waiver?," *MarineLink*, November 25, 2014.

58. John Frittelli, "Shipping under the Jones Act: Legislative and Regulatory Background," Congressional Research Service, R45725, May 17, 2019, p. 11.

59. Frittelli, "Shipping under the Jones Act."

60. Grabow, Manak, and Ikenson, "The Jones Act: A Burden America Can No Longer Bear."

61. Frittelli, "Shipping under the Jones Act," p. 9.

62. Frittelli, "Shipping under the Jones Act," p. 11.

63. Manuel Reyes, "A Shift Toward Murkiness: How Conflicting Transportation Policies Have Forced Unsupervised Oligopolies on Jones Act Trades in the Past 23 Years," chap. 8, in *The Case against the Jones Act* (Washington: Cato Institute, 2020).

64. "Comprehensive Economic and Trade Agreement, Article 14.1–14.4," Government of Canada, https://www.international.gc.ca/trade-commerce/trade-agreements-accords-commerciaux/agr-acc/ceta-aecg/text-texte/14.aspx?lang=eng.

65. "Comprehensive Economic and Trade Agreement, Article 14.3.2," Government of Canada, https://www.international.gc.ca/trade-commerce/trade-agreements-accords-commerciaux/agr-acc/ceta-aecg/text-texte/14.aspx?lang=eng; and "Coasting Trade and the Canada-European Union Economic and Trade Agreement (CETA)," Government of Canada, https://www.tc.gc.ca/eng/policy/coasting-trade-foreign-vessels-canada-european-trade-agreement.html. The procurement of dredging services from EU-flagged vessels by the Canadian government includes a number of additional restrictions. For example, government procurement of dredging services below the threshold of $5 million Special Drawing Rights (SDR) can still only be carried out by Canadian registered *and* manufactured (or substantially altered) vessels. What the trade agreement altered was the government procurement of dredging services at or above $5 million SDR. Here, EU-flagged vessels can be granted a temporary license under the Coasting Trade Act, as long as it is also of Canadian or EU manufacture, or has been predominantly modified in Canada or the EU and owned by a person located in Canada or the EU. The granting of the temporary license will not be subject to the condition that a suitable Canadian-flagged vessel cannot provide the service.

66. House of Commons Debates, October 31, 2017, Forty-second Parliament, 1st. sess., https://www.ourcommons.ca/DocumentViewer/en/42-1/house/sitting-226/hansard.

67. For example, Rep. Brian Babin (R-TX) recently made the ominous statement on the House floor that a "Chinese-built vessel, subsidized by their communist regime, operated by the Chinese and delivering Chinese goods all in the very heartland of the United States of America. But this could easily become a reality if the Jones Act is waived." See Colin Grabow, "Chinese Ships on the Mississippi River: Just Another Jones Act Tall Tale," *Cato at Liberty* (blog), May 21, 2019.

68. House of Commons Debates," October 31, 2017.

69. While foreigners are not barred from working on Canadian vessels, they do have to be permanent residents and have Canadian certifications. See "Questions Frequently Asked Regarding: Certification and Training," Government of Canada, https://www.tc.gc.ca/eng/marinesafety/mpsp-training-examination -certification-faq-1052.htm. The Emerson Report also went as far as to recommend that Canada improve its processes for recruiting and certifying foreign seafarers. See Transport Canada, *Pathways: Connecting Canada's Transportation System to the World*, p. 230.

70. Blank and Prentice, "NAFTA at 20."

71. Frittelli, "Shipping under the Jones Act," p. 10.

72. Mary R. Brooks, *The Jones Act Under NAFTA and Its Effects on the Canadian Shipbuilding Industry* (Halifax: Atlantic Institute for Market Studies, September 2006), p. 12.

73. *Vision and Balance: Report of the Canada Transportation Act Review Panel*, p. 146.

74. *Vision and Balance: Report of the Canada Transportation Act Review Panel.*

75. Grabow, Manak, and Ikenson, "The Jones Act: A Burden America Can No Longer Bear."

76. Grabow, Manak, and Ikenson, "The Jones Act: A Burden America Can No Longer Bear."

77. Frittelli, "Shipping under the Jones Act," p. 13.

78. The U.S. defense industrial base refers to the products and services that the Department of Defense uses to support its mission. Under U.S. law, Canadian persons or organizations that provide production, research, and services are part of this base. See, for example, Heidi M. Peters, "Defense Primer: U.S. Defense Industrial Base," in *In Focus* no. 10548, Congressional Research Service, February 6, 2020.

Chapter 16

1. In 2002, the U.S. International Trade Commission estimated that the annual economic gain from repealing the act for residents of Alaska, Hawaii, and Puerto Rico would be between $5 billion and $15 billion in current-value dollars. See U.S. International Trade Commission, *The Economic Effects of Significant U.S. Import Restraints: Third Update*, Publication no. 3519 (Washington: USITC,

2002); and Russ Kashian, Jeff Pagel, and Ike Brannon, *The Jones Act in Perspective: A Survey of the Costs and Effects of the 1920 Merchant Marine Act* (Honolulu: Grassroot Institute of Hawaii, April 9, 2017). For a more recent study that estimates the costs of the Jones Act, see, Karin Gourdon and Joaquim J. M. Guilhoto, *Local Content Requirements and Their Economic Effect on Shipbuilding: A Quantitative Assessment,"* Organisation for Economic Co-operation and Development, Science, Technology and Industry Policy Papers no. 69 (Paris: OECD, 2019), p. 6.

2. "The Big Q: What Do You Think about the Jones Act, the 1920 Law Designed to Protect U.S. Domestic Shipping Interests?," *Honolulu Star Advertiser*, December 1, 2012.

3. "Big Q: What Should Be Done about the Maritime Shipping Law, the Jones Act?," *Honolulu Star-Advertiser*, October 2, 2017.

4. "Big Q: What Should be Done about the Maritime Shipping Law, the Jones Act?," *Honolulu Star-Advertiser*, October 3, 2017.

5. Reeve and Associates and Estudios Técnicos Inc., *Impact of the U.S. Jones Act on Puerto Rico* (Ogden, UT: Reeve, 2018), p. 6.

Chapter 17

1. Douglas Irwin, *Clashing Over Commerce: A History of US Trade Policy* (Chicago: University of Chicago Press, 2017), p. 35; and John Frittelli, "The Jones Act: An Overview," Congressional Research Service, RS21566, July 8, 2003.

2. John Randolph Spears, *The Story of the American Merchant Marine (Illustrated Edition)* (Norwood, MA: Norwood Press, 1910), p. 29.

3. Winthrop L. Marvin, *The American Merchant Marine: Its History and Romance from 1620 to 1902* (New York: Charles Scribner's Sons, 1916), pp. 26–27.

4. Marvin, *The American Merchant Marine*, p. 31

5. Henry Hall, *American Navigation: With Some Account of the Causes of Its Recent Decay, and of the Means by Which Its Prosperity May Be Restored* (New York: D. Appleton and Company, 1880), p. 41.

6. Hall, *American Navigation*, p. 39.

7. Bryan Clark, Timothy A. Walton, and Adam Lemon, *Strengthening the U.S. Defense Maritime Industrial Base: a Plan to Improve Maritime Industry's Contribution to National Security* (Washington: Center For Strategic and Budgetary Assessments, 2020).

8. Andrew Gibson and Arthur Donovan, *The Abandoned Ocean: A History of United States Maritime Policy* (Columbia, SC: University of South Carolina Press, 2001), p. 16.

9. Irwin, *Clashing Over Commerce*, p. 37.

10. Gibson and Donovan, *Abandoned Ocean*, p. 23.

11. Constantine G. Papavizas and Bryant E. Gardner, "Is the Jones Act Redundant?," *U.S.F. Maritime Law Journal* 21, no. 1 (2008): 95–138; and Gibson and Donovan, *Abandoned Ocean*, p. 23.

12. Gibson and Donovan, *Abandoned Ocean*, p. 23.

13. "Second Annual Message of George Washington," December 8, 1790, Yale Law School, Avalon Project, https://avalon.law.yale.edu/18th_century/washs02.asp.

14. Gibson and Donovan, *Abandoned Ocean*, pg. 25.

15. John Frayler, "Privateers in the American Revolution," National Park Service, https://www.nps.gov/revwar/about_the_revolution/privateers.html.

16. David Ames Wells, *Our Merchant Marine: How It Rose, Increased, Became Great, Declined and Decayed* (New York: G. P. Putnam's Sons, 1890), pp. 62–65.

17. Wells, *Our Merchant Marine*, p. 68.

18. See, Gibson and Donovan, *Abandoned Ocean*, p. 25.

19. Gibson and Donovan, *Abandoned Ocean*, p. 40.

20. Gibson and Donovan, *Abandoned Ocean*, p. 40.

21. Gibson and Donovan, *Abandoned Ocean*, p. 40; and Papavizas and Gardner, "Is the Jones Act Redundant?," pp. 98–99.

22. See, Gibson and Donovan, *Abandoned Ocean*, pp. 43–63.

23. Gibson and Donovan, *Abandoned Ocean*, pp. 57–58.

24. Gibson and Donovan, *Abandoned Ocean*, p. 45.

25. "English Navigation Laws 1651–1849: An Exercise in Protectionism," in *Maritime Redevelopment: Hearings before the Subcommittee on Merchant Marine of the Committee on Merchant Marine and Fisheries, House of Representatives* (Washington: GPO, 1985), https://books.google.com/books?id=trVFAQAAMAAJ&lpg=PA625&ots=rrtTmBWchs&dq=English%20Navigation%20Laws%201651%E2%80%931849%3A%20An%20Exercise%20in%20Protectionism%2C%E2%80%9D%20Library%20of%20Congress&pg=PA625#v=onepage&q&f=false, p. 635.

26. "English Navigation Laws 1651–1849," p. 638.

27. "English Navigation Laws 1651–1849," p. 636.

28. John Lewis Ricardo, *The Anatomy of the Navigation Laws* (London: Charles Gilpin, 1847).

29. Ricardo, *Anatomy of the Navigation Laws*, p. 55

30. Wells, *Our Merchant Marine*, p. 104.

31. Wells, *Our Merchant Marine*, p. 104.

32. Wells, *Our Merchant Marine*, p. 102.

33. Gibson and Donovan, *Abandoned Ocean*, p. 62.

34. Wells, *Our Merchant Marine*, pp. 106–08.

35. Wells, *Our Merchant Marine*, pp. 106–08.

36. Gibson and Donovan, *Abandoned Ocean*, pp. 62–63.

37. Spears, *The Story of the American Merchant Marine*, p. 161.

38. C. G. Calkins, "Our Merchant Marine: The Causes of Its Decline, and the Means to Be Taken for Its Revival," in *Proceedings of the United States Naval Institute* 8, no. 1 (January 1882).

39. "Grover Cleveland: Second Annual Message (Second Term)," December 3, 1894, American Presidency Project.

40. Papavizas and Gardner, "Is the Jones Act Redundant?"

41. John Frittelli, "Shipping under the Jones Act: Legislative and Regulatory Background," Congressional Research Service, R45725, November 21, 2019.

42. Papavizas and Gardner, "Is the Jones Act Redundant?"

43. Papavizas and Gardner, "Is the Jones Act Redundant?"

44. *The Establishment of an American Merchant Marine, Hearings Before the Committee on Commerce*, 66th Cong. 2nd sess. (1920), p. 1381.

45. *Establishment of an American Merchant Marine*, p. 1430.

46. *Establishment of an American Merchant Marine*, p. 1430.

47. *Establishment of an American Merchant Marine*, p. 1442.

48. *Establishment of an American Merchant Marine*, p. 1456.

49. Papavizas and Gardner, "Is the Jones Act Redundant?"

50. Mark D. Aspinwall says that the Alaska trade was a "major factor in the inclusion of this wording," with Senator Jones recorded as stating that "we have a direct competitor with our shipping in Canadian shipping. It seems to me whenever we can legitimately give an advantage to our shipping, we ought to do it." See Mark D. Aspinwall, "Coastwise Trade Policy in the United States: Does it Make Sense Today?," *Journal of Maritime Law and Commerce* 18, no. 2 (1987): 243–62.

51. Paul Maxwell Zeis, *American Shipping Policy* (Princeton: Princeton University Press, 1938).

52. Paul Maxwell Zeis, *American Shipping Policy*.

53. Michael L. Grace, "History of the Alaska Steamship Company, Seattle, 1895–1971," Cruising The Past, March 10, 2010.

54. Walter J. Hickel, *Crisis in the Commons: The Alaska Solution* (Oakland: Institute for Contemporary Studies Press, 2002), p. 51.

55. Ernest Gruening, "Let Us Now End American Colonialism" (speech to the delegates of the Alaska Constitutional Convention, November 9, 1955), https://www.alaska.edu/creatingalaska/constitutional-convention/speeches-to-the-conventio/opening-session-speeches/gruening/.

56. U.S. Government Accountability Office, *The Jones Act: Impact on Alaska Transportation and U.S. Military Sealift Capacity*, RCED-88-107 (Washington: GAO, September 30, 1988).

57. "Senator Jones Defends His Bill at Tacoma: Declares that Law Will not Be Altered Unless Proven Injurious to American Trade," *Nautical Gazette* 99, no. 8 (August 21, 1920): 228.

58. Karin Gourdon and Joaquim J.M. Guilhoto, *Local Content Requirements and their Economic Effect on Shipbuilding: A Quantitative Assessment*, Organisation for Economic Co-operation and Development Science, Technology and Industry Policy Papers no. 69 (Paris: OECD, 2019).

59. World Economic Forum, *Enabling Trade: Valuing Growth Opportunities* (Geneva: WEF, 2013).

60. "Senator Jones Defends His Bill at Tacoma."

Conclusion

1. World Economic Forum, "Case Examples," chap. 6 in *Enabling Trade: Valuing Growth Opportunities*.

2. "By the Capes around the World: A Summary of World Cabotage Practices," U.S. Department of Transportation, Maritime Administration, https://www.hsdl.org/?abstract&did=455295.

3. Paul Bartlett, "Winds of Change," *Maritime Executive*, December 31, 2018.

4. Loren Thompson, "Trump Industrial Policy Likely to Target U.S. Commercial Shipbuilding and Merchant Fleet for Revival," *Forbes*, June 5, 2018.

5. United Nations Conference on Trade and Development, *Review of Maritime Transport, 2019* (Geneva: UNCTAD, 2019).

6. Organisation for Economic Co-operation and Development, *Peer Review of the Norwegian Shipbuilding Industry* (Paris: OECD, 2017), https://www.oecd.org/sti /ind/PeerReviewNorway_FINAL.pdf.

7. John Frittelli, "Shipping under the Jones Act: Legislative and Regulatory Background," Congressional Research Service, R45725, November 21, 2019.

8. United Nations Conference on Trade and Development, *Rethinking Maritime Cabotage for Improved Connectivity*, Transport and Trade Facilitation, Series no. 9 (Geneva: United Nations, 2017).

9. Robert Y. Cavana, "A Qualitative Analysis of Reintroducing Cabotage onto New Zealand's Coasts," *Maritime Policy Management* 31, no. 3 (2004): 179–98.

About the Editors

Colin Grabow

Colin Grabow is a policy analyst at the Cato Institute's Herbert A. Stiefel Center for Trade Policy Studies, where his research focuses on U.S. trade with Asia as well as domestic forms of trade protectionism, such as the U.S. sugar program and the Jones Act. His writings have been published in a number of outlets, including *USA Today*, *The Hill*, *National Review*, and the *Weekly Standard*. Prior to joining the Cato Institute, he performed political and economic analysis for a Japan-based trading and investment firm and published research and analysis for an international affairs consulting firm with a focus on U.S.-Asia relations. Grabow holds a BA in international affairs from James Madison University and an MA in international trade and investment policy from George Washington University.

Inu Manak

Inu Manak is a research fellow at the Cato Institute's Herbert A. Stiefel Center for Trade Policy Studies. She is an expert in international political economy, with a specialization in international trade policy and law. Manak's research focuses on the World Trade Organization, non-judicial treaty mechanisms, technical barriers to trade, regional trade agreements, and development.

Previously, she was a junior visiting fellow at the Center for Trade and Economic Integration at the Graduate Institute and a fellow at TradeLab, a Geneva-based association that assists developing countries, small to mid-sized enterprises, and nongovernmental organizations build legal capacity in trade and investment law. Manak is also a participating scholar in the Robert A. Pastor North American Research Initiative, a joint program between American University's Center for Latin American and Latino Studies and the School of International Service.

Manak earned a PhD in government at Georgetown University.

About the Contributors

Keliʻi Akina

Keliʻi Akina is the president and chief executive officer of the Grassroot Institute of Hawaii and is a public policy expert and politician in Hawaii. In the predominantly Democrat-controlled Hawaii government, he is the only philosophical libertarian elected to statewide office and one of the state's highest vote-getters. In 2016, Akina was elected to a four-year term as trustee-at-large for the state Office of Hawaiian Affairs. Akina has become a national advocate for reform of the protectionist law known as the Jones Act. He is also an expert in East-West philosophy and ethics, and has lectured at universities in Asia and the United States. Akina holds a PhD from Northwestern University and the University of Hawaii and has been published in national media outlets such as the *Wall Street Journal, Forbes*, and *The Hill*.

James W. Coleman

James Coleman is an associate professor of law at Southern Methodist University. He received two degrees from Harvard University—a JD (cum laude) and a BA in biology (magna cum laude with highest honors in the field). Upon graduation from law school he served as clerk for Eighth Circuit Judge Steve Colloton, and then practiced energy, environmental, and appellate law as an associate in the Washington, DC, firm of Sidley Austin LLP for three years.

Prior to joining Southern Methodist University, he was on the faculty at the University of Calgary, where he taught at both the law school and the business school. Before Calgary, he served on the faculty at Harvard Law School as a Climenko Fellow and lecturer on law.

Coleman's scholarship addresses regulation of North American energy companies, focusing on how countries account for and influence regulation of fuel and electricity in their trading partners and how global energy companies respond to competing pressures from investors and regulators in multiple jurisdictions. He publishes the *Energy Law Professor* blog and you can follow him on Twitter at @energylawprof.

Andrew G. Durant

Andrew Durant is managing director of Samuels International Associates, Inc., an international consulting firm that he cofounded 25 years ago. Durant has extensive experience in international trade and business matters. Prior to entering private practice, he worked on Capitol Hill for members who served on the House Energy and Commerce Committee and the House Agriculture Committee. Durant has written extensively on the U.S.-Japan economic relationship, economic interests in Vietnam and Burma, and on the financial crisis for the *Economist* magazine, published by Mainichi. He works in Washington on matters related to the environment, international trade, and business, and helps clients address problems and opportunities throughout Asia and Europe. Durant has advised and supported clients in international negotiations at the World Trade Organization, and in various plurilateral and bilateral forums as well as in negotiations for build-operate-transfer infrastructure projects.

He served as the senior adviser for international trade to Capital Insights Group, a private company providing advice on U.S. government policies to institutional investors.

Durant also served on the advisory boards of the Association for Interactive Media and the Japan Information Access Project. He is currently a board member of the U.S. Capitol Historical Society as adviser to the EU-Asia Centre, which is based in Brussels. Durant is a graduate of James Madison University.

Steve Ellis

Steve Ellis is president of Taxpayers for Common Sense (TCS), which he joined in 1999, overseeing programs and serving as a leading media and legislative spokesperson. A persistent critic of the mounting budget deficit and federal fiscal policy, Steve has testified before numerous congressional committees and has appeared on national network news programs, including those on CBS, NBC, ABC, Fox, CNN, MSNBC, PBS, and NPR. His expertise ranges from earmarks to flood insurance and a lot of spending issues in between.

Steve formerly served as an officer in the U.S. Coast Guard for six years, including tours of duty as a department head and deck watch officer aboard the U.S. Coast Guard Cutter *Sorrel*, managing the Coast Guard's inland waterway fleet, and managing a small boat acquisition contract.

Steve received a BS in government from the U.S. Coast Guard Academy. He has earned both the Coast Guard Commendation Medal and the Coast Guard Achievement Medal.

Timothy Fitzgerald

Timothy Fitzgerald is an economist appointed as an associate professor in the Rawls College of Business at Texas Tech University. He researches topics in natural resource and environmental economics, focusing on energy issues. From 2017–2018 he served as a senior economist and as chief international economist on the Council of Economic Advisers in the White House.

Thomas Grennes

Thomas Grennes is professor of economics and professor of agricultural and resource economics at North Carolina State University, emeritus since 2014. He was also a member of the founding faculty at the Stockholm School of Economics–Riga, in Riga, Latvia, where he was also visiting professor of economics from 1995–2001. He has done extensive research on the Jones Act and written articles that include "Does the Jones Act Endanger American Seamen?," *Regulation* (2017); *An Economic Analysis of the Jones Act*, Mercatus Research Paper (2017); "The Jones Act Revisited," Mercatus on Policy Series (2017); and "Sacrificing Safety Is an Unintended Consequence of the Jones Act," Mercatus on Policy Series (2018).

Daniel Griswold

Daniel Griswold is a senior research fellow at the Mercatus Center at George Mason University and codirector of its Trade and Immigration Project. Griswold is a nationally recognized expert on trade and immigration policy. He is the author of the 2009 book, *Mad about Trade: Why Main Street America Should Embrace Globalization.* He has authored numerous studies, testified before congressional committees, commented for CNBC, CSPAN, Fox News, and other TV and radio outlets, and written articles for the *Wall Street Journal,* the *Los Angeles Times,* and other publications.

Griswold holds a bachelor's degree in journalism from the University of Wisconsin at Madison and a masters in the politics of the world economy from the London School of Economics and Political Science.

Howard Gutman

Retired ambassador Howard Gutman is the managing director of the Gutman Group, an international consulting and investment firm with a primary focus on the United States, Europe, the Middle East, and Asia. His career has spanned the public and private sectors on both sides of the Atlantic and on both sides of the political aisle. Dubbed by European press as "the ambassador who makes us love America again," in mid-2013 he completed four years of service as the U.S. Ambassador to Belgium, the third-longest-serving ambassador in more than 100 years. In May 2017, Gutman was presented the Grand Cross of the Order of the Crown, the highest medal bestowed by Belgium.

Gutman brought a rich and diverse background to both the Gutman Group and the diplomatic corps. He previously was a senior partner with the Washington, DC, law firm of Williams & Connolly LLP, where his areas of practice spanned the full gamut of litigation, investigation, and counseling matters. During the Reagan administration, he served as a special assistant to FBI Director William H. Webster, focusing on counterterrorism and counterintelligence. He has also served as a law clerk to Justice Potter Stewart on the United States Supreme Court and as a law clerk to Judge Irving L. Goldberg on the United States Court of Appeals for the Fifth Circuit. Gutman was also an adviser to a variety of political candidates, assisting in races for president, governor, Senate, and Congress.

Gutman appears regularly on Fox News and Fox Business News (despite being a Democrat), speaking on such issues as American and global politics, terrorism, foreign affairs, the Holocaust, and geopolitical events. He is a frequent contributor to the *Washington Post*, *Politico*, and the *Huffington Post*, and appears regularly on Belgian television, including on the leading Flemish programs *De Zevende Dag*, *Van Gils & Gasten*, and *Terzake*.

Gutman is a 1977 graduate of Columbia University and a 1980 graduate from Harvard Law School. He is married to Michelle Loewinger, a dentist turned consultant, and has two grown sons.

Daniel J. Ikenson

Dan Ikenson is director of Cato's Herbert A. Stiefel Center for Trade Policy Studies, where he coordinates and conducts research on all manner of international trade and investment policy. Since joining Cato in 2000, Ikenson has authored dozens of papers on various aspects of trade policy, focusing his research on U.S.-China trade relations, bilateral and multilateral trade agreements and institutions, globalization, U.S. manufacturing issues, trade politics, and trade remedies such as the antidumping regime.

Ikenson has been involved in international trade since 1990. Before joining the Cato Institute in 2000, he was director of international trade planning for an international accounting and business advisory firm. In 1997 he cofounded and was a principal at an international trade consulting firm in Washington, and from 1990 to 1997 he was a trade policy and antidumping analyst at a few international trade law practices. In addition to his many studies and articles, Ikenson is coauthor of the book *Antidumping Exposed: The Devilish Details of Unfair Trade Law*. He has testified before congressional committees on a variety of policy matters and has appeared on numerous television news programs and networks, including PBS, CNN, CNBC, Bloomberg TV, MSNBC, ABC News, Fox News, Fox Business News, and NPR. His articles have been published in widely circulated newspapers and magazines, including the *Wall Street Journal*, the *Los Angeles Times*, *USA Today*, the *Chicago Tribune*, the *Washington Times*, the *Detroit News*, *Forbes*, and *National Review*.

Ikenson holds an MA in economics from George Washington University.

Taylor Jackson

Taylor Jackson is a Canadian public policy consultant and graduate student at Johns Hopkins School of Advanced International Studies. He holds a BA and an MA in political science from Simon Fraser University. Jackson is the author or coauthor of a number of studies on Canadian public policy issues spanning education, health care, taxation, economic policy, democratic reform, Canadian-American relations, demographics, energy, natural resources, and electricity.

Logan Kolas

Logan Kolas is a research associate at the Cato Institute's Herbert A. Stiefel Center for Trade Policy Studies. His work has appeared in the *Daily Signal* and the *Foundation for Economic Education*, among others, and he has been quoted in *Forbes*. Kolas holds a BS in economics and political science from George Washington University and is pursuing an MS in applied economics at the University of Maryland.

Ted Loch-Temzelides

Ted Loch-Temzelides is a professor of economics, a Rice Scholar in energy studies at the Baker Institute for Public Policy, and the master of Martel College at Rice University. He earned his PhD from the University of Minnesota and has taught at the University of Minnesota, the Tippie College of Business at the University of Iowa, the University of Pittsburgh, the Wharton School at the University of Pennsylvania, and the European University Institute. He has worked for the Federal Reserve and held visiting scholar appointments at the European Central Bank, the International Monetary Fund, and the Central Bank of Portugal. He currently serves on the editorial board of *Economic Theory* and on the board of directors of the French-American Chamber of Commerce—Houston Chapter.

Loch-Temzelides's current research concentrates on the intersection between macroeconomics, energy, and financial economics. He studies the effects of innovation in renewable and fossil energy production on economic growth and on energy independence. He also investigates the design of efficient environmental policies and that of European Union policies related to energy, banking, and financial markets. He has been published in some of the leading economics journals, including *Econometrica*, the *Journal of Political Economy*, the *American Economic Review: Papers and Proceedings*, and the *Journal of Monetary Economics*.

Nicolas Loris

Nicolas (Nick) Loris, an economist, focuses on energy, environmental, and regulatory issues as the deputy director of the Thomas A. Roe Institute for Economic Policy Studies and Herbert and Joyce Morgan fellow at the Heritage Foundation.

Loris studies and writes about energy supplies, energy prices, and other economic effects of environmental policies and regulations, including climate change legislation, energy efficiency mandates, and energy subsidies. He also covers coal, oil, natural gas, nuclear gas, and renewable energy policy and articulates the benefits of free-market environmentalism.

Loris has testified before House and Senate committees and been published and quoted in major newspapers, such as the *Wall Street Journal* and the *New York Times*. His radio and television appearances include CNN, Fox News, MSNBC, and National Public Radio. He is a prolific contributor to the energy and environment section of the *Daily Signal*, Heritage's multimedia news organization.

Loris was promoted to research fellow in March 2016. He had been a senior policy analyst since 2013, and was named Morgan fellow the year before. Before joining Heritage in 2007, Loris was an associate at the Charles G. Koch Charitable Foundation, where he immersed himself for a year in a market-based management program.

Loris received his master's degree in economics from George Mason University and holds a bachelor's degree in economics, finance, and political science from Albright College. Loris was born and grew up in Quakertown, Pennsylvania, and currently resides in Washington, DC.

Robert "Rob" Quartel

Rob Quartel is a multisector entrepreneur, a former member of the U.S. Federal Maritime Commission, an internationally recognized expert on U.S. national maritime and transportation security policy, and chairman and founder of NTELX, Inc.

As commissioner, Rob was the leading advocate for international shipping deregulation and reform of archaic U.S. maritime laws, taking on much of the maritime industry's encrusted interests, including unions, shipyards, and ship operators. After 9/11, he took an early role in shaping the public policy response to international container security and was the first to describe a breakthrough technological approach that merged commercially available data with intelligence information.

Quartel has been a business and policy entrepreneur and innovator throughout his career and has served as a member and adviser to the Army Science Board, is a life member of the Council on Foreign Relations, a former board member of the Wilson Council, and serves on numerous boards and advisory committees related to U.S. homeland security policy, including the board of the Northern Virginia Technology Council and the Commonwealth of Virginia's Innovation and Entrepreneurship Fund.

Rob was a senior policy adviser in two presidential campaigns and has run for federal office himself; he has written and testified extensively on maritime and security issues and modern technology challenges and is involved in numerous technology startups as an investor and adviser. He has a degree in biology and environmental science from Rice University and was a member of the charter class of Yale University's School of Organization and Management. He is married to Michela English and the couple have two adult children.

Manuel Reyes

Manuel Reyes Alfonso is the executive vice president and CEO of the Puerto Rico Food Marketing, Industry, and Distribution Chamber. He holds a BA in economics (magna cum laude) and a JD (cum laude) from the University of Puerto Rico. He also obtained the Spanish law degree from the University of Barcelona and has a master's degree in business and maritime law from the Pontifical University of Comillas in Madrid.

Reyes began his legal career as an attorney in his family's law practice in Bayamón, Puerto Rico. In 2000 he was recruited by the Puerto Rico Manufacturers Association (PRMA) as legal and legislative director. In 2001, Reyes worked as special aide to the executive director of the Puerto Rico Industrial Development Company and in 2002 was appointed director of the Puerto Rico Commercial Office in Madrid. In 2003, he was again recruited by PRMA and served until 2007, when he was offered the position of executive director for the Society for Human Resources Management Puerto Rico Chapter.

Reyes has defended the interests of the Puerto Rico business community in public and private forums, including the legislative, executive, and judicial branches of both the Commonwealth and the federal government. In 2007, he represented PRMA as amicus before the Puerto Rico Supreme Court in a leading labor law case, *Jimenez Marrero vs. General Instruments*, and has also overseen litigation challenging the constitutionality of taxes and the container scanning initiative by the Puerto Rico Ports Authority, among others. He has served on the board of directors of national trade organizations such as the Council of State Manufacturers Associations and the Food Industry Association Executives, as well as serving as an advisory board member of educational institutions on the island.

Reyes has taught at the University of Puerto Rico Law School, its business schools in Humacao, and in the Río Piedras campuses, as well as in the criminal justice program of the American University of Puerto Rico. Reyes is a frequent spokesperson for the corporate sector in local, national, and international radio, television, and print media.

Bryan Riley

Bryan Riley is director of the National Taxpayers Union's Free Trade Initiative. Riley's background includes years of research on the impact that trade has on people in the United States. He has led grassroots campaigns in support of initiatives such as the North American Free Trade Agreement (NAFTA) and in opposition to special-interest efforts to get the government to pick winners and losers in the U.S. economy.

Riley has been quoted in publications including the *Washington Post*, the *New York Times*, and the *Wall Street Journal*. He is also an in-demand speaker who travels the country explaining the benefits that international trade and invest-ment bring to Americans. Riley grew up in Manhattan, Kansas. He holds a bachelor's degree in eco-nomics from Kansas State University and a master's degree in economics from the University of Southern California.

Riley first came to Washington, DC, as an National Taxpayer Union intern during the Reagan administration, and he continues to champion Reagan's pro-trade vision for America.

About the Cato Institute

Founded in 1977, the Cato Institute is a public policy research foundation dedicated to broadening the parameters of policy debate to allow consideration of more options that are consistent with the principles of limited government, individual liberty, and peace. To that end, the Institute strives to achieve greater involvement of the intelligent, concerned lay public in questions of policy and the proper role of government.

The Institute is named for *Cato's Letters*, libertarian pamphlets that were widely read in the American Colonies in the early 18th century and played a major role in laying the philosophical foundation for the American Revolution.

Despite the achievement of the nation's Founders, today virtually no aspect of life is free from government encroachment. A pervasive intolerance for individual rights is shown by government's arbitrary intrusions into private economic transactions and its disregard for civil liberties. And while freedom around the globe has notably increased in the past several decades, many countries have moved in the opposite direction, and most governments still do not respect or safeguard the wide range of civil and economic liberties.

To address those issues, the Cato Institute undertakes an extensive publications program on the complete spectrum of policy issues. Books, monographs, and shorter studies are commissioned to examine the federal budget, Social Security, regulation, military spending, international trade, and myriad other issues. Major policy conferences are held throughout the year, from which papers are published thrice yearly in the *Cato Journal*. The Institute also publishes the quarterly magazine *Regulation*.

In order to maintain its independence, the Cato Institute accepts no government funding. Contributions are received from foundations, corporations, and individuals, and other revenue is generated from the sale of publications. The Institute is a nonprofit, tax-exempt, educational foundation under Section 501(c)3 of the Internal Revenue Code.

Cato Institute
1000 Massachusetts Avenue NW
Washington, DC 20001
www.cato.org

www.ingramcontent.com/pod-product-compliance
Lightning Source LLC
Chambersburg PA
CBHW070801280326
41934CB00012B/3009